D0539812

THE HOOLIGANS ARE STILL AMONG US

MICHAEL LAYTON & BILL ROGERSON

AMBERLEY

First published 2017

Amberley Publishing
The Hill, Stroud
Gloucestershire, GL5 4EP

www.amberley-books.com

Copyright © Michael Layton & Bill Rogerson, 2017

The right of Michael Layton QPM and Bill Rogerson MBE to be identified as the Authors of this work has been asserted in accordance with the Copyrights, Designs and Patents Act 1988.

ISBN 978 1 4456 6588 7 (print)
ISBN 978 1 4456 6589 4 (ebook)

British Library Cataloguing in Publication Data.
A catalogue record for this book is available from the British Library.

Typesetting and Origination by Amberley Publishing
Printed in the UK.

CONTENTS

FOREWORD

The police in the UK have a long, rich history of policing football supporters at stadiums, in towns and cities, and on the rail network. That history stretches from before the two decades synonymous with football-related disorder – the 1970s and 1980s – through to the present day.

While recognising that the vast majority of citizens who attend games every weekend during football seasons, in support of their favourite team, are decent, law-abiding members of the community, there is nevertheless an acknowledgement that hooliganism, and violence linked to watching football, has not been totally eradicated. The response to this phenomenon has been developed through strategies such as more structured intelligence-gathering processes, better use of high-quality CCTV, and legal measures such as Football Banning Orders. All have had a positive impact; however, those who have a taste for violence and disorder are nothing if not determined. As with most forms of criminality, offenders adapt and change tactics in order to pursue their objectives. The reality is that law enforcement agencies, and their partners, are constantly challenged in order to maintain an effective response to an ever-changing threat.

While football stadiums are no longer generally the preserve of the organised hooligan, city centres remain attractive battlegrounds and, inevitably, railway stations and key transport hubs provide suitable arenas for such groups to engage in their 'sport' – that of inflicting gratuitous violence on the innocent or, in some cases, the not-so-innocent.

During my lifetime, I have witnessed the impact of football violence from a number of different perspectives:

- Firstly, as a youth going to watch football on the terraces, where the potential for violence inside stadiums, as well as outside, was almost taken for granted.
- Secondly, as an operational police officer, during which time it was a rare 'football' Saturday that did not result in physical confrontations between 'supporters', with arrests invariably following. I well remember as a CID officer being involved in the arrest of a hooligan on a train between Witton and Birmingham for committing criminal damage. Rather than getting a 'pat on the back', I got a 'kick up the backside' as my boss at the time was of the opinion that this was not proper CID work! As is still the case today, senior police officers often have differing views about how best to tackle issues, and sometimes these do not always appear to make sense to operational officers who have to make decisions based on what they are facing in real-time, rather than by reference to some strategic plan.
- Thirdly, as a senior manager of a train operating company, where I discovered that our ability to restrict certain categories of lower-priced tickets, in an effort to deter undesirable elements from travelling for certain fixtures, was restricted by the complex regulatory structure around tickets that had been imposed by the government. Well-intentioned arrangements to protect consumers after the privatisation of the railways had a perverse impact when it came to trying to manage the risk of importing disorder onto the network. While, in theory, it was possible to seek dispensation from the relevant government department to suspend the sale of certain tickets, in practice it was never given.
- Finally, in retirement I have myself witnessed the poor behaviour of fans on trains through the eyes of a middle-aged member of the public, and I can tell you that it was a horrific experience that left me feeling angry, frustrated, and helpless. There seems to be a view that, provided that there is no direct threat of physical violence, it is okay to sing and shout, use obscene language and

consume large amounts of alcohol, irrespective of the impact it has on ordinary people, be they in a bar, on public transport, or shopping in a city centre.

In April 2016 the British Transport Police recognised the emergence of routine anti-social behaviour, much of it fuelled by alcohol and by individuals engaged in football-related violence. Fortunately, incidents of serious injury are still relatively rare, but the impact on the travelling public and members of rail staff is huge, and disproportionate to the numbers involved. In highlighting the difficulties that the force faced, they raised the profile of the issue to make tackling football-related incidents one of their priority targets, second only to tackling terrorism.

This book, the latest of a welcome series covering the great work undertaken by the British Transport Police, and Home Office police forces, seeks to map some of the positive progress that the police have made, while at the same time recognising that there is still a big job to be done to tackle the parts of the so-called English Disease, which still disproportionately affects the police and communities to this day. Recollections and accounts are used throughout the book, some of which are from retired officers. Many can recall what it was like to police football hooligans during their early years of police service, and compare this with the nature of the problem as it stood at the completion of thirty years' service.

Are the hooligans still among us? – You will have to ask yourself that question at the end of the book!

Paul Robb QPM
Former Assistant Chief Constable &
President of British Transport Police History Group (2016)

THE EARLY YEARS

Being a national force, the British Transport Police are well placed to regulate the numerous football supporters that travel the length and breadth of Britain. The force has been escorting football supporters for over 100 years. Years ago, football traffic was mainly confined to Saturdays and a couple of evenings during the week. However, today, with over 130 professional football clubs, it is a seven-day-a-week operation.

Bill Rogerson, co-author of this book, is a native of Morecambe, Lancashire, and is a self-confessed Preston North End supporter. Preston North End – or 'The Lilywhites', formerly known as 'The Invincibles' – are founding members of the Football League. In the inaugural season, they were unbeaten and became the first League champions. In the same season they won the FA Cup without conceding a goal to become the first club to achieve the English double. The motto of the City of Preston is 'Proud Preston'; however, one achievement of which Preston North End is not proud is their dubious distinction of becoming involved in the first recorded example of football hooliganism. This was in 1835, when they beat Aston Villa in a so-called friendly game. Following the match, there was a confrontation, which could only be described as bloody, between the supporters of the two teams when they fought between themselves with sticks and stones along with brutal kicks and punches.

The contemporary history of the world's favourite game spans more than 100 years. It began in 1863 in England, when rugby football and association football branched off on their different courses, and the Football Association in England was formed, becoming the sport's first governing body. In 1872 the FA Cup was launched, and in 1888 the Football League was formed.

Around this time the railways of Great Britain were being built at a phenomenal rate. As people got the confidence to travel on this new 'iron horse', it was inevitable that there were would be more and more people using the trains, as they were quicker than the stagecoach and people could travel around a lot easier. As the football leagues were formed up and down the country, football supporters started to travel by train, due to the fact that a number of football grounds were situated very close to the railway stations.

There are a few recorded stories of football hooliganism on the railway during those early years.

One such incident was recorded in an extract courtesy of the *Derby Daily Telegraph* of Monday 4 March 1912, via the British Newspaper Archives, and reported on as a riot at Burton-on-Trent:

> Riotous scenes followed a football match between Burton All Saints and Birmingham Gas Works in the Birmingham Cup competition at Burton on Saturday, 2 March 1912. The visiting team had a contingent of between two hundred to three hundred supporters. There were fisticuffs in the ground, and after the match on the canal bank adjoining the ground. Three or four of the combatants fell into the water but were rescued. The trouble was renewed when more than one hundred of the Birmingham supporters missed their return excursion at 6.40 p.m. and tried to rush the station barrier to return on a later train without paying their fares.
>
> The Midland Railway Police and the station porters were overpowered and had to have assistance from the Borough Police. By the time they arrived a crowd in excess of one thousand had gathered in the neighbourhood to witness the struggle. A Constable received a severe injury from a kick over one eye.
>
> The railway station approach was left in a shambles and many clay pipes were lying about. Eventually seven men were arrested.

A large number of the visitors ultimately paid their excess fare and went home. But around 2am on Sunday some twenty to thirty were still at the station, but could not pay the excess fare and most returned home by road.

During the early evening several publicans sent for the Borough Police for assistance due to the rowdyism.

On 21 March 1936, Arsenal fans travelled on a special train from London King's Cross to Huddersfield for an FA Cup semi-final match with Grimsby. On 9 April 1938 a Home International match between England and Scotland was played at Wembley Stadium. Twenty special trains, seven of which came from Scotland, arrived at London Marylebone station. There were no recorded incidents.

During the outbreaks of the two world wars, Football League matches were suspended. Shortly after the cessation of hostilities following the Second World War, football specials resumed on the rail network. People used these and ordinary passenger trains to travel to support their teams, as cars and coaches were far few and between.

From the 1960s we had the dubious distinction of developing a worldwide reputation for football violence – the phenomenon was dubbed the 'English Disease'.

* * *

Mike Spoors was born in Sunderland in 1949. His family were all, and still are, avid Sunderland supporters, so it went without saying that Mike also became a Sunderland fan.

From a very early age Mike recalls going to see Sunderland play, and one game remains firmly planted in his memory:

I was around twelve years of age at the time, so it would have been around 1961. It was a local derby between Newcastle United and Sunderland, which was played at St James' Park Newcastle. I went to the game on the train with my uncle Jimmy. On arrival at Newcastle Central station the fans on the train were escorted to the ground, and I remember being put into a caged area, and that we were not allowed to leave. I can recall men rolling up newspapers and urinating through the tube. At some point a goal was scored and a bottle came from out of the crowd, in another part of the stadium, and struck me on the head causing a cut and bleeding. I was attended to by members of the St John's Ambulance Brigade and then taken to the local Infirmary for treatment. I still have a scar to this day on my forehead.

* * *

From the 1970s, many organised hooligan firms sprang up, with most Football League clubs having at least one known organised hooligan element. Hooliganism was often as its worst when local rivals played each other. Supporters of teams including Chelsea, Leeds United, Millwall, Tottenham Hotspur, Portsmouth FC and West Ham United were among those most frequently linked to hooliganism.

Bob Cook, now a youthful ninety-two years of age, retired in 1977 as a British Transport Police inspector at Hull. He recalls an amusing incident regarding arriving football fans at Hull Paragon railway station:

In the early 1970s whenever Hull City were playing at home we used to meet the fans arriving by train, this could have been a football special with visiting fans on, or an ordinary service train with local fans on. As they went through the ticket barrier onto the concourse we stopped and searched them for weapons, i.e., knives, and knuckledusters. Some even carried hairdressing combs with the handle sharpened to a point.

On one particular occasion I stopped two youths with shoulder-length hair, dressed alike in denim jackets and trousers. To me they looked like two brothers. I searched one youth, then the other and was beginning to run my hands down 'his' body when 'he' spoke to me. To my horror, it was a young woman. I stopped my search and handed her over to a female police constable, even though the girl did not object when I put my hands on her! In those days a lot of the male fans had very long hair – it was all part of the fashion at the time.

Bill Rogerson joined the British Transport Police in 1971 at Birmingham New Street, at a time when football hooliganism was at its height. During the 1950s and early 1960s, football hooliganism on the railway system was at a fairly low level. It began to increase in the late 1960s and continued at high levels well into the 1980s.

He recalls that the British Railways Board had a reserve fleet of rolling stock for exclusive use on football specials, but that the damage caused to the stock ran into many thousands of pounds. This was due to seats being slashed, light bulbs being thrown out of the windows or smashed in their holders, windows being shattered, interior doors being broken, and fire extinguishers being let off and thrown out of the windows, together with anything else that was moveable – even down to the toilet rolls in cubicles.

In an effort to combat the vandalism, the British Railways Board embarked on a joint initiative with the Football League and, on 27 January 1973, a train called the 'League Liner' was launched. This train consisted of a number of coaches that incorporated a bar and a discotheque, complete with flashing lights in the hope that the supporters would have something to take their minds off vandalism on their long journeys. In the end, it was not very successful and was withdrawn three years later.

Wayne Clayton-Robb retired from the BTP as an inspector in September 1992. He has his own memories of football policing on the railway in the 1970s, and early 1980s:

On Sunday 24 April 2016, I travelled, in company with my son Max, from Watford High Street station to Wembley, to watch the FA Cup semi-final between Watford and Crystal Palace.

On entering the station, the atmosphere was friendly and jovial, the station staff were helpful, and access to the platforms was straightforward. Our train was modern, immaculately clean and comfortable. The train had an escort of British Transport Police (BTP) officers, who were relaxed, approachable and quietly in control.

As the train progressed towards Wembley, my mind drifted back to 1973, when I joined the BTP at Euston station. Those were the days of the so-called 'football special', with large numbers of football supporters travelling into London, out of London, and across London. It was also the time when most football clubs attracted a hooligan element, whose major joy in life was to lock horns with those of a similar mindset from other clubs.

A typical Saturday duty in those days would be a twelve-hour spell on the station meeting arrival trains from Manchester, Liverpool, Wolverhampton, etc., and marshalling up to 500 football supporters per train onto the London Underground system, or out of the station premises. There would also be several London teams heading north on football specials or, in some cases such as London-based Manchester United supporters, on normal service trains. With such large numbers moving about the railway system, there were inevitably occasions when the hooligan elements bumped into each other, or actively sought each other out, and serious disturbances would often result, with public order arrests being made.

The first large-scale disturbance I experienced, as a probationary constable, was on the day of the 1974 cup final. Liverpool was playing Newcastle United at Wembley. A considerable number of Liverpool supporters had travelled into Euston and several hundred were assembled on the concourse area. A similar number of Newcastle supporters had travelled into King's Cross, where a faction of them decided to visit Euston to check the Liverpool fans out. As they arrived at the Eversholt Street side of the station, there was a roar, a charge, and the air was filled with an array of missiles of biblical proportions. A swirling mass of fans engulfed Euston Gardens, pursued by each other and the police. The situation was brought under control with the aid of our colleagues from the Metropolitan police and a number of arrests were made. I would add that the vast majority of genuine supporters of both teams chose not to involve themselves in this confrontation.

When not deployed at Euston, officers would either be deployed at outstations that had local football traffic; for instance Watford and Luton were both policed by our division, or would either travel on 'football specials' or service trains where it was known that large numbers of football supporters would be travelling.

It was on static duty at Luton Station that I came face to face with Brian Clough, and several rather ferocious police dogs. Luton was playing Nottingham Forest in the old First Division and a considerable number of Forest fans had travelled by rail. After the match, the Forest team and fans arrived back at the station, only to be met by a volley of missiles thrown by the Luton hooligan element, which had taken a shortcut from the ground and had waited in ambush.

A general disturbance then took place at the front of the station and, as an acting sergeant, I had my officers escort Mr Clough and his team to a safe area of the station and then onto the train. His parting words to me, in that well-known voice, were 'Thank you very much sergeant, for all your help'. On returning to the front of the station, the situation had deteriorated as the increasing volume of returning football supporters added to the general throng. We were then joined by Bedfordshire officers and shortly afterwards by about three police dog vans. Unusually, the vans were shaking and the sound coming from the rear of the vans was a hideous, roaring, growling noise. As the dog handlers opened the rear doors, out burst the most malevolent looking dogs I'd ever set eyes on. They were Rottweilers and they launched towards the brawling fans, who sensibly fled in all directions. A large number of arrests were made.

On another occasion, in early 1975, when I was still a fairly new constable, Luton was playing Chelsea and several thousand Chelsea supporters had made the short trip up to Bedfordshire. After the match, Luton station was swamped with returning Chelsea fans and a number of extra trains had been laid on. I was allocated to a train that was loaded to the brim, but was 'closed stock'. Quite simply, this meant that my group could police the carriage that we were in, but couldn't walk right through the train as one could on an 'open stock' train. So in essence, we had sight and control of everything in the carriages with officers on board, but had no way of knowing what was occurring in the unpoliced carriages. Still, all could have gone well. It didn't!

On the outskirts of London, we became aware that the train was on fire and more experienced officers advised the rest of us that we were heading towards a tunnel, which could potentially have an extremely serious outcome. Fortunately, the train came to a halt in what appeared to be a large railway yard, with numerous sets of railway lines. We got off the train, which was well alight to the rear, and started decanting the Chelsea fans closest to the fire.

We had little option, and no time to liaise with the proper railway authorities, but to run them across the track and then to return to decant the next group. We weren't expecting what happened next, which is that the first group, whom we had escorted to safety, proceeded to bombard us with everything that wasn't nailed down. This group and many others then fled from the railway and into the back streets of North London. This drama received the full treatment in the Sunday newspapers and an investigation was set up headed by Detective Inspector Tommy Baker.

One particular football special that stayed in my memory was one that involved escorting West Ham United supporters to Carlisle, who were playing in the top division at that time. We knew it was to be an early start and a long day. The railway carriages provided for this lengthy away day were very old stock and probably insured against Viking raids. The fans boarded the train, with many of them carrying six and twelve packs of liquid, that the other parts couldn't reach and settled down into various card-schools, drinking-schools and play-schools. Most, of course, just relaxed with the sports pages of the morning papers and discussed their probable line-up for the match. Those were the days of Billy Bond, Frank Lampard snr, and Trevor Brooking; the latter two, along with many other famous players and managers, I had the pleasure of meeting when I was the press steward at Watford FC in the mid-1990s.

After a long and winding trip to Carlisle, I went up to the ground, where an exciting game ended one each. Having never previously been to Carlisle, the view from the ground was spectacular, with sheep grazing from the hillsides. I felt a little sorry for the local police, who were marched into position around the ground to the accompaniment of a loudly whistled Laurel and Hardy theme tune.

Our return journey was uneventful, until we shuddered to an unscheduled halt at Stafford station. Our train was in the 'middle road' – that is, not standing at a platform. On the platform opposite, a large wedding party were peacefully posing for photographs. I was hoping that we would continue our journey before the inevitable happened but alas no, and, very soon, the carriage door windows were wound down and the happy couple were being given some rather ribald advice on how the evening should progress, to the accompaniment of well-known hand gestures. The journey continued without further incident and, after a very long day, the train snaked its way into the platform at Euston.

One football journey that I found particularly memorable took place in March 1978. By this time I was a sergeant and was in charge of the police serial escorting Tottenham Hotspur supporters to Oldham. In what was a rarity for Spurs, they had experienced relegation from the top division, which was then the first division, to division two. The team was littered with many top players, including Peter Taylor, Glen Hoddle and Steve Perryman, among others, and were pushing extremely hard for a prompt return to the top layer of the game.

We took about 500 Spurs fans and, after an uneventful journey, we arrived at Oldham Werneth station. Having never been there before, I was surprised to see that Werneth was very much a countryside halt, consisting of just two platforms. As the train shuddered to a halt, it became clear that only the middle section of carriages was alongside the platform, and several of the front and rear carriages were well clear of it. This resulted in the fans from both ends of the train converging on the central section and a rather squashed, push-and-shove departure from the train. The fans then made their way onto the main road and, as the local police hadn't met the train, we escorted them up towards Boundary Park – Oldham's ground.

On arrival at the ground, I liaised with the local Greater Manchester Police (GMP) commander and he asked me if my serial could escort the Spurs team on and off the pitch. Being a football fan, this was quite a treat. Ironically, in the mid-1990s, having left the police to attend university, I worked for Watford FC as the match-day press steward, and one of the management teams I worked with was Steve Perryman and Peter Taylor. Other Spurs players from the Oldham match included Colin Lee (Watford manager 1990) and Gerard Armstrong (Watford player 1980).

One unusual experience I had occurred in the early 1980s. Tottenham Hotspur had signed the two wonderful Argentinian players Ossie Ardiles and Ricky Villa, and the Spurs supporters had adopted the Argentinian trait of a massive ticker-tape welcome as the teams came onto the pitch. On the day of the match, I had been on duty at White Hart Lane station, which Spurs supporters will know is actually in White Hart Lane, whereas the football ground isn't. Following a very busy duty at the station with thousands of Spurs fans passing through, my sergeant, who was a passionate Spurs fan, suggested that we go up to the ground during our break of duty, so that we could see some of the game. We arrived at the ground and he pointed at a door, told me to go through it and gave me a series of directions for where I had to meet up with him in the ground, as he was going to liaise with the Metropolitan Police match commander.

By the time I'd passed through the door, I'd completely forgotten my sergeant's directions and wandered up and down various passages trying to find my way up to the stands. I finally elected to walk down a particular passage that joined up with a tunnel; this was followed by the 'clunketty clunk' of football boots on concrete as the Spurs team followed me down the tunnel and towards the pitch. There was nowhere to go. I kept walking forward and left the tunnel to a huge roar and a massive ticker-tape reception as I led Spurs onto the pitch! It was with a mixture of pride and embarrassment that I scuttled back down the tunnel to find my sergeant.

Following a number of serious disturbances, Mobile Support Units (MSUs) were introduced in the BTP in 1981. There were twelve nationwide, with three of them based in London. I was the first sergeant on the Anglia Mobile Unit and served with it for three years. We had the dual role of proactively providing reassurance to staff and travellers, and reactively responding to a wide range of public order situations. Strongly featured among these was providing a visible police presence on stations where large numbers of football supporters were travelling from or returning to London. Generally speaking these incidents would be noisy and clearly of concern to the general public; however, on some occasions, large numbers of hooligans would go out of their way to attack travelling fans who they knew would be gathered at one of the London stations. On one such occasion in the early 1980s, Portsmouth and Millwall fans clashed at Waterloo station and my unit were on hand to make a large number of arrests.

Wayne Clayton-Robb concludes his recollections:

On 6 August 1994, I got to meet Ossie Ardiles more formally. He was by then the manager of Spurs and had signed Jürgen Klinsmann two days earlier. By this time, I had left the police and, after a year at the University of Hertfordshire, I had become a primary school teacher in Enfield. My part-time job was as press-steward at Watford FC. Jürgen's debut was in a pre-season friendly at Watford and my job was to facilitate press interviews with Jürgen and Ossie; so, of course, I got to meet both of them. Jürgen was charming, well-spoken and a model professional. Ossie was also charming, approachable and a thoroughly nice man. For a football fan, like me, I had just met two legends – great memories!

Andy Hunt joined the British Transport Police in 1980 and reached the rank of chief inspector before retiring in 2011. His early recollections are as follows:

Around 1985 I was working on one of the Mobile Support Units with the British Transport Police in Birmingham. One of the officers I worked with was Jim Rentell, who went on to become a dedicated football intelligence officer. In the early years I think that the force were very much the 'pioneers' in football intelligence, as we logged the numbers of fans travelling and then passed the details on to local police forces, and submitted intelligence reports.

We escorted football fans on trains all over the country, mainly the Blues – Birmingham City, and Aston Villa. The escorts usually consisted of a sergeant and four PCs and with hundreds of fans travelling you quickly learnt the art of good communication. We built up good relationships with many of the decent fans and I think that a lot of them respected the police.

You need to remember that in those days there were no mobile phones and on the trains we generally had no radio reception – we were on our own! Fortunately the fans didn't know this and I remember on one occasion being on a train with Sergeant Eddy Breakwell, after a Birmingham City versus Watford game, when the fans started to get a bit lively. We went into one of the toilets and put the radios on 'back to back' and then had a conversation, which we knew could be heard outside, in which we made arrangements for other officers to meet the train. It was a complete trick but they calmed down at the thought of a reception committee waiting for them.

You never quite knew what was going to happen on a football train. On one occasion I recall that we had tried to arrest some 'glue sniffers' on the station and one of them had run off. Shortly afterwards I did a football train to Shrewsbury and there he was sat in one of the carriages. Justice was done!

The routine at New Street station on a Saturday, when one of our teams was playing at home, was always the same. At around 5 p.m. home supporters would come to the railway station looking for some sport, with visiting fans going home by train. The Zulus were particularly active and would do constant circuits of the station looking for trouble. As fast as we moved them off through one set of glass doors, they would re-emerge a short time later through the others and back onto the station concourse.

On one occasion I recall having problems with a lad who was a known Zulu. He was with a group of others and for twenty minutes he would just not take 'no' for an answer and leave, so finally I took the unusual step of arresting him for trespass and loitering on the station. He put up a bit of a show for his mates, trying to resist arrest, but there was no rolling around the floor. It was a railway bye-law offence not normally used for this purpose and when we got to court he pleaded not guilty, but the Stipendiary Magistrate Bill Probert thought differently and convicted him.

We also had to bear in mind that opposing fans would often find themselves disembarking from trains on opposite platforms at the same time, or simply passing through north and south, and confrontations would frequently occur. On one occasion I was on duty at Coventry Railway station on my own, when I found myself in one such situation with two groups of up to thirty fans facing off each other. Fortunately the local police came to the rescue pretty quickly!

Chris Hobbs was a police officer, and served for thirty-two years before retiring from the Metropolitan Police Service as a detective sergeant in 2011. He has some early childhood memories of football, before getting into the serious business in later years:

We did things different then. I was escorted the one mile from my home in Hackney on my first day at infant's school and after that I had to make my own way. After taking a belated interest in football, from the age of eleven, I used to take the 236 bus across Hackney Marshes to watch Leyton Orient alone. At twelve years of age I was following my team across the country by supporter's coach, alone, though I quickly made friends over the next few months.

At the ages of fourteen and fifteen, we young 'O's fans formed a football team that played on Sunday mornings in a man's league where we were hammered every week. Sometimes we asked for the hammering, having got back from an Orient away game in the early hours of the morning. By the age of seventeen I had visited half the grounds in the Football League.

Running parallel with my interest in football was a growing interest in the crowds that followed our national game. The transition from friendly scarfed, rattle-waving, smiling fans to mass chanting and singing, involving swaying groups of thousands, was a gradual one.

A visit to Millwall, even in pre-war days, was never for the faint hearted but it was the singing, chanting thousands in Liverpool's Spion Kop, and Manchester United's Stretford End that set the trend. Not only did they lend their extraordinary support to home matches, but legions also travelled away and formed up on the terraces of clubs throughout the country. Gradually other clubs too formed their own choirs of chanting fans, who congregated in their own sections of the ground, such as the Shed at Chelsea, the Park Lane at Tottenham and the North Banks at Arsenal and West Ham. Perhaps inevitably, when home and away supporters ended up in the same part of the ground, disorder began to take place. Arguably one of the most serious occurred at a West Ham versus Manchester United match in the late 1960s, where fighting using flag poles continued throughout the entire match.

Although singing groups of away fans were not uncommon, matters started to change as friendly banter became more sinister, as the 'choirs', in addition to those from Merseyside and Manchester, began to travel away. These 'choirs', however, consisted of youths in their late teens and early twenties, and part of the day out consisted of attempting to 'take' the home side's end.

Travelling away with the Orient became a more precarious business – but then fate intervened. I had long wished to represent my school at football on Saturday mornings, but it was only when in the lower sixth that I was able to fulfil that ambition. A late drop-out saw the 2nd XI captain approach me, and my ambition was fulfilled.

I was asked again the following week, when Orient were playing away. I voted for the school and the die was cast – well, almost. I still went to London derbies and away games during the school holidays. However, many Saturday afternoons were now free and so, after playing and eating pie and mash, I'd pick the most attractive game in London and go and watch it; there was no all ticket hassle then; you just had to turn up, queue and enter.

As it happened, the attractive games would also, in policing terms, be those that today would be classed as high risk. The whole football violence issue became as fascinating as the matches themselves, as did the policing. I witnessed some legendary incidents that have since gone into football hooligan folklore and saw that policing was really struggling to get a grip.

After a thoroughly enjoyable sixth form, I trotted off to Borough Road College to train as a teacher. In my final year, a dissertation in relation to the now headline-catching problem of football hooliganism achieved a straight A and voluminous praise.

A short period of teaching saw me also sign up as a special constable, my brother having joined the regular force. Shortly after joining, I policed my first football match, which was Brentford versus Charlton. The PC I was assigned to seemed less than impressed initially to be lumbered with me but was full of praise at the end of the evening, concluding that 'I seemed to know what I was doing.'

I still trotted along to some high-risk matches and was on reasonable 'acknowledgement' terms with some of the hooligan groups, purely because I was a familiar 'face', but a number of Saturday afternoons were taken up with playing rather than watching. Joining the regular force as a young PC saw more policing of football. An England versus Wales match at Wembley saw carnage as, for once, Cardiff, Swansea and Wrexham hooligan elements forgot their differences and took on England's finest. My mate, who is now a judge in Wales, and I were given the internal concourse to patrol, and we spent the entire match running round it to the numerous fights that were taking place on the terraces.

Simon Pinchbeck joined the Metropolitan Police in 1976 and completed more than twenty-three years' service before leaving the force. He recalls some of his football-related experiences:

Between 1976 and 1986 I was based at Holloway in North London and worked in uniform as a beat officer. Highbury Stadium, the home of Arsenal Football Club, was situated on the division and, as such, I did regular football duties. They used to start officers off by posting them to the quieter areas of the ground, where the young kids used to gather, and then ultimately you would find yourself in the thick of it.

They used to have a squad to deal with rowdy behaviour on the North Bank home end, and another team of officers for the Clock End to deal with away supporters. I was regularly in one of these two teams.

Arsenal had a hooligan firm called The Herd, and the fun always began when Arsenal played another big London club. They were generally not violent towards the police. I had a big moustache at the time, and eventually the supporters gave me the nickname of 'The Walrus'. Being 6 foot 3 inches tall, I thought that I could look after myself.

Every time that Arsenal played Chelsea, West Ham or Tottenham Hotspur, there was a lot of trouble. One of the problems was that the fans all had the same accents and, as none of them wore club colours, it was sometimes difficult to tell who was who. Before I joined the police I used to go to matches myself and developed a sixth sense for trouble. It often happened just before kick-off and would frequently erupt into mass fighting on the terraces. I never feared for my safety and was often one of the first to get in among them.

I can describe one game in particular, on 2 May 1982, when Arsenal was playing at home to West Ham. I remember it well as it was just three weeks before I was to get married. There was something different about the day. The atmosphere was different and we were dealing with fans at the height of the activities of West Ham's so-called Inter City Firm, who were notorious hooligans.

On this day the ICF infiltrated the North Bank from several directions in a pre-planned attack, and trapped a number of Arsenal fans in the middle in a pincer movement. Someone let off a big red smoke bomb and I found myself right in the middle of it. As the smoke swirled around, there was fighting everywhere on the terraces. The game was stopped and trouble spilt over onto the pitch. Foolishly I thought everyone was going to follow me but I found myself isolated and, on this occasion, some of the fans decided to attack me. I was literally fighting for my life. I was at one stage the police heavyweight boxing champion for the Metropolitan Police and, before that day, I had thought that the blue uniform could save me from anything – but at that moment I felt very vulnerable and it did have an effect on me.

Eventually the cavalry arrived and we managed to restore some sort of order inside the ground. About an hour after the end of the game a young Arsenal fan was surrounded by a group of West Ham fans and was stabbed to death.

I got to know a lot of the hooligans over a period of time and that helped a great deal because they understood that whatever they did they would not be able to get away with it. We were fair with them but very firm.

I remember one occasion in the 1980s when I got my dad and my brother some tickets for Arsenal at Christmas for a game with Chelsea. I was on duty and waved to them as they went off to get something to eat before the game started. I suddenly became aware of a confrontation on the terraces and, within a short space of time, found myself with my truncheon in one hand trying to separate the main Chelsea lad, who actually was a black lad with one arm, and one of the main Arsenal boys, as they squared up to each other.

In 1986 a book was written called *WPC Courage* by Norman Lucas. The book recounts numerous incidents of bravery by female police officers, including a number related to football violence during this period, when officers routinely found themselves fighting with hooligans to restore order, often outnumbered and regularly receiving injuries. Three specific incidents are referred to in this book.

In October 1977 Brighton played Crystal Palace at Hove, Sussex. Rival football fans began fighting between themselves as they made their way to Hove railway station. Police officers, including PC Sheena Rankin, who was aged nineteen years and had only been on the beat with Sussex Constabulary for three weeks, intervened. She was kicked and punched, receiving a brutal blow in the back from the thugs. She had to be taken to hospital. The ambulance conveying her to the hospital had to crawl along at a walking pace, as it was thought that her injuries were very serious. After a series of X-rays, it was established that her spine had not snapped but was badly bruised. Over a period of weeks she managed to move and walk again.

On 23 February 1980 Bristol Rovers played Chelsea at Rover's Eastville Stadium, Bristol. A group of football supporters began fighting between themselves. The youths started to throw stones and hurl road signs and cans – in fact, anything upon which they could get their hands. The police officers who attended the scene were heavily outnumbered. One officer, PC Monica Harris, was one of the officers, who in total numbered around a dozen. She noticed a large mob of around thirty fighting under the motorway bridge and saw a motorcycle officer, PC Brandon, among the thugs and on the ground, being kicked and battered. His head and body had been viciously beaten. PC Harris pushed her way between the thugs and threw herself across him to protect him from further injuries and waited for help to arrive. She received nothing more than a few bruises.

The crowd began to disperse and made their way to the nearby railway station, smashing windows and causing general mayhem and havoc on the way. A number of fans were arrested. It transpired that PC Brandon had attempted to arrest one of them for throwing stones, and other fans had jumped and attacked him. At the subsequent trial, one of the youths finished his evidence by saying that, if it hadn't been for the female police officer intervening, PC Brandon would have received more serious injuries.

In 1982, PC Sarah Rogers, who joined the Staffordshire Police in March 1980, was on duty in Stoke-on-Trent after a match between

Stoke City and West Ham United. At around 5 p.m., she was on duty alone when she saw two large groups of rival supporters who were obviously about to clash. She tried to turn each crowd away, as she anticipated and feared the violent consequences. She coolly displayed a complete and utter disregard for her own safety during the mêlée.

Sarah was punched in the face, which resulted in her nose being smashed by a powerfully built football hooligan aged around nineteen. Despite bleeding profusely she gave chase, but he escaped into the crowds. Following the incident Sarah was off sick for more than three weeks. Fortunately she didn't suffer any permanent ill effects from her injury.

The chief constable awarded her a commendation for her action and her 'meritorious and courage devotion to duty'.

When Mark Whitehouse was about five years old, together with his classmates, he listened to a Lewis Carroll 'nonsense' poem called 'The Hunting of the Snark', which struck a chord with some of his friends. From that moment he became known as Mark 'Snark', and it stuck with him in later life. Mark is one of the co-authors of *Sons of Albion*, which was published in 2009; to use his own words, it recalls the history of the 'casual' culture of West Bromwich FC followers. In respect to football hooliganism, he says, 'I agree that the hooliganism of the 1980s should not be glorified, but it was an important part of the British Youth Movement and, as a twenty-year-old growing up in the 1970s and 1980s, I would say that it did affect a lot of young working-class lads.'

In 1981 Desmond Morris wrote a book called *The Soccer Tribe*, in which he alludes to this phenomenon in the following terms:

Sociologists studying the background of offenders have found that, time and again, it is the young men from the more deprived areas of the city or the town, living out their daily lives in crowded slums, or boring, soulless housing estates, who are the typical offenders. Their outbursts of violence have little to do with the Soccer Tribe itself, which merely acts as a dramatic stage on which they can perform. Since society has given them little chance to express their manhood in a positive or creative manner, they take the only course of action left to them apart from dumb subservience and strike out in a negative and destructive way. They know that at least they will not then be ignored and that they will be able to make their mark on society, even if it is only a scar on someone else's body.

Mark Whitehouse further recalls,

My great-grandad Sammy Richardson played for Albion and England, and my great-uncle Bill Richardson was also a player at the Albion. My dad took me to my first Albion game when I was just fourteen months old and I have been going ever since.

With hindsight it was probably a mistake to do the book as it put a label on me. Even these days I come in for some attention from the police, filming me and that, but I keep telling them I'm just not into that sort of thing, and avoid any form of aggression.

I've never been one to say that I was actually a criminal or a football hooligan. I would never call myself that. I think that a 'football hooligan' is an all-encompassing way to describe, on the one hand, someone who might get involved just once in hooliganism, and the psychopaths who get involved in the serious stuff. I have never done what I would call a crime like a burglary, or a robbery, stuff like that.

I did find myself in trouble a couple of times in the 1980s for public order, and a Section 18 wounding, which was not football related, plus I was arrested in Japan in 2002, the first time I went to an away England game, but was released after three days. I hadn't done anything wrong – I just got scooped up with a load of other people over an allegation of theft.

The Section 5 Public Order charge was after a home game with West Ham. I was walking home with my cousin and some West Ham fans smacked him in the mouth. There was a group of West Bromwich fans nearby, and I shouted to them to come over and help us. I got nicked by a copper and got fined about £160, which was a lot in those days, as I was only earning £17.50 a week at the time and had to pay it off in instalments.

My problem in the 1980s was that I wouldn't back away from anyone. Back then I belonged to a group of 'casuals' who supported West Bromwich Albion. We used to go to away games in a coach that we hired ourselves. We used to call ourselves 'The Clubhouse', because we always met to travel away at the Throstles Club next to the ground. It's true that we did sometimes get involved in fights with the opposition, but it was always with like-minded people. It wasn't organised stuff in those days. We had no mobile phones. Every team had a 'firm' attached to it and confrontations were inevitable.

At the time I was interested in the Mod scene, Ska music, and bands such as The Jam and The Specials. Clothing at the time was all about early Fred Perry jumpers. This was all part of the culture I was involved in.

I formed close relationships with all of these lads, which even to this day are still very strong. I was in my twenties then, and I'm fifty-five years old now, but we still keep in regular touch. It was about having a sense of belonging and looking after each other. Some used to say I was a 'leader' but I don't look at it that way. I was just good at organising and keeping us together to stay safe.

Over the years we developed a healthy respect for some of the main characters in some of the other firms and, nowadays, when we meet up it's all about socialising and reminiscing at boxing events and stuff like that. West Bromwich Albion is a huge part of my life. It's a family thing. If someone insulted my wife or someone close to me I would want to do something about it. West Bromwich Albion for me invoked the same sort of feelings as a twenty-year-old. It probably sounds daft now but that's how I felt. In those days we were mainly white working-class kids and being part of the scene gave us a purpose.

Steve Burrows completed thirty years' police service in the West Midlands Police and Warwickshire Police before retiring. His recollections serve to provide examples of events that occurred in the 1980s during the height of football hooliganism in city centres and stadiums across the UK, week in and week out.

I began my police career on 3 October 1983 at Acocks Green police station, on the E3 sub-division, which was one third of the 'E' Division, the other two sub-divisions being Bromford Lane and Stechford. The 'E' Division had the dubious honour of hosting St Andrew's football ground, home to Birmingham City FC.

The outcome of this was that I regularly spent many 'happy' hours on the touchline and terraces of St Andrew's during my first eighteen months of service. My abiding memory is that it was the coldest I had ever been. The joke was that there was nothing between St Andrew's and the Ural Mountains, and much of a match would be spent taking turns warming up in the hot air from the outlet vent on the hot-dog stand. The football tended not to warm anything and, being an Albion fan, I steadfastly ignored the seduction of watching the local rival's efforts.

In those days there were not many stewards, and we policed both inside and outside the stadium. It was thought to be good experience for young officers to police the football and it certainly resulted in a good grounding in the handling of public order situations. One became quite skilful at sensing tension and discerning between good-natured obscene chanting and that which preceded the 'You're gonna get your fuckin' heads kicked in' pre-scuffling war cry. It was also possible to spot a likely troublemaker in the crowd, and to 'nip a problem in the bud' by way of a fast two-man raid into the crowd and an ejection before anyone around them became sufficiently aroused to care.

One also came to know the troublesome clubs in terms of supporters. Blues were one of the worst, The Zulu Warriors being at their peak of mischief in the mid-eighties. One of the others was Leeds United, a club on the descent from the glory days of Don Revie. On 11 May 1985, Leeds was due to play at St Andrew's, in the old division two – the final match of the season. It was rumoured that the Leeds 'firm' intended to stop the match, thus pissing off the Zulus. One should remember that this period was at the peak of football violence: fences had gone up at the grounds; trouble was always expected as the rival 'firms' vied for the perverted glory of causing the most trouble; and they were often pre-arranging fights with each other, inside or outside the ground. More trouble than usual was thus anticipated by us regulars at the ground.

I recall that, a couple of days before the match, I was sent to Sheldon police station to pick up some paperwork. I bumped into the football intelligence officer, who asked me if I was going to be at the Leeds match on that Saturday. He then confirmed that he had seen reports to suggest that there were going to be big problems, and that the Leeds fans were going to attend *en masse* to mark the end of the season with a massive fight.

He delighted in telling me, however, that the 'gaffers' didn't believe the intelligence and had decided not to put any more officers on duty than they would for a normal Category A match, especially as they were expecting trouble at the West Bromwich Albion versus Arsenal match a few miles away, and had deployed the Operational Support Unit there.

The OSU was the crème de la crème of public order policing in West Midlands Police. They were specialist units, trained in public order techniques and formed into serials of one sergeant and ten constables per van. They were renowned for playing practical jokes, especially the dark art of 'spinning', which involved attracting the attention of anyone passing by, and causing them to turn round, at which point the 'spinner' would look away and general guffawing would ensue. All fine juvenile stuff, but it no doubt got them through long hours sat in a van, waiting to be deployed. The OSU could always be recognised by the fact that they wore their helmet chinstraps down and their black gloves when entering combat.

They were bloody useful in pitched battle, though, and it was not music to my ears to find that they were going to be several miles away on the Saturday of this match.

Steve continues the story of events as they unfolded on the actual day:

'Ours was not to reason why,' as Tennyson once said, and so it was that I found myself sat in the Railway End stand at St Andrew's that Saturday morning for the match briefing, looking around at what appeared to be far too few officers scattered in the seats, and thinking that this could be an interesting afternoon.

The briefing began. All the usual stuff I had heard many times before, including the essential information regarding being fed. The briefing then detailed 'Contingencies'. From memory, the plans went thus. Plan A was standard policing at the ground. Plan B was that, in the event of trouble, we were to get in between the opposing fans and keep them apart – a tactical masterpiece! I can recall a fair amount of muttering from my colleagues about our numbers and the anticipated trouble as we left the stand following briefing.

Following the essential feeding and watering, I took up my duty post on the touchline at the Railway End. This was where the family enclosure was situated, a 'safe area' in which rosy-cheeked young Blues fans could come with their parents to follow the generally depressing fortunes of Birmingham City. Thus there was no fencing at this end of the ground. This was before the Hillsborough disaster, when the caging of fans was common at football grounds. The visiting fans end had a full security fence and this is where the Leeds fans were to be housed for the match, and for some time afterwards.

I said that tension could be sensed after policing many matches and, as I took my place on the touchline at about one-thirty, I could taste it, never mind sense it. As I looked around the ground, the situation was not looking promising. I could see that there were already several thousand Leeds fans in the ground and they appeared to be in a volatile mood. They had an awful reputation and lived up to it that afternoon. They were already throwing missiles. A speciality I had encountered at Elland Road, following the Albion several years before, was the skimming of coins, some with sharpened edges; on this occasion I recall parts of seats flying over the fence, together with sundry other objects. They then put in a spot of team effort and proceeded to remove the roof from the hot-dog stand, pass it down the terraces over their heads and throw it over the fence. Still, at least they were fenced in.

The situation at my fenceless end of the ground also began to deteriorate. I had spent much of the previous eighteen months policing the Gospel Oak Estate in Acocks Green, together with parts of Tyseley and Sparkhill. I had learnt to recognise by sight many of the troublemakers that would frequent the pubs of Acocks Green and The Gospel, often ending their drink-fuelled nights out by kicking in a few windows and fighting.

A number of well-known delinquents also specialised in assaulting police officers if they saw a chance of outnumbering a lone officer. Thus, as I viewed the gathering crowd in the seats at The Railway End, I started to spot familiar faces. Not excited youngsters, but a selection of those local troublemakers with whom

I had regularly crossed swords, many of whom were members of the infamous Zulu Warriors. Such were their numbers that it gradually dawned upon me that they had arranged to infiltrate the Railway End, where there was no fence. To this day I believe that the day's subsequent events had been orchestrated to some extent between the Zulu Warriors and the Leeds fans in advance.

The match began and, for much of the first half, the situation remained tense but without incident. The half-time whistle was the signal for the first pitch invasion and – surprise, surprise – it came from the Railway End. In the light of what came later, this was, I suppose, a minor skirmish, but half time was a lengthy affair, accompanied by missiles and some robust policing that eventually restored order.

This was clearly just a scouting mission, the lull before the storm. The second invasion at the end of the match involved hundreds of youths, all Birmingham fans, and all from the Railway End. Seats were ripped up and skimmed as missiles. I recall being hit on the arm by one; it was thrown from such close range that I saw who did it. Being a resourceful cop, I assessed my surroundings and realised that a large white net would be of use in this situation. I found the goal very effective to shelter from several volleys of missiles; in fact I probably spent more time in it than the ball had that season.

We were clearly losing the battle, heavily outnumbered and in possession of no riot gear. One of my clearest memories was the sergeant in charge of my section running along the touchline shouting, 'That's it lads, fuck Plan A and Plan B, it's Plan C, every man for themselves.' It was time for a tactical withdrawal, as being left alone in the goal was looking increasingly risky.

An irony not lost upon me, even as I fought on the pitch, was that the other end was by now policed by the OSU in full riot gear, including NATO-style crash helmets with visors and shields. They had been diverted from the Albion versus Arsenal match at half time; someone had made a good decision after the half-time ruckus. The OSU were in line, on the touchline, facing the fence in front of them and, if you watch the film of the riot, they can be seen discouraging the Leeds fans from climbing over the fence and onto the pitch with as good a display of synchronised 'truncheoning' as ever seen. I don't think many Leeds fans got over that fence.

If they had done so in numbers, there would have been very serious consequences as we would have been caught between the fans with nowhere to go – Plan B in all its glory!

Meanwhile, on the other half of the pitch, we had no riot gear, no shields, wooden truncheons and no fence. The battle lines between us and the pitch invaders ebbed back and forth and, at one stage, I was nearly in the centre tunnel, thinking that, if we got backed into there, we would get a good hiding.

The day was saved by the affectionately termed 'donkey wallopers'. In those golden days, before budget cuts, the West Midlands Police still had a large mounted section. Whenever I watch a historical film depicting battle with cavalry, I'm reminded of that moment. I quickly appreciated the effectiveness of horses against foot soldiers. It was like the Charge of the Light Brigade, especially in relation to the white horse who continually rode backwards and forwards, knocking the hooligans over like ninepins, and was later immortalised in an oil-painting. The horses drove the mass of the invaders inexorably back towards the stand.

Encouraged by this development, we were formed into a line with pegs drawn and mounted a ferocious foot charge. I remember an assistant chief constable was next to me, laying into marauding fans like a 'good 'un', and, in a beautiful moment of poetic justice, I came face to face with the seat thrower who had injured me earlier. I am afraid that he enjoyed our reunion a lot less than I did.

We finally beat – and I mean 'beat' – the hooligans on the pitch back. They had to be encouraged all the way, while they threw missiles and kicked and punched any police officer to whom they could get close enough. We beat them back into the seats and I can remember a number of them being hauled up onto the upper tier by others in order to escape our advance.

Their resistance and momentum broke, and they fled the ground. A kind of peace descended – time for a breather! I could see that the ground was clear, bar the Leeds fans penned behind their fence by the OSU. They were not to be released until the Birmingham fans had been dealt with and marshalled away from them, the ground and the railway station. 'Job done', I thought. The chief inspector, quite rightly, had other ideas.

He formed us up on the centre line, praised us, and then transmitted the unwelcome news that trouble outside the ground needed sorting out and that we were the only ones available to do it. There were about thirty of us I guess, in various states of injury and exhaustion, none of us having any riot gear as yet. We exited the ground into Garrison Lane. In those days you came out onto a road that led to a children's playground, set at a much lower level than was visible from where we were standing.

About 100 yards away I could see thirty to forty 'scufflers' milling about, and the CI decided that another baton charge would be appropriate. We formed into a line, drew our pegs and, with a blood-curdling cry, of which William Wallace would have been proud, off we went. As we got closer, the hooligans began to run, disappearing out of sight over the edge and down the drop into the playground.

Encouraged by this success, our momentum increased, fuelled by a touch of red mist – it had been a long day by then. As we drew closer to the playground, which was a large tarmacadam area, it began to become visible. This revealed a daunting prospect. I was right next to the chief inspector, and I can remember shouting, 'Gaffer, gaffer, can you see what's down there?' He was in full charge mode, but eventually realised that the playground was actually occupied by several hundred youths busily ripping the swings out of the ground to use as weapons. As we appeared a primeval roar went up and, as one, we skidded to a halt at the edge of the drop. The CI shouted, in true Monty Python fashion, 'Fuck me, right lads, retreat,' and we retraced our charge at about the same speed. Our pursuers stopped to turn over a police van, which probably saved us, as reinforcements arrived in the form of a phalanx of police motorcyclists known as 'scruffies', who had the advantage of crash helmets and full leathers. As luck would have it, the overturned van belonged to the OSU and was full of shields that we joyfully liberated, joining our rescuers in chasing the crowd off.

Saturday afternoons at the football did not end there. The next stop after any home match for the Zulus was traditionally Birmingham city centre, and I can remember having to walk from the ground into Birmingham, shield before me, chasing football hooligans. It took a further hour or so before we could be sure that the majority of troublemakers had either gone home, or begun their normal evening of drinking, a curry, a fight and a night in the cells. The 'F' Division, Digbeth and Steelhouse Lane, had plenty on duty as it was a Saturday evening, including extra resources due to trouble being anticipated after the match, and so we were glad to finally hand the task of keeping order over to them for the rest of the evening.

I arrived back at Acocks Green police station at about half-past seven, with a bruised arm and enough war stories to last for the next few months. When I got home I expected to have been part of big news, but it was the same day as the Bradford Fire Disaster, which rightly overshadowed an event that was probably one of the worst instances of football violence ever seen in England.

I must not conclude without mentioning the tragic death of fifteen-year-old Ian Hambridge at his first ever football match, when a 12-foot wall collapsed at St Andrew's at the height of the riot. It is believed that he was sheltering from the violence under the wall – a truly innocent victim of football hooliganism.

Steve Burrows concludes his recollection with an encounter that was typical of its time:

I left the 'E' Division, St Andrew's, and the Zulu Warriors behind in November 1986 and became a response (999) shift sergeant at Steelhouse Lane, Birmingham city centre.

Saturday afternoons were always chaos, with shoplifters galore queuing up to go into a cell, and tying up valuable officer time. Most were just kids and were cautioned, but it still took a much-needed resource off the streets. It was always busy and, for some reason, we always seemed short of staff. That was the situation on 21 November 1987 as I grabbed a ten-minute break at 6.30 p.m. With me in the rest-room were two female police officers, likewise attempting to eat as quickly as possible before the next job came in. We managed fifteen minutes before being turned out to a report that a large crowd of Zulu Warriors were rampaging along Digbeth High Street towards the city centre, damaging cars and fighting.

On this date Birmingham City played away to Manchester City at Maine Road in a match that Birmingham lost 3-0 in a League division two game. My recollection is that this group had been playing up on a train that had just got back from Manchester.

The three of us jumped in a Panda car and, while we were driving, an assistance call came over the radio. This meant that an officer was in trouble and the rule was that one dropped everything and made for the scene to help them. The location given was Stephenson Street, next to the ramp from the Pallasades shopping centre. As we arrived, I saw two officers struggling with a fighting youth under the walkway that ran along Stephenson Street and adjoined the ramp.

I got out and ran towards them. As I did so, a large group of youths rounded the corner at the Hill Street end of the road. They were chanting 'Zulu, Zulu', yelling obscenities and behaving in a disorderly manner; I knew that meant trouble unless nipped in the bud, and they did not look amenable to reasoned argument. A large crowd of shoppers had already gathered on the ramp and walkway, clearly intent on watching the forthcoming spectacle from a safe distance. This was one of those moments to grit your teeth, stand up to be counted, and pray!

One youth in particular seemed to be leading this group and egging them on to attack the police officers present, shouting, 'Come on, let's get the cunts.' I could see that his efforts at rabble-rousing were having an effect and the group began to square up against us.

The ringleader was some 10 yards ahead of the rest of the group and, as we approached each other, he shouted to me, 'Come on you bastard, let's have a go.' This was accompanied by another round of Zulu chants from the group.

It was one of those moments in my police service when the world stood still for a second or two. You realise that you are the 'thin blue line' and it's down to you to sort it out. My mind raced through options, although there were not many really to consider, and I confess that I'd well and truly lost my temper with this idiot. I decided that taking him out was the only option: it might give the rest pause for thought, or I might get a good kicking. I knew from the radio that lots of other officers were en route, so it was a calculated risk and I really wanted to sort him out in front of the watching crowd, to dissuade the others.

As I approached, he threw a punch at me and we had a good old-fashioned scuffle. My favoured option in these circumstances was the full nelson, and I managed to get the hold on as we both fell forward onto the pavement. He softened my fall beautifully and this had the effect of taking some of the fight out of him for a moment or two.

I pinned him to the floor and he started screaming to a youth nearby, 'Get the bastard off me, come on, and help me.' Luckily the other youths seemed rather taken aback by the turn of events, and did nothing; by this time my two fellow female officers had reached us and he backed off. Other officers began arriving and battle behind me began in earnest.

My opponent was screaming at the top of his voice for help and struggling so violently that he had to be lifted bodily by four of us and carried to a nearby police vehicle. What amused me was the round of applause from the spectators on the walkway above. I returned to the fray where, by now, over thirty youths were in combat with officers, several of whom were on the floor struggling. Traffic had stopped and shoppers were screaming and running for cover. There were about 200 people watching from above. Eventually it took over 100 officers and fifteen minutes to restore order.

My arrestee was taken to Digbeth police station and later charged with violent disorder.

As we walked back to the Panda car, one of the female officers said, 'I've never seen you lose your temper before Sarge, but you did then, didn't you?' I said, 'What makes you think that?', to which she replied, 'I could see the vein in your forehead throbbing and knew he was going to have it!'

My second and final close encounter with the Zulus.

Deirdre 'Dee' Cobley retired from the British Transport Police in May 2008, with twenty-eight years' service, having acted as a constable on the London South Division, one of the busiest areas for football policing in the capital. Her recollections of football-related incidents between 1994 and 1998 are as poignant and relevant now as they were then. Some are good; most are bad; and a couple are ugly.

In one instance she recalls being attacked on a train:

I was with Barry Castle policing a football train that was coming into East Croydon. It was in the days when we frequently escorted trains with very few officers. I think that we may have been policing Brighton fans but I am not totally sure. The train was heaving with supporters, and Barry and I were the only officers on the train. The fans started playing up and we radioed in asking for officers to meet us on the platform. Just prior to arriving at East Croydon, the supporters managed to separate us. It was a very deliberate pincer movement and a very determined effort. I knew something was about to happen, so I tried to get to the door so that I could get off the train as quickly as possible. In those days it was the old 'slam-door' stock.

As I did so, and as the train was pulling into the platform, several of the supporters indecently assaulted me. Their hands were all over the place, up my skirt, touching my breasts; I just had to do whatever I could to protect myself. I was determined not to 'go down without a fight', with one or two of them receiving some nasty scratches, that's for sure, and I pulled quite a lot of hair. I actually jumped off the train while it was still moving!

Needless to say there was no one waiting for us on the platform. It shocked me to the core, I must admit. I did report it but nobody seemed that interested, so it was just left. In those days it was all just seen as part of the job. I learned a valuable lesson that day!

On another occasion, again at Croydon, I was standing on a platform as a fast train went through with loads of football fans heading into London. I had my back to the train, when suddenly I felt a full can of lager go whistling past my ear, which then exploded on the floor in front of me with some force. It had been thrown out of the window by one of the fans and the thought of what might have happened had it hit me on the head scared me more than when I was attacked.

Dee goes on,

On another occasion I was posted to Watford to assist with visiting fans from one of the Manchester clubs. While at the station, a train came in, and one of the passengers on board became ill and collapsed on the platform. He stopped breathing. An officer by the name of 'Slim' Townsend, who had been in the Ambulance Service, but is sadly no longer with us, started doing CPR on him, while I started doing mouth-to-mouth resuscitation. We were on the floor with him when a train with football fans arrived and, as they got off, several of them kicked out at us as we were trying to revive the man. It was unbelievable. I was right by the side of the track. They made their way into town and there were fights all over the place. It later turned out that the man's pacemaker had stopped working and he survived. We later got a certificate for our actions on the day.

On another occasion I was on a train with football fans travelling through Millwall country, a couple of stops outside London Bridge. I was in the guard's brake with a number of other officers, when suddenly we were showered with bricks and rocks in what was clearly an ambush. We literally had to hit the floor to avoid the bricks coming through the glass.

Dee Cobley recalls another incident, which restored her faith in human nature somewhat:

I was at Fulham Broadway with some other officers, including a DC by the name of Jeff Hull. A train came in with some Leeds fans on. As we were trying to get them up the stairs and off the platform, a load of Fulham fans arrived on another platform on the LU Overground section. We put a line of officers between the two sets of fans to try to keep them apart and, while this was going on, Jeff saw one fan take a metal tail-comb out, which he was obviously going to use as a weapon. It was impossible to hold them back and, for our own safety, the sergeant told us to break the cordon. As we did so, I got swept towards the track just as another train came in.

I found myself squashed up against the carriages of this train – it was unbearable and I was really frightened about what would happen if the train started to move off. Suddenly this arm came one side of me, followed by another arm on my other side. I looked around in the crush and it was a man wearing a Fulham scarf who had actually put himself between me and the crush, and was holding his hands against the carriage to give me space to breath.

I always remember him saying 'You're alright love. I'll look after you.' I couldn't thank him enough.

Andy Hunt, retired BTP officer, continues,

In 1999 I went to London Underground as an inspector and, within a short space of time, I developed a great deal of respect for the control room staff, who were experts at predicting where and how fans would travel on the network. It was a game whereby fans would try to avoid travelling on services with a police presence, whereas we wanted to be one step in front all the time.

When I was working at Baker Street I used to liaise closely with the management of the Globe pub and the Metro Bar. This location was a crossover point for fans travelling to Wembley, and thus it was a flashpoint. Likewise, when I was OIC at Finsbury Park, I was closely involved in monitoring travelling fans visiting the Arsenal ground. As a crossover for the Piccadilly and Victoria lines, Saturdays proved to be extremely busy as many of them made use of Arsenal tube station.

Former PC Simon Pinchbeck recalls Euro '96:

I left the Territorial Support Group in 1995 but, in 1996, for Euro '96 I was involved with intelligence gathering and prevention. I was in one of five teams performing this task. We were all billeted in a section house in South London and deployed from there to the games. Our job was to find the potential troublemakers for the England games before they found the trouble.

The one game was the Scotland game. All the London clubs were meeting in the Edgware Road, while the Midlands clubs were meeting at the Swiss Cottage. I was aware that Chelsea's top guy was putting himself forward as the leader of England, but not everyone was in agreement. We knew that Scotland's fans, casuals from Aberdeen and Dundee United, were somewhere in the Barnet area.

In a pub in Cockfosters, North London, we found hooligans from Carlisle, Shrewsbury, and Grimsby, and took them to Wembley to avoid disorder. At Trafalgar Square later there was major disorder, but it was actually the Category B and C supporters in drink more than the main boys. Any German-made car got wrecked and we spent the whole of the night with our truncheons out going from incident to incident.

On 15 June 1996, England played Scotland in a UEFA Euro '96 match in front of a crowd of 76,864. It was a game that England ultimately won 2-0 but, off the pitch, London was the focus for disorder.

'ED' was a police officer based in London at the time and recalls the following:

I was part of a serial driving around in a plain white minibus. We were on spotting duties. I remember pre-match we were observing a Middlesbrough group in The Allsop Arms, near Baker Street, and they suddenly moved off *en masse* onto Euston Road, literally in the road, with us following. All of a sudden they began to run and were heading towards The Globe to attack it. Someone shouted to the driver to stop the van. For some strange reason, he wanted to park it properly, but we shouted at him to stop in no uncertain terms and jumped out. We had the Boro group just in front of us and we managed to stop a confrontation – but only just. There were some serious-risk fans about. Later on we ended up at Leicester Square, where the atmosphere was extremely tense. I recall seeing a very well-known risk supporter called Andy at the entrance to Leicester Square tube and, just after that, a group came round the corner from The Porcupine Pub – I believe that they were Chelsea. Next thing we see the Middlesbrough lot coming towards us from the Covent Garden direction. I remember jumping out of the van and confronting a huge guy called Neil and shouting at him to get back as they moved towards the Chelsea group. Again, we were in the thick of it! Post-match we were in the Strand, and there had been very serious disorder in Trafalgar Square, with cars set alight. There was disorder between England and Scotland fans and, as we turned into one of the streets, we suddenly noticed shops being looted. Heavily outnumbered and with no shields, the reality was that there was not a lot that we could do. It was a really scary moment, and another disgraceful night of football violence.

Finally, Dee Cobley remembers some lighter moments, when police humour came to the fore:

> In April 2002 an organised fight occurred at Maze Hill railway station between a number of Charlton Athletic fans and Southampton fans. A post-incident investigation was launched called Operation Fabric*, which I was a part of. We had about 2,000 exhibits and lots and lots of mobile-phone records. DI Karl Skrzypiec was the senior investigating officer and, at one stage, we had to go to a meeting with the senior prosecuting barrister, who was a real character. It was raised during the meeting that one of the defendants was going to say that he had a lot of hooligan books in his room because he was doing a thesis on the subject. I quipped 'So what was Maze Hill then, his practical exercise?', and everyone laughed. The court case went on for months at Kingston Crown Court in 2004 and one of the defendants was called 'Billy'. He insisted that no one had contacted him in advance to tell him about the fight and the prosecuting barrister said to him, 'Are you sure that your name is not Billy-no-mates?'
>
> At the end of the trial Karl was outside trying to do a live television interview with Sky News. We could see him from a window inside and someone suggested phoning him on his mobile. It was a bit naughty really, but it was funny to watch as Karl was desperately trying to turn his phone off while live on camera. That's police humour for you!
>
> * *Operation Fabric is dealt with in the book*, Tracking the Hooligans – A History of Football Violence on the UK Rail Network.

Despite seventy-six football banning orders being obtained by the BTP in 2009, football-related violence increased on the rail network during the 2009/10 football season, with sixty-eight serious incidents recorded, and 582 incidents classified as anti-social behaviour. Twenty-one BTP officers were assaulted.

The number of persons dealt with for offences increased by 49 per cent.

Andy Hunt concludes,

In 2010, I was in London when I saw PC Jim Rentell at Charing Cross railway station. He was involved in some sort of force operation targeting football hooliganism. I was struck by the fact that, after twenty-five years, there he was still grappling with the same issue as we had done in the mid-1980s. In those days things were much more overtly violent. The problem has not gone away but, in my opinion, it is now more isolated, and technology has changed the face of hooliganism with the availability of mobile phones and social media. As long as the potential for groups to confront each other continues to exist, whether that is on religious, political, or sporting grounds, the police will continue to face huge challenges.

The responsibility for policing events on the rail network does not rest totally within the domain of the BTP, with large numbers of trained security staff playing a key role in ensuring the safety of passengers and the smooth running of trains. It can sometimes be routine work, and occasionally mundane, but it is nonetheless important. Carl Jarvis describes one such experience of managing the movement of football fans in 2011:

I am a railway enforcement officer for Southeastern Railway. My primary roles include high-visibility patrols on trains and stations; I deal with low-level crime, and tackle anti-social behaviour around the Southeastern network. The role includes operations working alongside British Transport Police and Kent Police.

I came onto the railway from an educational background; it was like stepping into a totally different world, with a complete set of new rules to be learned. Some people expected to travel for free and, if questioned, threats and violence quickly followed. There were the chancers, who, if found without valid authorisation, would make up a story that was usually the same as everyone else's – vary rarely did I hear something original, or even entertaining. Lastly, there were also the genuine passengers who just wanted to get from A to B on time and with as little fuss as possible.

Every week, as rail enforcement officers, we received a weekly brief on where to patrol. Occasionally an event would be on, which would mean crowd control and standing around waiting for something to kick off – more often than not, it did.

I remember the first time of seeing GLM F/B on our roster. This meant a football match at Gillingham. After asking the obvious question of who they were playing, the reply was Millwall. I was nine months into the job at the time in 2011, and this was to be a new experience for me. My experience of football was very limited. In my teens I had been to a few games, and felt the boots on my toes as I entered and the scary excitement of being escorted out and away from the ground at the end – what got me the most was the sheer numbers of people.

On the day of the Millwall game, our team of enforcement officers made our way to Gillingham, and all I could think of on the way was, 'we're Millwall, no one likes us, and we don't care' – the favourite chant of their fans. After an hour, we arrived at Gillingham station; for some reason, I was expecting loads of football fans to be hanging around. I was glad to be wrong.

Trains arrived, and people got off, walked up the stairs and out of the station. Nothing to worry about: there was just the odd bit of singing, but nothing to write home about. Then the game started. You could hear the crowd from the Priestfield Stadium at the station, and there was a lot of cheering going on; however I had no idea of the score and, to be honest, I had no interest in knowing it.

I was more concerned with the return of the fans, due to the reputation that preceded them; I was not looking forward to it. However, it turned out that all my concerns were for nothing. When the fans did arrive back at the station, the numbers were fewer than I had envisaged, with some singing and chanting on the platform. To this day I still don't know who won.

There were a few little issues with crowd control, which were more along the lines of 'keep away from the edge' (this was greeted with a volley of abuse), but all in all it was acceptable. The only scuffles that took place occurred when people decided to hold the doors open for 'mates' who weren't ready to board. This impacts on the running times of the trains and, if held, can damage the doors themselves. If asking politely not to hold the doors didn't work, a choice was given: either get on or be removed and get the next train. Some chose the latter, and then jumped back on afterwards, throwing abuse – they played the game and got away safely in the end.

I

HOOLIGANS ON THE MOVE, 2015/2016

During the 2012/13 and 2013/14 football seasons, the British Transport Police dealt with a total of 1,027 football-related incidents – of these, a total of 100 recorded incidents were said to involve an allegation of racism. Leeds United fans were top of the list, having been involved in seventy-seven recorded incidents.

On Friday 3 April 2015, just before 10.30 p.m., a forty-one-year-old man from Bradford was returning by train from Bradford City's game against Doncaster Rovers at the Keepmoat Stadium in Doncaster. He was one of a group of disorderly fans who was asked to calm down by an off-duty Virgin Trains East Coast staff member.

The Bradford fan, who had been drinking all day, threatened the man, before head-butting him in the face, resulting in the loss of two front teeth, which required dental surgery costing £2,500. The offender was subsequently given a twelve-month suspended prison sentence; ordered to carry out community service, attend anger management classes, pay compensation; and given a three-year football banning order. BTP Superintendent John Conaghan said, 'This type of drunken loutish behaviour by a minority of football fans is completely unacceptable.'

On Monday 6 April 2015, a huge clear-up operation took place in Sheffield city centre after Grimsby fans stopped off on their way to a bank holiday fixture with Alfreton. Some 300 'Mariners' fans descended on the city after arriving by train, throwing missiles before clashing with the local police. At 12.20 p.m. the fans headed back to the railway station, where they attacked two British Transport Police officers, punching and kicking them, before order was restored.

On Saturday 11 April 2015, Leicester City and West Bromwich Albion fans clashed just yards away from New Street station in Birmingham. As Leicester City fans prepared to head to the station from the nearby Shakespeare pub in Lower Temple Street, fighting broke out. Five men aged between eighteen years and forty-one years were subsequently arrested in Leicestershire, as part of a post-incident investigation.

Again, at 6.46 p.m. on Saturday 11 April 2015, a group of football fans hurled abuse at passengers on a train travelling to Stoke, which had departed from Euston, including at a boy in a wheelchair, who was travelling with his parents. They also abused a woman and her two daughters, who were so upset that they left the train at Nuneaton.

On the same date Birmingham City FC played at home in a local derby match with Wolverhampton Wanderers. There was trouble after the game in the streets around the ground, as fans made their way back into the city centre; the tactics adopted by the local police received a lot of negative comments in response to an article in the *Birmingham Mail*. One anonymous reader kept his comments for the BTP: 'Rookie police officers treating the normal train escort as hooligans. Blues fans get 100 per cent more protection at Wolves than Wolves do at Blues.'

On 17 April 2015 the British Transport Police held a summit involving passengers, clubs, train operators and other interested parties to address the effects of football-related disorder on the rail network. It had already been acknowledged that alcohol was a major contributory factor to this behaviour, as 630 football-related incidents were recorded by the force up to that point in the season.

During the course of the conference, delegates heard from a rail passenger Dawn Parkinson about her experiences. The forty-three-year-old head teacher described an 'absolutely terrifying' journey, which started at Euston as drunken football fans overran the carriage she was in with her eight-year-old daughter, who was reduced to tears by their behaviour. Mrs Parkinson said, 'Football is a sport based on good values. How can it be that one of the big rich industries in this country is at the heart of corroding social norms of behaviour?'

It was universally agreed that a 'cultural change' was needed to change the view that football-related ASB was low-level in nature and, as such, should be acceptable and tolerated. The BTP declared that they would be looking to examine academic research and to review best practice from around the world, as well as being informed by behavioural science and analysis in the search for new incentives and sanctions. Chief Constable Paul Crowther also said, 'I don't think that it is an issue we can arrest our way out of'. He went on, 'My message to anyone – passenger or staff – who find themselves in an intimidating, or worse, frightening situation because of the behaviour of fans is: don't accept it. Report it and together let's change it.' During an interview on BBC Radio 4, Paul Crowther estimated that about 10 per cent of incidents reported contained a 'racial element'.

On social media 'CC' commented about the summit:

Well done. It seems these days the police are more concerned with job preservation than giving praise where it is due. I have travelled season after season by train for a decade of matches and the only incident I have ever seen was when the train company cancelled a train up to Manchester on one of the busiest fixture days (Manchester United versus Liverpool), which resulted in a chronically overcrowded train. Football fans are one of the last remaining prejudiced groups in our society and the police are institutionally prejudiced at football fans ...

On social media in one newspaper article, 'JM2' put forward a somewhat more extreme point of view:

The problem is – as with all crime – there is simply no deterrent. Your average sub-human criminal hooligan simply does not care, and is not intimidated by the punishments currently on offer. The courts need to have the power to declassify all criminals as humans, removing all their human rights ...

Following the summit the Midlands edition of the *Express & Star* carried an article on the outcome of the meeting and conducted an online survey that asked the simple question, 'Is enough done to reduce violence in football?' The results were 30.2 per cent for YES and 69.8 per cent for NO.

Officers from Paddington covering the Underground to Wembley for the Arsenal versus Reading FA Cup semi-final on Saturday 18 April 2015 reported that the mood of fans was 'good humoured'. On Sunday 19 April 2015, 800 BTP officers were deployed for the FA Cup semi-final game between Aston Villa and Liverpool at Wembley Stadium.

On the same date, after a large group of supporters put a number of travellers in fear for their safety, four persons were detained at Euston railway station and kept in custody overnight. Virgin Train services were declared 'dry' out of London.

On Saturday 25 April 2015, at about 2.10 p.m., a woman was travelling on a Northern Rail service between Leeds and Bradford Forster Square with her four-year-old son, when, it was alleged, racist abuse was hurled at them by a group of Barnsley FC fans. The fans were reported to have been singing racist football chants on the train as they headed to watch their team play Bradford. As she stood up to leave the train at Shipley railway station, she had the courage to take a photograph of the group and informed BTP.

PC Craig Virco from BTP commented to the media, 'As is understandable, the mother left the train hugely upset, shocked and disgusted at the vile abuse directed at her very young son and promptly contacted the police.' Operating in an environment that is rich with CCTV, the force was able to release images of eight people that they wanted to speak to in connection with the incident.

Chief Constable Paul Crowther later referred to the 'casual thuggishness' that had become an all-too-common fixture on trains and tubes, and said of this incident, 'I applaud the mother of the young child at Shipley who had the bravery and presence of mind to challenge those singing, and to take a photo.'

In a further incident on this date, two men who had been refused entry to a football match earlier in the day were arrested for making racist comments towards two other men on a London King's Cross–Doncaster train.

Over the weekend period of 25/26 April 2015, BTP officers covering the Lancashire area reported making a number of arrests for football-related disorder. Officers were involved in escorting Swindon fans from Preston to Blackpool, and also monitored fans for the Bradford versus Barnsley fixture.

In the North East, officers arrested two fans for being drunk and disorderly in York and dealt with two people for bye-law offences at Sheffield, while two arrests for public order were dealt with at Barrow-in-Furness, and abusive behaviour was reported at Preston. In Scotland, disorder was reported at Glasgow Central railway station and at Helensburgh Upper railway station. In the Midlands, disorder was reported at Derby, with one arrest, as well as at Stafford, where another arrest for drunken behaviour took place, and Wolverhampton. In the south, disorder occurred at Reading and Southampton Central, with an arrest for assault taking place on a train between Brighton and Southampton.

Across the force as a whole, BTP officers dealt with twenty-one recorded incidents, resulting in fourteen arrests, including one case wherein a forty-eight-year-old man was detained for assaulting a sixteen-year-old boy at Milton Keynes railway station, who was punched as he waited on a platform for a train.

On Sunday 26 April 2015 a man was arrested at Birmingham New Street station for racial abuse directed towards an officer engaged in football duties. In London a flare was set off at Arsenal Underground station, and one of the exits was blocked. BTP received a 61016 text from a member of the public complaining about drunken behaviour on a train between Liverpool and London Euston.

On Monday 27 April 2015, 'RG' posted on a social media site about how he felt football fans were sometimes treated:

Went to a game against the Chavs yesterday with a mate who I have been going to Arsenal with for 15 years ... After the game we headed back to Euston. We got there about 7.30 p.m. ... Then spotted a bar on the station concourse and suggested a beer while we waited for the train. After asking for two pints I was told by the barmaid, 'I am sorry I can't serve you because you are football hooligans.' I add at this point that we were not wearing Arsenal shirts, just subtle Arsenal jackets with a club badge on. Also we were neither pissed, loud, nor abusive.

In 2015 BTP estimated that the cost of policing football supporters each season on the railway was in the region of £4 million.

On Saturday 2 May 2015, officers on duty during a bitterly cold evening at Carlisle railway station arrested one football supporter for being drunk and disorderly. During the weekend of 16/17 May 2015, ACC Mark Newton announced that, after a weekend where 'for a few hours football brought violence and fear to the public', offenders could expect to receive an 'early call' from the police and asked the question as to whether 'football should show greater social responsibility'.

In the same month Chief Constable Paul Crowther announced that, in the future, BTP would routinely film carriages and platforms to identify fans using offensive chants and that a smartphone app would enable passengers to upload their own videos. It was intended to help police make swift arrests instead of having to wait for videos to be spread on YouTube. Throughout the latter part of the month of May, the BTP in Scotland were heavily engaged in policing travelling football fans, with commitments on more than seven days, some of which were consecutive.

The Premier League finished on Sunday 24 May 2015. On Saturday 30 May 2015, the FA Cup final took place at Wembley between Aston Villa and Arsenal in a game that Arsenal won 4-0. Following the game, at around 9 p.m., fans clashed at Kilburn Underground station, with reports of assaults and persons fighting on the tracks. Transport for London was obliged to suspend services on the Jubilee Line until the situation was brought under control.

On Saturday 11 July 2015 a number of Blackpool's 'Seasider' fans travelled to Lancaster to watch a so-called friendly game with Lancaster City. A dispersal order was later served on one fan to leave Lancaster, and he travelled back by train with other fans, escorted by BTP officers.

Extra officers were on duty at Preston railway station for a number of pre-season friendlies, where this same individual was warned about his language. When he got off at Poulton, he gesticulated at the departing train and went to a stairway, where he set off a canister that filled the station with tangerine-coloured smoke. The whole incident was captured on CCTV and the individual was subsequently traced and arrested. He was later sentenced to complete eighty hours' unpaid work, with costs awarded.

On Saturday 18 July 2015, officers monitored more than 200 visiting supporters through Preston railway station. At one point a BTP officer was bombarded by fans with bottles, cans, and coins, but fortunately escaped uninjured.

On Saturday 25 July 2015 a thirty-seven-year-old man from Grangemouth attended a friendly fixture between Celtic and Stade Rennais. He subsequently travelled on the 22.22 train service between Glasgow Queen Street and Falkirk. Shortly after the train departed from Glasgow, he started swearing and singing offensive songs, and, when asked to desist by the train conductor, he refused. He also punched a female passenger several times, which led to a number of members of the public intervening. BTP officers met the train at Gartcosh and the offender was arrested and charged. Several months later, he pleaded guilty to a charge under the Offensive Behaviour at Football and Threatening Communications (Scotland) Act 2012, and was subsequently sentenced to an eleven-month Restriction of Liberty Order, as well as being banned from going to matches for a year.

On Wednesday 29 July 2015, BTP monitored Newcastle fans travelling to York and Sunderland fans travelling to Doncaster for pre-season 'friendlies'. Virgin Trains decided not to impose 'dry trains' for the Magpies and Black Cats supporters.

On Saturday 1 August 2015, at about 7.35 p.m., Richard Powell, aged thirty-nine years and from Higham in Kent, suffered serious head injuries following an altercation at London Victoria station. He was a Crystal Palace fan on his way home after seeing his side draw 1-1 with Fulham in a pre-season friendly. He died three days later in St Thomas' Hospital. The BTP arrested one man, aged twenty-one years and from South London, on suspicion of causing grievous bodily harm, and released him on bail. Detective Superintendent Gary Richardson appealed for witnesses to come forward who may have seen a disturbance involving three men on the main concourse. During the course of the investigation, leaflets were distributed to passengers and BTP also used Bluetooth technology via handheld devices to highlight the appeal.

On Sunday 2 August 2015 an FA Community Shield match took place between Arsenal and Chelsea. At about 5.40 p.m. a train en route to Tring from Harrow & Wealdstone station pulled into Watford Junction. The train was crowded with fans returning home from Wembley. A group of Arsenal fans were on the platform singing songs and, as a group of four Chelsea fans got off the train, one of them started throwing beer cans at the Arsenal group. He then proceeded to charge at the group, hitting one of them over the head with a bag full of cans. The forty-one-year-old victim was dragged on to a train by his friends, while his attacker, who sported a distinctive European Cup tattoo, fled. DC David Peck said, 'We are committed to tackling this thuggery ...'

On the opening day of the new season on Saturday 8 August 2015, when Cardiff City were playing at home to Fulham, a Cardiff fan spat in the face of an officer while being arrested for assaulting other passengers. On the same day an Ipswich fan set off a smoke bomb in a train on the opening day of the season, away to Brentford.

On Sunday 9 August 2015 some post-match football-related disorder took place at Mill Hill railway station in Blackburn, and an off-duty BTP PCSO was able to point out an offender, who was arrested by Lancashire Police.

On Friday 14 August 2015 Aston Villa played Manchester United at home. A group of Manchester United fans travelling by rail started harassing a young man and, when another supporter intervened, three fans confronted him and he was struck three times. In an incident on the same night, another Manchester United fan was arrested for 'causing harassment, alarm or distress' after trying twice to kiss a BTP officer.

On Saturday 15 August 2015, a number of Cardiff fans, known as the 'Bluebirds', travelled to London for an away game with Queens Park Rangers. An incident was recorded wherein a group of five of them used abusive language while forcing their way through platform barriers without tickets.

In the preceding week, it was announced by BTP Inspector Richard Price that Grand Central services between Sunderland, Teesside and York would operate 'dry' trains for the match between Hartlepool and York on 15 August 2015. On that day, at 9 p.m., a fight took place between two groups of Leicester City fans as they returned to Leicester railway station after watching an away match at Upton Park in London against West Ham, which Leicester won 2-1. The two groups, numbering between ten to fifteen men, became involved in a mass brawl and a forty-nine-year-old man was arrested.

Just after 7 p.m., West Ham fans travelling back from the same match by train caused problems, as a man boarded at Watford Junction and took his seat in a first class carriage. A number of fans already in the carriage started chanting anti-Semitic songs as the train pulled out and, despite his protestations, they refused to stop. The fans were believed to have left the train at Northampton and BTP released images of five men that they wanted to trace. PC Michael Botterill told the media, 'This sort of casual racism has gone unchallenged for too long …'

On the same day, on the 09.27 service from Rotherham to Sheffield, a woman and her two teenage sons were verbally abused by a group of Rotherham fans on a journey to Nottingham. The woman and her fifteen- and nineteen-year-old sons were left shaken and intimidated after asking the group to quieten down, upon which they were met with a barrage of abuse.

When the victims got off the train at Sheffield to board the front carriages to continue the journey to Nottingham, the group followed them and threw beer cans at them. One of their attackers, described as in his mid-forties, pulled earphones from the ears of the nineteen-year-old. PC Emma Williamson from BTP said, 'The victim asked the group of football supporters who were behaving in a rowdy manner to quieten down. Her request was met with a barrage of foul language and abuse.'

On 19 August 2015, Assistant Chief Constable Stephen Thomas announced a new 'dry trains' policy whereby, in addition to the station of departure being declared 'dry', stops en route would also be given the same status. While he did not envisage an increase in arrests as a result of the policy, he did expect to see a rise in the number of people being refused travel.

'NW' responded on social media: 'It will be interesting to see whether the BTP start using common sense. I have seen a businessman who had just flown in from Heathrow with a bottle of duty-free in an airport bag that he was obviously taking home being told that he couldn't get on a train with it.' 'BA', another user, responded, 'They have nothing at all against the public enjoying themselves. They have a great deal against drunks preventing other passengers from enjoying themselves.'

On Tuesday 25 August 2015, all the internal lights on a train carriage were destroyed by Aston Villa fans, leaving glass shattered over the seating.

On Wednesday 26 August 2015 three incidents involving Manchester United fans were reported, as fans travelled for the away visit to Belgian side Club Brugge as part of the Champion's League Group stages. One man was kicked on a train as he tried to retrieve his luggage, and the following day an incident of racist abuse was reported. The latter incident was dealt with at Manchester Piccadilly on Thursday 27 August 2015, when BTP officers arrested a fifty-one-year-old man who was under the influence of alcohol, as a train carrying Manchester United supporters pulled into the station. The suspect was pointed out by a fellow passenger on the train, while a second man, thought to be in the same group, was arrested for common assault after kicking the witness. Inspector Michelle Wedderburn said, 'Anyone who finds themselves in an intimidating or frightening situation because of the behaviour of football fans should not ignore it ...'

On Friday 28 August 2015 Blackburn Rovers played Bolton Wanderers during an evening fixture. BTP special constables escorted some eighty fans from Mill Hill railway station in Blackburn and subsequently made two arrests for drunkenness at Lancaster and Blackpool.

On Saturday 29 August 2015 a female passenger reported to a train guard a case of 'sexual touching' as Everton fans made their way to London for a game with Tottenham Hotspur. On the same date, a group of some fifteen to twenty Aston Villa fans making their way through a railway station shouted racist chants at members of staff. Also on Saturday 29 August, a Preston North End fan inexplicably dropped his trousers and began to wipe his buttocks with baby wipes when travelling to the club's away game with Hull City. A group of Preston North End supporters came to notice on the same date when, at about 8.10 p.m., they became involved in an argument with a Manchester City fan, who was then repeatedly kicked and punched. As the incident unfolded on platforms 13 and 14 at Manchester Piccadilly railway station, frightened passengers were caught up in the fighting.

The alleged offenders caught a TransPennine express service to Preston at about 8.30 p.m. after the train was delayed due to the disturbance. Two men, aged nineteen years and twenty-six years, were subsequently traced and reported for an offence of affray. PC David Cawley from BTP appealed for witnesses and CCTV pictures of two suspects were released to the media. He stressed the additional dangers posed by the fact that the disturbance took place on so-called satellite platforms, with trains passing on either side.

One of the media reports, however, attracted an alternative view on the paper's social media website from 'WFL', who said:

> Fact one the PNE fans were on the station in high spirits singing and having fun. The Man City fan took offence and started shouting his mouth off. Fact two the Preston fans didn't attack him he pushed people out of the way including myself to attack the Preston fans. Fact three if he had kept his mouth shut, just got on his train and gone home nothing would have happened.

On 7 September 2015 BTP special constables supported regular officers in policing fans travelling for the Scotland versus Germany game at Hampden Park, and a dry train policy was implemented from Glasgow Central railway station to Mount Florida and Kings Park for the evening fixture.

Home Office statistics revealed that, as of 8 September 2015, a total of 2,181 football banning orders were in force across England and Wales. This figure included those applied for through the courts by BTP. The figures revealed that there had been a steady decline in the overall use of FBOs during the preceding five years. In contrast, the figures also revealed that there had also been a steady decline in the number of football-related arrests over the last five seasons. For the 2014/15 season, there had been 1,873 arrests, of which 31 per cent were connected to Premier League games. In keeping with the trend on the rail networks, an increase was noted in the use of pyrotechnics.

On Saturday 12 September 2015, a small group of drunken Swansea fans travelling to Watford were reported by the escorting officers after repeated warnings about their behaviour. On the same date a large group of Derby County fans, returning from an away match at Preston North End, were being loud and abusive on a train travelling between Stoke and Derby. When a sixty-eight-year-old man from Swadlincote approached them and asked them politely to calm down, he was met with threats of violence from one twenty-year-old man. The train was met at Derby by BTP officers, who obtained details and later arrested the offender for an offence under Section 4 of the Public Order Act. He was later given a three-year football banning order and PC Wayne Mitchell, one of BTP's football intelligence officers, said after the conclusion of the case, 'This man's behaviour was disgraceful. Trains are not extensions of the football terrace or a pub ...'

On Sunday 13 September 2015, a nineteen-year-old Aston Villa fan, who had already been ejected from a match at Leicester for gesturing at home fans, arrived back at Birmingham New Street station at 7.45 p.m. While walking along one of the platforms, he was observed by BTP officers throwing a beer can, which struck a West Midlands Police officer on the back of the neck. He was arrested and charged with assaulting a police officer, and subsequently received a five-year football banning order. BTP football intelligence officer Jim Rentell said, 'Thankfully the police officer was uninjured in the assault but this in no way makes his loutish and aggressive behaviour acceptable.'

The result of the case drew some interesting comments on social media, with 'RK' saying, 'Uninjured yet in court the copper said he had lost sensation in his neck and needed to use deep heat every day to and I quote to cope with the pain!' 'AS' said, 'Never see Old Bill rest of the week ... throw a can on a Saturday afternoon and you hit one on the head ... amazing.' 'R.Mc' said, 'If you were convicted of throwing a beer can in a non-football related incident would your punishment last five years.'

On Saturday 19 September 2015 a fight took place on the 6.45 p.m. service train from Birmingham to Worcester, involving up to thirty people, who were believed to be a mixture of Aston Villa, Wolverhampton, and West Bromwich Albion fans. The violence began after the train stopped at Droitwich and continued until they got off the train at Worcester Foregate Street station. During the course of the fighting, belts were used as weapons. One of the alleged offenders was captured on a phone image taken covertly by a member of the public, and an appeal was made via the media for the suspect to come forward. A thirty-one-year-old man subsequently surrendered himself to police and was interviewed under caution, before being released at Castle Street police station in Worcester.

On the same day, three women wearing Islamic-style clothing reported being racially abused by Leeds United supporters travelling by train on the day of their away game with MK Dons. A forty-seven-year-old Leeds United fan was arrested on suspicion of a racially aggravated public order offence after being removed from a train by BTP officers at Stoke-on-Trent railway station. The man, from Bolton, had been travelling among a group of supporters who were drinking aboard a Virgin train service running between London Euston and Manchester Piccadilly when it was alleged that he made derogatory remarks to a female Muslim passenger about her traditional dress. He was interviewed and given police bail, pending further enquiries.

Again on 19 September 2015, BTP in Nottingham announced that they had dealt with three persons for football-related violence during the preceding week.

On Tuesday 22 September 2015 an evening League Cup fixture took place between Aston Villa and Birmingham City at Villa Park. A total of eleven men were dealt with on the night by BTP officers for public order-related matters, six of whom were issued with fixed penalty tickets, and four others were reported for process to be decided. One twenty-one-year-old from Hednesford was charged with breaching a football banning order.

On 24 September 2015 Chief Constable Paul Crowther announced at a rail industry conference that the force was 'taking a new tougher approach.'

On Saturday 26 September 2015, up to forty Swansea fans in drink were witnessed to be taking part in racist chants and making monkey gestures towards a family sitting on a platform as they made their way to an away game with Southampton. On the same day six incidents occurred in one day involving Manchester City fans, as their side was beaten 4-0 by Tottenham Hotspur at White Hart Lane. In one instance fans racially abused a fourteen-year-old boy on a train when he was in company with his father and brother. Fights were reported with other fans on board trains as communication cords were activated and rail staff abused by drunken hooligans. Again on the same date, officers escorting football fans back to Wolverhampton, equipped with body-worn video, removed two fans at Crewe railway station and dealt with them for unacceptable behaviour under Bye-law 6.

In Scotland, on the same day, BTP officers started an investigation into the behaviour of Heart of Midlothian FC fans travelling by train from Edinburgh Waverley railway station to Glasgow Queen Street for a match with Celtic FC. On one train, up to ten fans, who boarded at 10.30 a.m., were alleged to have been involved in drunken and sectarian behaviour, and other passengers complained to police.

In a separate incident thirty Hearts fans boarded a train to Glasgow Central railway station at 1.15 p.m. at Haymarket station. Passengers alleged that the group swore continuously and used religiously offensive language. BTP Chief Inspector David Marshall described their behaviour as 'appalling and totally unacceptable' and Hearts FC released a statement condemning their actions and reiterating that they were committed to working with the police to identify offenders.

Andy Bryson works as a train driver, based at Edinburgh Waverley station, and recalls some of the behaviour of fans:

I had a load of Hearts fans fighting outside, and on my train at Glasgow Central, after the Hearts versus Celtic game in Glasgow. Hearts fans were fighting among themselves. About thirty civilian police came running up through the barriers as there was no British Transport Police. The main instigators struggled with police and were handcuffed and arrested. I refused to take the train load of Hearts fans back to Edinburgh without police on board. The local civilian police sergeant said she was having trouble locating BTP officers to go with the train. Eventually two arrived and they refused to go without more police to accompany them. Eventually we had four or five on board and we then took the train out after being delayed for about twenty minutes. There was loads of chanting all the way back to Edinburgh by the fans. As they left the train, en route at Westerhailes, Kingsknowe, and Slateford, they shouted abuse at the police.

On 3 October 2015 BTP officers were deployed at Witton station in Birmingham to assist with football traffic to Villa Park.

On Saturday 17 October 2015, following a match at Livingston, a group of St Mirren fans caused trouble at Livingston South railway station. A group of ten men then boarded the 17.47 Edinburgh Waverley–Glasgow Central service, chanting and singing religiously offensive songs throughout the service, leading to eventual delays.

On the same date Manchester City fans played Bournemouth at home and, during the course of the day, a fight on board a train was reported, leaving one man with cuts to his face and back of the head. Again on the same date, BTP officers escorting Bolton Wanderers fans acted swiftly when a smoke canister was set off in a subway at Preston railway station and a fifteen-year-old youth was detained. Also on Saturday 17 October 2015 BTP officers commenced an investigation into an allegation of criminal damage on a train carrying Fulham fans from Darlington to Middlesbrough. Some fans complained to the media, as a number were filmed and questioned by police.

On 23 October 2015, a Derby County fan was reported to have received a three-year football banning order for threatening an elderly passenger on a train. On Saturday 24 October 2015, on the day of their home game against Everton, two Arsenal fans verbally abused someone for speaking Arabic, before then assaulting their victim. On Sunday 25 October 2015 a Newcastle fan threw a sparkler onto the railway tracks on the day that their side went to Sunderland for the Wear and Tyne 'derby' game. On Wednesday 28 October 2015, Celtic fans were reported to have been singing sectarian songs while on board a train.

On Saturday 31 October 2015 at 6.40 p.m., a fight broke out between Nottingham Forest fans and fans from another club on platform 8 at Sheffield station. Five men were arrested. On the same day Manchester City beat Norwich 2-1 at the Etihad Stadium and a group of travelling Manchester City fans were reported to be behaving in a drunk and disorderly manner towards rail staff.

In London a Fulham supporter who works on the railway commented on the social media website Friends of Fulham on an incident he had witnessed at about 8.35 p.m. that day:

> I work on the railway at Paddington. The police were called to deal with fighting on the train from Bristol. They took a couple of 'muppets' away. When I asked what had happened I was told my lot had been fighting and caused loads of trouble on the way back – embarrassed to wear my Fulham badge on my uniform last night.

On the day that Fulham FC had faced Bristol City FC, he went on, 'Saw two twenty somethings being led away by police, while swearing at them … I counted about eight police officers on the platform as the train came in.'

Again on 31 October 2015 extra officers were on duty at Preston station for the game between Preston North End and Bolton Wanderers. They had a busy day and were particularly challenged by the return traffic. At about 8.30 p.m., rival fans from Bolton, Blackpool and Leeds, who all arrived on the station at about the same time, clashed and BTP officers, together with Lancashire Constabulary, struggled to maintain control as fans chanted and scuffles broke out on various platforms.

A lady travelling with her eight-year-old son commented, 'I've never seen anything like it. The front of the station was over-run and there was a line of police and dogs trying to hold them off the platform but a fair few were breaking through. At one stage officers were physically pushing people back onto a train, which left twenty minutes late.' The rest of the story is told in the words of social media responders to a *Blackpool Gazette* article on the disturbances. 'TT' said,

> I was at the station from 7 p.m. until I got the Blackpool train at 7.30 p.m. There were large groups of police there and regular passengers were asked to wait at the other end of the platform. Once on the train it was a very unpleasant journey with football fans swearing, shouting, drinking and chanting – even though there were some transport police officers on board … As a regular train

traveller, football 'fans' are the bane of my journeys. I've had beer thrown over me before now because I dared to stand up to them and ask them to tone it down. As I'm a 5 foot nothing female it must have made them feel very 'macho'. I'm appalled that we are continually subjected to this kind of anti-social behaviour every football season. I hope that cash-rich football clubs are paying for the police presence that has to be committed to scenarios like the one at Preston – if not why not. I think that there needs to be football trains laid on or at the very least certain coaches that are just for them with dedicated security guards to keep them in order. If they can't behave like civilised people then they should be kept apart from regular travellers. Pathetic behaviour from grown men.

Meanwhile 'PF' commented, 'There is a video of the police separation and action at the station on social media. Batons were drawn and used. The police I have to say appeared to quell the violence and maintain order very quickly indeed where stun grenades and pint pots were being thrown around.' 'PG' also observed,

I was there at 8.30, having just got off a train from Manchester – which was also filled with shouting and singing football fans. A massive crowd were pushing and shoving anybody in sight, while shouting, swearing and throwing bottles. I managed to escape the mob and then they started setting off fireworks! Luckily I got out just as the riot vans arrived but it was a horrible, scary experience and I am disgusted with the behaviour that I saw. These people are grown adults getting worked up over a game with an inflatable ball. There was no consideration for the people going about their daily business – completely out of order. Props to the police/transport officers for their quick response.

'TH' concluded, 'There was a massive police presence on the station. It started kicking off at 7.30 p.m. when a train arrived from Manchester en route to Blackpool. I travel a lot on Saturdays watching my own team and there is definitely an upbeat in trouble leading to a return to the bad old days of the seventies and eighties. Not so much in the grounds but on public transport and pre-arranged meets for a punch up between rival "fans".'

Mobile phone footage of the incident was downloaded onto a hooligan video website and 'LC' commented, 'Another singing contest', while 'DH' said, 'Waste of time and space, all bouncing and giving it large and nobody makes a move.'

On Sunday 1 November 2015, Rangers fans were reportedly singing sectarian songs before throwing beer cans at a train on the day of their away game against Hibernian. On 3 November 2015, fireworks were set off by football supporters in Preston station.

On Saturday 7 November 2015, a group of some twenty Glasgow Rangers fans boarded a train at Lancaster, at around 10.15 a.m., on their way to Glasgow Central station for a match with Alloa Athletic in the SPFL. It was alleged that they sang religiously offensive songs until they arrived at their destination at 12.30 p.m. PC Gordon Anderson from the BTP appealed for witnesses.

On Saturday 21 November 2015, at about 4.45 p.m., a twenty-three-year-old woman on a Metro train service travelling between Newcastle to Whitley Bay was racially abused by a man who said that she was 'going to bomb the train' and that she should get off. A number of travellers, including a number of football fans, rallied round and instead insisted that he leave the female alone, before forcing him to get off. As he did so, passengers clapped and cheered. The victim said that she had 'never felt more proud of being a Geordie'. The incident was reported to Northumbria Police.

On 2/3 December 2015 Assistant Chief Constable Stephen Thomas from the BTP gave a keynote speech on football violence at the Transport Security Expo event. In December 2015 figures released by the BTP under a Freedom of Information request hit the media headlines, as it was stated that a total of 276 incidents of a football-related nature had been reported to the BTP between 7 August and 7 November 2015.

In one instance logged by BTP, a Cardiff City fan spat in the face of an officer after being arrested for assaulting another passenger. On another occasion drunken Newcastle fans were reported to the BTP for being abusive to a mother and daughter and making sexual comments, while on another date damage valued at £500 was caused when a Leicester fan forced his way through the station barriers without a ticket, breaking the 'paddles' and leaving shattered glass on the floor.

The top twenty clubs for incidents of anti-social behaviour during that period were named as Aston Villa (22 incidents), Manchester City (12), Celtic (12), Newcastle United (11), Leeds United (10). Birmingham City (10), Rangers (9), Manchester United (9), Leicester City (8), Coventry (8), Portsmouth (7), Millwall (7), West Bromwich Albion (6), Stoke (6), Chelsea (6), West Ham (5), Tottenham (5), Sheffield United (5), Arsenal (5), and Wolverhampton Wanderers (4).

In other incidents, Bolton Wanderers and Celtic fans were reported to have been involved in setting off smoke bombs on trains and in stations. In one instance an officer observed a flare being thrown onto a railway line and yet another was thrown onto a platform, which at the time was packed with Polish supporters. The attitude of some football supporters was summed up when one Celtic fan approached an officer and said, 'Why don't you go and deal with car crashes. Why don't you answer phones and not let people die?'

With Aston Villa supporters at the top of the so-called league, one social media fan 'DL' posted on the Avilla Fan forum on 8 December 2015:

> Not much really is it 22 incidents over 15 games. I'm not defending it but I come at this from the point of view of somebody who was on the trains in the 70s on match days and without exaggeration I think what I have read here in those 22 incidents would once have been regarded as low level for one game ... our dickheads have been caught acting like dickheads more than the dickheads elsewhere.

Also at the end of December 2015 it was announced by the BTP in Scotland that they were going to create a joint taskforce of uniform and CID officers to deal with an increase in football-related anti-social behaviour. In the previous season, eighty-six incidents had been recorded that were linked to football supporters, whereas thus far in this season alone fifty-six incidents had already been recorded, which included assaults of a physical and sexual nature. BTP insisted that the problem was not limited to Scotland's 'central belt', with clubs in all Scottish leagues having been identified as being involved in anti-social behaviour in places such as Glasgow, Edinburgh, Motherwell, Bathgate, Stirling, Paisley Kirkcaldy, Falkirk, Dumfries, and as far north as Brora.

Fans of English Premier League teams returning north also sometimes posed problems on the network, with supporters travelling back from Lancaster having to be escorted on arrival back at Glasgow's Central station. Chief Superintendent John McBride, divisional commander for the BTP in Scotland, condemned the behaviour of a minority who made life intolerable for others.

At its launch BTP announced that the team were already making an impact with three men – two believed to be affiliated with Partick Thistle and another with Tottenham Hotspur – arrested for alleged disorder at Glasgow's Queen Street station in recent days.

It was stressed that, while BTP would work closely with Police Scotland's football operation codenamed 'FOCUS', their tactics would vary given the specialised environment of working on trains. At the same time, ScotRail placed BTP 'Text 61016' stickers on their entire fleet to ensure that customers knew how to contact police, and Dave Scott, campaign director for the anti-sectarian group Nil by Mouth, welcomed the initiative.

On Monday 28 December 2015 at 1.15 p.m., a thirty-three-year-old woman boarded a train at Hebden Bridge station and sat in one of the rear carriages, where she found a group of ten to twelve Wrexham fans travelling to Halifax for a game in the Vanarama National League. The group were singing sexist and offensive songs, and she later said that was 'offended and disgusted' by their conduct. The fans were rowdy, drunken and abusive, and one of them climbed into an overhead luggage rack, throwing his shoes about, which just missed other passengers. They were also reported to have mocked recent flood victims, chanting 'where are your houses gone' at flood-ravaged Hebden Bridge.

PC Jo Kellert from BTP circulated the images of six people that they wanted to speak to in connection with the incident via the media, and all six came forward for interview. 'MJ' commented on a social media site about the incident: 'Races crowd, rugby fans, music festival goers, stag/hen do = high jinks. Football fans = police over-reaction.'

The previous weekend, BTP officers from Guildford travelled on trains between Southampton and Waterloo, monitoring football traffic.

PC Andy Baxter retired from the British Transport Police on 31 December 2015, and recounts an experience from his early years of policing football fans, as well as one of his final escorts before retiring. He describes it, 'warts and all':

I joined BTP at Brighton in July 1986. Back in the 1980s policing was a much simpler affair. You'd have a roster published weeks in advance and you'd know exactly what you were doing and who with. Football days were normally either a 6 a.m.–6 p.m. early or a 6 p.m.–6 a.m. night, either in the thick of it or mopping up afterwards.

I was based down at Brighton, where at the time just about every night was 'fight night' and football Saturdays could be very interesting indeed due to very limited resources. I recall one Saturday, possibly in either 1987 or 1988; I think I was possibly still in my probation. We were rostered to work a 6 a.m.–6 p.m. early shift – so that would be the long hard slog, meeting all the trains, recording fan movements and numbers, and then passing them on to the relevant parties, the local control room and our boss. I recall it was a warm day so possibly towards the end of the season, with lots of tourists arriving for a day at the seaside, as well as the football fans. It was busy, very busy; just about everyone was heading straight out of the station towards the sea front. Not ideal as, once they left the rail system, we couldn't keep tabs on their movements. Sussex Police had numerous units out and pretty soon it became apparent that the fans were looking for trouble. Police or local fans, it didn't matter, all were fair game!

Pre-match, there were several skirmishes within the town, and Sussex Police were being run ragged trying to corral these 'oiks' and get them to Hove, where the ground was situated. Eventually they brought a posse back to the station, having lost goodness knows how many in the town. I honestly can't remember who it was that Brighton was playing that day but there were a lot of them. A day out at the seaside, beer, and a football match was too much of a temptation. I think some of these folks have a different

DNA to the rest of us human beings! I'm thinking it was probably a London-based club as they were arriving quite early.

We received these fine young chaps, and old geezers, with open arms, giving them polite and informative directions to the trains. Their journey was only three minutes by rail so hopefully they couldn't get up to much prior to their arrival. They piled on; tickets weren't normally checked as the numbers were just too many to make it viable. Get them in, get them there, and then get them out of the system. Off they went; some officers were there to receive them and point them towards the Goldstone Ground. Once they were there they were no longer our problem, and we could stand down, grab some food, a brew, or a snooze in some cases, and prepare ourselves for the return.

This was a standard old school, pre Sky TV, football Saturday. The match started at 3 p.m., finished about 4.45 p.m. Any time after that the fans would start to appear. We were waiting at Hove station for their return. We'd been paired with a view to each of the pairs being detailed to accompany the busiest trains back into Brighton. We'd got serials of officers standing by to take the away fans directly back to London. Our responsibility was the Brighton bunch. My partner was my shift partner, Bob Cager. He was not a big chap but was someone who'd saved my backside on numerous occasions and someone who I'd follow through thick and thin. He always had the right answer for whatever the situation and for him this was just another Saturday.

It was always a hectic time, an hour or so of being ready for anything. Bearing in mind that, in this era of policing, our equipment consisted of a truncheon, which was near useless, handcuffs, which were only useful afterwards, a whistle, which was just nice and shiny, and our bobby's 'nous' – a.k.a., common sense!!

These delightful chaps returned, obviously they'd won as they were in good spirits and loud voice. The trains were filling up quite quickly and leaving for Brighton. A particularly vocal group were shoehorned into four carriages; they'd been causing problems outside and Sussex Police had rounded them up and pushed them into the station to get rid of them. This group had a number of well-known faces among them, so we knew it was potentially our risk group. They were bouncing, shouting, swearing, pushing and shoving. It was so bad that a dog handler was summoned to try and get his very vocal German Shepherd, 'Land Shark', to quieten them down. He was an experienced dog man and not one to back down; very old-school. He approached the train and went to put his dog in through the door, more to threaten than anything. He stood there, about 2 feet from the open door, looked back at the assembled group of BTP officers who'd gathered and were expecting to see blood, and said 'You're fucking kidding me. I'm not putting my dog anywhere near that lot!', before withdrawing.

Our inspector looked at the waiting group of BTP and selected myself and Bob to accompany this group. The train was rocking; Bob and I looked at each other, shrugged and forced our way inside the carriage. Doors shut and we were off. As I've previously mentioned, it was a three minute trip. Three minutes standing in a carriage full of bouncing football fans can feel like a lifetime. The type of train we were on had doors at every set of seats; they had internal, chromed handles, which just needed a pinch grip to open them. We had our backs to one of these doors.

Then it started – coins being thrown, spitting, chants of 'Kill the bill, kill the bill' repeated over and over again. Then they started unscrewing the lightbulbs and throwing those. They were climbing over the seats, onto the luggage racks, getting closer. Bob told me to get my truncheon out and just hit anyone who came within striking range; I did as I was told. Bob wasn't easily ruffled but this was different. They were trying to open the door handle behind us; Bob and I looked at each other, as numerous hands got hit in that three minute trip.

Bob looked at me, and spoke quietly, 'Pick your man; we're going to have one of these for this.' I looked at the baying group and locked onto one in particular. I spoke to Bob, 'Him there, he's most vocal; he's stirring them up the most.' Bob agreed.

We watched and listened: if we were going to do this properly, we needed to stay focused, keep him in our sights and also to listen to exactly what he was saying. We had to get something called 'evidence'! That was potentially the scariest three minutes of my life to date, inches from the door being opened and with possibly fifty or sixty fans chanting 'Kill the bill, kill the bill'.

Eventually the train slowed and pulled into the platform. Radio communications at that time were pretty diabolical, so no one knew at that time what had been going on.

Even before the train stopped, the doors were opening. We'd got our mark and we made it our business to keep him within arm's reach. The noise of the fans arriving at Brighton was deafening; that's the thing with old railway stations, they were designed for the crowd to make the most noise. I looked towards the ticket barrier, where there was a wall of police, both BTP and Sussex – the reception committee, whom I was so relieved to see!

The fans were oblivious to Bob and me now. They were heading for the next big confrontation at the ticket barrier. Bob looked at me, looked at the mark, and nodded. We took an arm each and took the guy to the ground. No ceremony, no technique, no consideration for anything else – just getting our man. He hit the platform like a ton of bricks, face first. Our adrenalin levels were off the scale, and we weren't going to lose this one. He put up quite a struggle and a couple of his mates started to come back to rescue him, but they were intercepted and kept away from us. We finally got him controlled and cuffed.

Our next problem was getting him to custody; the station was heaving with members of the public and fans. Our detective sergeant came to the rescue; there was a staff entrance at the far end of the platform, which was accessed from a railway yard. He took the car there and we bundled this male into the back of it. Once deposited, the drunken fan was left to sober up prior to being charged. No question he was going to appear before the magistrates – back then it was more or less a given under these sorts of circumstances.

Back at the office it was time for a cuppa and a written statement. Get it done while it's fresh in your mind. Pen and paper, sit down and begin to write. I couldn't, my hand was shaking, it looked like a spider had been thrown at the page. No matter how I tried it just wasn't happening. I looked at Bob. For the first time in my life I'd been truly scared, and I was still coming down from the adrenalin high. Bob looked at me and said, it'd be okay, he'd do his, that's all that was needed to charge, I could do mine the next day – my work dad was looking after me.

Football in those days was a whole different ball game!

Roll forward to 2015, my last year in the job. I'm now based in Manchester, a motorcycle officer, mainly! No easy numbers for us 'old boys'. Football escort on the roster, where will we end up I wonder?

'Barnsley', came the reply from one of the youngsters on my serial of a sergeant and six officers. I could barely contain my excitement! Another long day of being stood on my aching feet, body armour weighing me down along with telescopic baton, speed-cuffs, captor spray, and everything else a twenty-first-century cop was expected to carry.

Off we go – Preston North End were paying a friendly visit to Barnsley, there would be no issues, we were told.

They lied.

We travelled on a train service via Sheffield to Barnsley. It was a miserable, dark, damp day and, to be fair to Barnsley, it didn't do anything for the tourist trade in the town. We had a little time to kill before the fans returned, so off we went in search of something to eat. The normal diet on football consisted of kebab, chips, burger or perhaps a Subway sandwich, if you were a healthy sort. I can't remember what I had but I fancied a little snooze to aid the digestion. It was not going to happen. Local bobbies turned up, telling us that they were on the way back.

We positioned ourselves on the overbridge where we could see the action unfolding below. The fans arrived. There's a railway level crossing at the end of the platform; the barriers were down so the fans were being directed to technically the wrong platform, and they'd have to come up over the bridge, past our position. Obviously one or two didn't like being told where to go and what to do. Our Home Office colleagues weren't the patient sort and the batons came out! It was actually quite entertaining, watching from our lofty position. Batons twirling, somewhat more medieval techniques than you might see in a marching band! Seconds later they came running into the station, again met by the friendly face of the BTP, who were as ever, informative, tolerant and only too pleased to welcome them with open arms.

Certain things in my experience of policing football fans never change. They're always noisy, mostly obnoxious towards the police, and occasionally have to be spoken to in a manner that would make your mother blush!

The platform was full, and they were all complaining about the locals; for once, we BTP were classed as fair-minded, reasonable, friendly cops. That's a rare thing and it was later to change. We got them on a train, absolutely full to the brim, barely a cigarette paper's width between anyone. Very noisy, no idea what the result was, didn't really care, nearly thirty years of this had beaten any interest out of me. Unfortunately, the trains being what they were, we landed at Leeds with nearly an hour to wait for the connection to Preston. Beer-o'clock for the fans, and more standing around on near-fifty-year-old legs again.

The train arrived and the fans trooped on. It was ridiculous, there was barely room to move, the aisles were 'chokka' and every seat was taken. My younger colleague Julian, forty-eight years old, and I were jammed into the rear vestibule, along with possibly ten other human beings. The smell had to be experienced to be believed – body odour, cheap aftershave, stale beer and one clown who insisted on farting constantly! We'd got over an hour to put up with this – roll on retirement.

This little two-carriage train was trundling along at a sedate pace with its cargo of fans and general passengers, seemingly stopping at every gate post and taking forever to get there. My feet were aching; this wasn't fun anymore. I was tired of it.

We finally started getting to stations whose names I recognised. Burnley Manchester Road, several fans wanted to get off. This necessitated most of the standing folks getting off and then getting back on again. Among the new arrivals was a young mum with at least three kids, a pushchair and numerous bags. I could see the look of concern on the face of the bloke who'd seen her onto the train. I told him we'd keep an eye on them, which he appreciated.

The train was again full. From my position in the vestibule I couldn't see directly into the carriage; I had to lean to one side. Julian and I exchanged small talk. He'd transferred into BTP from Greater Manchester Police, and he'd been a very well-regarded detective with a lot of experience in that field of policing. Football trains were not his natural operational environment.

The general noise of the carriage under these circumstances normally remains the same until the beer takes hold and the fans start to fall asleep. Bless! You can normally tell by the volume what's going on. Sometimes there's one noisy person who has to be spoken to but on this occasion it was just a dull drone.

So it was until I heard the volume rise and individual voices begin to shout. I leant sideways to see fists flying about halfway down the carriage. Strange, as they were all Preston fans! I forced my way through the folks who were standing in the aisle – no mean feat, as I'm 6 foot 2 inches tall and, fully kitted, I probably weighed in at about 17 stone. There was a lull in the scrapping as I was about 6 to 8 feet from someone with a raised fist, and then it started again. I reached in and, using all my strength and training, picked the protagonist up in a headlock. It was all I could do to control him; the space was confined and people were coming at him from three sides. Thankfully, he was somewhat smaller than me and lighter. I lifted him and rotated him back towards Julian, who was about a pace behind me. He was struggling but, with a good push from me and some serious assistance from Julian, he was dragged away from the crush of people.

It was then that I felt something wet on my hand. I looked down to see both hands covered in blood; my clothes were covered, my arms, my face, even my glasses had blood on them. I didn't feel any pain so I presumed it was off the lad I'd taken hold of. The train had by now arrived at Accrington, I think. I made my way to the exit; Julian was already on the platform with the lad. He'd got a large gash in the side of his head above his right ear. Julian was busy trying to put a bandage on him so I went back into the carriage and removed the one lad he'd been going to punch. This lad had in fact been the protagonist; he subsequently got arrested for several offences.

I subsequently got an account from the young lad.

He was a Royal Marine with the weekend off, going to the football with a couple of mates. He was standing up but there was an empty seat and a young woman standing nearby. He spoke to three lads who were sat at a table of four seats. He asked if it was taken; it wasn't, so being a Royal Marine with standards, he asks the young woman if she'd like to sit down and she accepted. There then begins a tirade of comments by the two sitting opposite concerning the young lady's looks, assets, and what they'd like to do to her if she wanted them to!

Our Royal Marine basically told them to shut up and leave her alone, as inappropriate remarks to a single woman were not acceptable – a decent young Marine. One of them then made a move to stand up. The Royal Marine reacted instantly and gave him a tap on the left side of his head! A sort of 'sit down and shut up' kind of tap. Obviously not understanding this, the male stood up again and the carriage erupted, which is where I'd come in. While I was en route through the crowded carriage, this individual had then taken a bottle and hit the Marine in the side of his head – hence the blood.

I could see exactly why he'd done what he did, and said we'd do our best to make sure he was treated correctly. There was, however, going to be a full investigation so he'd better be prepared. I spoke to any number of witnesses, who all blamed the Marine until I asked who'd heard the young woman being abused and who'd seen the bottle incident. There was silence.

I rolled off the train at Preston station to a chorus of abuse from my colleagues, mostly about a man of my age getting involved in a fight – I should know better etc, etc. One or two came up to me and asked if I was okay. One or two even complimented me on the fact that I'd 'taken out' a twenty-five-year-old Royal Marine! I still had it, the ability to survive!

I just considered myself bloody lucky to have got the jump on him; any other day of the week he'd have probably killed me! I would add that, the following day, my shoulders were aching and my feet were ready to get up and leave. It made me realise my own mortality and just how lucky I'd been over the length of my service to have escaped with only a few bumps and bruises. It also made me realise that my time at the 'pointed end' was drawing to a close. All that fighting was a young man's game and I was no longer young! To quote the character of Murtagh in the *Lethal Weapon* films: 'I'm too old for this shit!'

My time within BTP has been varied and interesting and I've seen and done things, like most cops, that most folks would have turned and gone the other way if confronted with. I've learnt so much from the people I've worked with and I hope that I've passed on some hints and tips to those who follow on behind me.

On Saturday 9 January 2016, after fighting at about 3 p.m. between Manchester United and Sheffield United fans, dozens of

Sheffield fans were corralled together in Manchester by officers in nine vans, accompanied by police dogs, and escorted back to Piccadilly station to be put onto trains. Film of the incident was uploaded onto a hooligan video website with the heading 'Sheffield United all wrapped up in Manchester on Saturday', to which 'AW' commented, 'All twenty of them by twice as many plod.'

In a separate incident fifty Bradford fans were escorted to Manchester Victoria station and put on trains after trying to make their way into the city centre post an early kick-off game against Bury. On the same day for the Scottish Cup tie between Hearts and Aberdeen in Edinburgh, service trains were declared dry of alcohol from 19.15. Also on 9 January 2016, BTP officers monitored Newcastle and Sunderland fans travelling south for FA Cup clashes, with Newcastle playing Watford and Sunderland meeting Arsenal at the Emirates Stadium in London. Returning northbound trains were declared dry for alcohol purposes.

On 12 January 2016 BTP officers from Guildford were engaged in covering football traffic for the Bournemouth versus West Ham game but reported no incidents. On 15 January 2016 BTP announced a new partnership approach between themselves and Leeds United FC in an effort to combat football violence and ASB on stations and trains. Inspector Pete Kooper said, 'It's great that we are now linking in with Leeds United to all work towards one goal, which is to show football-related crime and ASB on the rail network the red card.' To mark the new approach, stewards from Leeds United were expected to be on hand at Leeds station for the following day's game, in order to meet and greet fans.

The new agreement meant that any fan reported, arrested, fined or convicted of an offence while travelling to or from Leeds United football fixtures could be punished by the club as well, with penalties ranging from having their account with the club suspended to a lifetime ban, depending on the nature of the offence.

On Saturday 16 January 2016 two trained BTP football spotters were deployed at Birmingham New Street station, while Virgin Train services at Euston enforced a dry train policy as part of Operation Stronghold, with no alcohol on board trains allowed. On Sunday 17 January 2016 a thirty-seven-year-old West Ham fan was travelling home by train after attending a match at Newcastle the previous day. While waiting at Darlington station for a train, he was refused service after asking for four cans of beer, having purchased another four just fifteen minutes earlier. The man started shouting and swearing, and then went into the ladies' toilets, where he was asked to leave by the female cleaner, who was then threatened with violence. He later received a twelve-month community order after pleading guilty to two public order offences.

On 18 January 2016 a new station at Coventry Arena for the Rioch Stadium, home of Coventry City FC, on the Coventry–Nuneaton line was opened. It would be served by London Midland services but not on match days, as the single-car units would not have enough capacity to cater for supporters. With the station opening one hour after major events, many local fans were perplexed by the advice to use road transport.

On Saturday 23 January 2016 eight men in their mid-to-late teens sang religiously offensive songs on the 17.28 Dunblane–Edinburgh service. They all left the train at Linlithgow station and were believed to have been returning from a match between East Stirlingshire and Fife SPFL. On the same date at least five BTP public order vans were visible outside Euston railway station in London. Additional BTP officers monitored football traffic, as Virgin Trains declared that from 19.00 all trains heading to Manchester Piccadilly would be dry, with no alcohol allowed or consumed on board.

On Saturday 30 January 2016, a group of men who styled themselves as the 'South Yorkshire Casuals' were intercepted at Leeds station and spoken to by BTP officers. They were on their way to a Britain First demonstration in Dewsbury. The SYC are linked to another group called Yorkshire's Finest, who on their social media website proclaim, 'This is a closed group of patriots from around Yorkshire who have formed to stand with other patriotic movements and football groups in the UK. Yorkshires Finest are football lads and patriots who have come together to take on anything we see as a threat to our country or our way of life'.

Officers were concerned about the group's behaviour, as a result of which they were told that they would be prevented from attending the demonstration and were issued with dispersal notices to return to South Yorkshire. They subsequently boarded a train that was escorted by a number of BTP officers. During the journey several people began chanting and, despite being asked to desist by police officers, three men in particular continued to behave in an anti-social manner on the busy train. As the train pulled into Barnsley station, two men, aged forty-two years and thirty-five years, began singing religiously offensive songs loudly; they were arrested, together with a thirty-three-year-old man.

All three were charged with public order offences and were later fined and ordered to pay costs. At the end of the prosecution case, Inspector Granville Sellers from BTP said, 'The train was extremely busy and the behaviour of these three men was very uncomfortable and distressing for the other passengers on board, who should not have to be subjected to such abhorrent conduct.'

At 7.50 p.m. on Sunday 31 January 2016, a group of Chelsea fans, travelling back from an FA Cup game with MK Dons, boarded a Euston-bound train service at Milton Keynes. The carriage was crowded; they began using foul language and then turned their attentions towards an Orthodox Jewish man, who was subjected to anti-Semitic chants and abuse to such an extent that he decided to move to a different carriage. DC David Peck from the BTP appealed for witnesses and released a CCTV image of a man that they desired to locate.

Kevin Marshall retired as a chief inspector with the British Transport Police in January 2016 and has his own recollections of policing football, initially with a Home Office force, and more latterly with the BTP.

I first joined the Metropolitan Police as a cadet in 1982. Being a Devon boy, my only experience of anything like football hooliganism had been the occasional trip to St James' Park in my youth, to watch the mighty Exeter City. I still remember one of the chants that the Cowshed Boys used to sing – 'we're the boys in red and white, love to sing, love to fight, Exeter la-la-la, Exeter la-la-la' – though to be honest I never witnessed a huge amount of disorder.

I became a PC in July 1984 and, as a young officer, in addition to many tours of duty policing the News International dispute at Wapping (where we were affectionately referred to as Maggie

Thatcher's boot boys), I policed a variety of football matches, mainly around South and West London. One that sticks out in my memory was a Millwall versus Leeds United fixture, probably around 1985 or 1986. As we travelled to the ground in our battle bus, we all knew it was likely to be a fairly lively affair, and the fixture lived up to our expectation. I recall several skirmishes during the match and, although I can't remember the result, I do remember the disorder that followed!

As was often the case, the Leeds away fans were kept back at the end of the match to allow the Millwall fans to leave the area. This process was clearly taking too long for some of the Leeds fans, and they decided that their plight would improve if they started ripping up the seats and throwing them towards the police lines! Order was eventually restored, largely thanks to the dog section, and a number of arrests were made.

In March 2000, after several years of policing London, I decided to transfer to the British Transport Police at Bristol. This transfer not only allowed me a move back to the West Country, but it also enabled me to see football policing from another perspective – i.e., how to police football fans with limited or sometimes hardly any resources!

Not long after transferring, I was on duty at Bristol Temple Meads when one of the London teams, QPR I think, came down to play Bristol City. The away fans appeared to be pretty relaxed on the forward leg of the journey from London Paddington to Bristol Temple Meads but, during the course of the afternoon, something changed.

After the match, we could hear over the radio that Avon & Somerset Police were having real problems with some of the away fans, and the decision had been made to escort them back to the railway station. We took up our positions at the front of the station and, after a short while, we could see the front of the escort appear at the bottom of the approach road. The local police appeared well-prepared for this fixture, with a helicopter, horses, dogs, and seemingly more police officers than you could shake a stick at! I was a sergeant at this stage in my career and my task was to take these 'characters' back to London, using the six – yes, six – BTP officers who were at my disposal. 'Hey Sarge, welcome to the BTP', one of them chuckled!

With the help of First Great Western, we managed to segregate the thirty to forty football fans from the general travelling public, which I learnt was always a good move, unless you wanted to spend the rest of the following week resolving complaints! Our BTP style of policing was quite different from that I had experienced in my previous force, not least because there were only seven of us and we were hurtling through the countryside at 125 mph.

I don't know whether it was due to our presence, our finely polished communication skills, or that the fans were simply too tired to fight anymore, but in general terms we managed to keep the lid on things until we reached London Paddington, where a 'welcoming committee' had been laid on for us.

One typical example of how hooligans behaved was on Saturday 6 March 2010. I remember I was directed by Mike Layton, with other officers, to intercept a train at Westbury railway station that had up to ninety Newport fans on board who had been to Weymouth. There was a female train manager who done her best to cope with their obnoxious behaviour during the journey.

As I stepped onto the train at Westbury, I was confronted by what might be best described as carnage! The group of Newport County fans were drinking, smoking, chanting and generally being abusive. Among the group were some fairly tasty-looking individuals, some of whom had tattoos on their necks, and they weren't spring chickens either! We decided that a couple of the worst offenders would be arrested when the train arrived at Bristol Temple Meads, as the group would need to change trains, and we could also muster a healthy amount of police officers with the support of our colleagues in Avon & Somerset Police.

We escorted the train into Bristol Temple Meads and, as the train pulled onto the platform, a confrontation took place as a number of the supporters threatened police officers. As was routinely the case, there were more of them than us and officers were obliged to draw batons and deploy captor sprays in what can only be described as a running battle. We made four arrests before things calmed down, but it was by no means an unusual situation to face.

In addition to the arrests that were made on the night, there was a post-incident investigation led by the CID wherein at least another half-a-dozen fans were subsequently brought to justice.

Rolling on to 2015 (my last year in the police service), and I ask myself whether much has really changed in terms of football hooliganism? Well, on a personal level, I'm slightly more rotund than I was at the age of nineteen; I've developed a beard to try to hide the ageing process; and I've managed to move a couple of rungs up the promotion ladder. But I don't think football fans have changed that much. Police officers are clearly better equipped, better trained and arguably more intelligent than we were back in the 1980s – but of course, back then, we didn't have the benefit of CCTV to the same extent, or the opportunities given by social media.

From a policing perspective, I think the whole thing is generally more organised than it was back in the 1980s. That said, of course policing has never been an exact science and sometimes things would not go the way you had them planned. For example some football supporters would travel to a fixture by coach. If they played up, the coach drivers would sometimes refuse to take them home, and they often ended up in some far-flung destination on the rail network, with no train tickets. Equally it was not uncommon for two sets of fans travelling to two very different destinations, who by rights should have had no contact with each other on the network, to find themselves on a broken-down train, and then unexpectedly boarding another train that contained their arch-rivals.

This was all commonly known as copper's luck!

The railway continues to be a very popular mode of transport for football supporters. I guess for some it's the convenience and the flexibility, but for others it's the ability to be able to consume large quantities of alcohol. For ordinary members of the public, who are just going about their normal business, enduring one of those 'Saturday nights from hell' even now can be a very daunting experience.

On Monday 1 February 2016, football-related disorder took place at Preston station and, after order was restored, a knife was recovered. On Tuesday 2 February 2016, Scunthorpe United played Doncaster Rovers. After the game, an eighteen-year-old Scunthorpe man threw a smoke bomb in the direction of Doncaster fans as they waited to board a train at Scunthorpe station. The device landed at the feet of police officers. He was later convicted of a public order offence and was given a five-year football banning order.

On Wednesday 3 February 2016, BTP officers were on duty at Aberdeen railway station ahead of the game between Aberdeen and Celtic. On Saturday 6 February 2016, a group of Nottingham Forest fans, under the influence of alcohol, started to behave in a disorderly manner on 19.05 train between Leeds and Nottingham. Three men were subsequently arrested by BTP officers for being drunk and disorderly, with two men aged twenty-two years and twenty-nine years from Ilkeston, and a twenty-nine-year-old man from Ripley in Derbyshire. A fourth man, aged thirty-six years and from Alfreton, was arrested for assaulting a police officer, and charged and bailed to appear in court at a later date. PC Wayne Mitchell from BTP appealed for witnesses to the incidents to come forward.

'WSFN' commented on a social media site in relation to the incident: 'It's funny that you never see a headline asking for witnesses to a copper rapping his stick round the back of your knees or letting his dog take a bit outta ya calf. Wankers'. On the same site 'MH' said, 'BTP are wankers of the highest order'.

Also on the same date, a female BTP officer in Manchester was spat at and punched by a drunken Manchester City fan, who was arrested. The thirty-four-year-old fan was returning from a home game against Leicester, when he attacked the officer and her colleague at Manchester Piccadilly railway station. He had been asked to produce his ticket by a member of rail staff carrying out a routine check, but had become abusive and pushed him out of the way.

The two BTP officers, and a PCSO, attended and, when asked to provide his details, the fan continued to be abusive and aggressive. As they tried to arrest him for the earlier assault he responded by punching the female officer in the face with such force that the blow knocked her to the ground in what was later described as a 'sickening attack'. He was later banned from attending football matches for three years, as well as being made the subject of four-month curfew that included wearing an electronic tag.

During the lead-up to the Wales versus Scotland rugby match on Saturday 13 February 2016, BTP Superintendent Andy Morgan, based in Cardiff, made a comparison between rugby and football supporters travelling on the rail network, when he said that rugby fans could be more difficult to deal with than football fans, who 'pushed boundaries' but generally listened to the police.

By comparison he described rugby supporters who drank all day as follows: 'On any other day of the week they will be perfectly law-abiding family people who know how to behave. Today they won't listen. They won't take advice or warnings. They will be a nightmare.' On the same date BTP officers conducted additional patrols for football at King's Cross station.

On 18 February 2016 the British Transport Police released the results of a national consultation exercise involving more than 6,000 rail users, more than a third of whom identified one of their three priorities as being the prevention of anti-social behaviour, which included that relating to football. During the weekend covering 20 and 21 February 2016 the BTP deployed more than 150 officers to football-related duties.

On Monday 22 February 2016 Shrewsbury FC hosted Manchester United in an FA Cup game. Under the operational name 'Claudius', BTP officers worked jointly with officers from West Mercia Police, Warwickshire Police, and mounted police officers from Thames Valley to ensure that the game passed off peacefully.

On Saturday 27 February 2016, at about 10.30 p.m., West Yorkshire Police dog handlers were called to Bradford Interchange station to support BTP officers as a train arrived with some fifty to 100 Bradford fans on board, returning from a match with Blackpool. A small number had been acting in an abusive manner on the train and, when they alighted from the train on arrival, minor disturbances broke out on the platform between them. Police made two arrests and the remainder of the fans were dispersed.

At about 12.30 p.m. on the same day, a fifty-one-year-old man who walked with the aid of two walking sticks boarded a train at Carntyne station. He was originally reported to have asked a group of Hibs fans, who were believed to be travelling to watch their team play at Dumbarton in an SPFL match, if he could sit down in a seat designated for disabled passengers.

After initially refusing, it was alleged that they allowed him to sit down; however, as he alighted from the train at Glasgow Queen Street, the group verbally abused him, making references to his disability. PC John Paul O'Kane from BTP later appealed for witnesses. After further enquiries by the BTP a fifty-one-year-old man was reported to the Procurator Fiscal for allegedly wasting police time.

Also on 27 February 2016 another sports-related incident occurred as a fifty-eight-year-old man was assaulted by two men, who had boarded a train at Clapham Junction after attending the England versus Ireland rugby match at Twickenham. DS Sarah Garden said, 'The victim was attacked after taking issue with one of the men who was vomiting on the carriage floor. He was punched and kicked to the floor by the men, who only stopped when other passengers intervened.' The victim suffered cuts and bruises and was treated in hospital.

On Wednesday 2 March 2016, prior to an evening Premier League match between West Ham and Tottenham, groups of fans clashed outside Upton Park tube station, close to the West Ham Stadium. Lines of officers and mounted police struggled to separate fighting fans, and bottles were thrown. One onlooker likened it to something like football violence in the 1980s and one tweeted, 'The trouble has started at Upton Park, Police calling for medics, fights on the streets. Silly people. It's only football.'

In the same month Assistant Chief Constable Mark Roberts, the national lead for football policing in England and Wales, announced that forces would begin operations in the coming months to ensure that up to 2,000 persons subject to banning orders would not be allowed to travel to France for Euro 2016. At the same time it was announced that, after years of falling levels of football-related violence in the UK in and around grounds, it was on the rise again. During the 2011/12 season, one or more incidents occurred at 509 of the almost 3,000 football fixtures across England and Wales. By last season this figure had increased to 910 games – almost one in three.

The UK Foreign Office issued eleven-point guidelines for British fans travelling on how to behave and stay safe, but it was acknowledged that vast numbers were expected to travel by various means, including by train from London St Pancras travelling to Lille, Paris, Lyon and Marseilles on Eurostar services.

Between 8 and 8.22 p.m. on Saturday 5 March 2016, a group of five football fans, believed to be Sheffield Wednesday 'Owls' supporters, were involved in racist chanting on a Northern Rail train between Sheffield to Lincoln. At the time, the train was packed with families, and BTP subsequently released images of an individual in a baseball cap that they wanted to locate in relation to the incident. On the film a man stands tapping out the chants against the train vestibule wall with some sort of stick, completely oblivious to innocent members of the public around him.

A witness who was in the same carriage described a group of men singing football songs for about twenty minutes, before making racist chants on two occasions that included derogatory remarks about Pakistanis. The witness described how another passenger had challenged the group's behaviour, but they had basically ignored him before alighting at Retford station. They had also chanted about the IRA, and one had commented that he hoped that the Rotherham manager, Neil Warnock, who had previously managed Sheffield United, got cancer.

Also on Saturday 5 March 2016, Hamilton played at home to Motherwell in a game that they lost 0-1. A photograph published on a football hooligan social media website showed police officers containing two groups of opposing fans at Hamilton station, which was headlined 'Spot the little firm of Hamilton wrapped up at the end of the platform'. It attracted the following comments, which tell you something about the mentality that still prevails;

'SD' said, 'Fair play not about numbers. It's about no runners.'

'AD' said, 'Little firm stood proud!'

'PB' said, 'Lol. A group of fifteen year-olds standing behind the OB (Old Bill) they absolutely shit themselves when we arrived on the platform.'

Also on the same day, Tottenham Hotspur played Arsenal in the North London derby game. In one incident on the railway, a Tottenham fan kicked a man in the head after some 'good-natured' chanting between rival fans got out of hand.

On Saturday 12 March 2016, BTP in Scotland faced a busy day with Hibs and Ross County football fans travelling to the League Cup final at Hampden Park, while on the same day Scotland played France in the Six Nations Championship. Chief Inspector David Gray from BTP appealed for fans to be well behaved, as plans were put in place by ScotRail for alcohol restrictions to apply on trains, with extensive queuing arrangements put in place at a number of stations.

Also on Saturday 12 March 2016, at 6.30 p.m., some thirty Derby County supporters were on a train, which was stationary on a platform at Rotherham station, when they got involved in a verbal dispute with a group of Rotherham United fans on the opposite platform. A number of the Derby supporters then left the train and ran across the tracks to platform two, and a fight lasting several minutes took place, involving up to ten people, before they finally dispersed. BTP later released ten CCTV images of men that they wanted to speak to in relation to the incident.

Again on Saturday 12 March 2016 Bournemouth played at home to Swansea in a game that they won with a score of 3-2. Two twenty-two-year-old Swansea fans became involved in disorderly behaviour during the course of their return journey. Having already been ejected from an earlier train by police officers at Temple Meads due to their behaviour, they then caught a Swansea-bound service at Bristol Parkway, which contained some Welsh rugby fans returning from Twickenham.

During the course of this journey these two men were shouting, swearing and singing offensive songs, completely oblivious to the impact that they were having on normal passengers and, in particular, a woman and her young child. Their behaviour degenerated as the journey progressed, to the point where, after spraying a can of beer into the faces of a young couple in the same carriage, they began chanting anti-Cardiff songs before throwing a can of beer towards the group of rugby supporters.

The two men then ran down the carriage aisle and started attacking the rugby fans, during the course of which an elderly passenger was struck, and other passengers were spat on. Upon arrival at Cardiff Central, police met the train and arrested the pair, who subsequently received three-year football banning orders as well as receiving substantial fines. A third Swansea fan, aged twenty-three, was also arrested for two separate public order offences and received a fine of £1,000. Inspector Jonathan Cooze from BTP said, after the case was finalised, 'The behaviour of these men was nothing short of pure thuggery. A number of passengers – including children and young women – were terrified by what they had been forced to endure during the journey, with some of them tearful and visibly shaking with fear.' He went on, 'Alcohol clearly played a part in their actions. One man admitted afterwards he was so drunk he couldn't even remember what had happened during the game or who had won'.

On Sunday 13 March 2016, Manchester United played West Ham in an FA Cup quarter-final match at Old Trafford. It was a 4 p.m. kick-off and 9,000 fans were estimated to have travelled to the game, with up to 3,000 by train. Thousands of returning fans were caught up in chaotic scenes at Manchester Piccadilly, as people tried to catch the last train heading towards London and found themselves in a queuing system, mixed together with ordinary passengers, including women and children. As chants rang out across the station concourse, one man was arrested for a public order offence. Amid reports of children crying, and the situation being like a 'rugby scrum', police and rail staff struggled to contain the huge crowds within the cordons which had been set up, and complaints were made that passengers were only being allowed to use one entrance to get onto the platforms.

Two people gave differing views in response to some of the media reports, with 'TB' commenting, 'There is a tragedy waiting to happen here. Have we not learnt from Hillsborough? I was at a game against Spurs at Upton Park and the same thing happened there on the platform, it was quite scary, supporters/passengers could have ended up on the tracks. The police are doing their usual rubbish in herding fans like cattle using these kettling tactics.'

In contrast, 'JNC' said, 'Why should my family and I have to tolerate these dummies. Standing in the station with my wife and ten-year-old daughter with autism, I was disgusted by this hooligan behaviour. Couldn't tell what they were attempting to sing, didn't get a single word. Drunken bums, barking dogs, hooligan scum'.

Passengers reported that fighting broke out on the train, which left at around 9 p.m. and was subsequently held up at Stockport station for fifteen minutes, as Virgin Train staff made tannoy announcements appealing for the fighting to stop before they would take the train any further. An announcement was made on one of the trains returning to London that the buffet bar would not be opening during the journey south. A group of men, who were believed to be West Ham fans, made their way to the buffet and broke into the fridge, stealing a large amount of alcohol. PC Michael Natavio said, 'We know the vast majority of West Ham fans are law-abiding people and that most of those on the train behaved impeccably and were a credit to their club, but the actions of this group were unacceptable.' Costs resulting from the damage, and the theft of the beer and wine, were estimated to be in the order of £5,000 and the BTP subsequently circulated CCTV images of six men that they wanted to speak to in connection with the incident.

A man was punched in the face, resulting in a broken cheekbone, shortly after 11 p.m. on Saturday 19 March 2016 at Sheffield station. As a group of some fifteen Sheffield United supporters, returning home from a fixture in London, walked past the Café Ritazza on the station as they headed towards the taxi rank, a fifty-seven-year-old man was assaulted and knocked to the ground. PC Stephen Slocombe said, 'The victim attended hospital and was treated for the injury which required him to have a metal plate fitted.'

At 7 p.m. on Sunday 20 March 2016, two eighteen-year-olds were attacked by a man wearing a Guinness St Patrick's Day hat while they waited in a taxi queue at Leeds railway station. The two friends, both from Leeds, were returning from the Tyne and Wear derby game in Newcastle when three men wearing hats approached them. One of them started to abuse one victim, before punching him in the head. As his friend tried to stop the assault he was also attacked and punched to the ground. DS Tom Eastwood said, 'This was completely unprovoked and violent behaviour displayed by men who were simply returning home from a day out watching football'.

On the same date, eighty-five-year-old Alice Austin was knocked to the ground while waiting in the taxi rank at Newcastle Central station as fists flew among opposing fans. She had to be rescued by other family members and later received treatment in hospital.

At 5.30 p.m. on Friday 25 March 2016 a group of Scunthorpe United supporters, travelling to Sheffield from Barnsley, ended up fighting with Barnsley supporters travelling on the same train between Barnsley and Wombwell. As a result, one Scunthorpe fan sustained head injuries that required stitches and a forty-two-year-old man from Barnsley was arrested. DC Ian Grice the investigating officer said, 'This was a nasty fight that broke out in the middle of a busy train at peak time.'

On Saturday 2 April 2016 Norwich played at home to Newcastle and won the game with a score of 3-2, exposing Newcastle to the threat of relegation. An eighteen-minute-long film was subsequently posted on YouTube, which was titled 'Newcastle United Fans singing on train back from Norwich.' Within five weeks it had been viewed 2,413 times. The term 'singing' was something of a misleading statement, as a group of men behaved in a totally anti-social manner in one of the coaches. As they drank from beer cans and bottles, they engaged in endless rounds of clapping, chanting, swearing and screaming at the tops of their voices. Did they care about the impact of their behaviour on others on the train? Absolutely not!

In the comments section on the social media site, 'TJ' commented on the film,

> Feel a bit sorry for these blokes, most of them probably wish they had a nice home and a nice girlfriend and kids and good jobs that earnt a good wage. Bet most don't wanna be hanging out on a train with a load of drunken men howling out these chants, waking up the next day feeling shit in their own sick. But I don't blame them, without all that, is there much else they can do.

Also on 2 April 2016, Birmingham City played away to Charlton and Birmingham City fans were reported to have been involved in chanting racist comments towards other passengers. On Monday 4 April 2016, at 10.30 p.m., a thirty-one-year-old man was attacked at Canada Water Underground station in London. The victim and his friend were leaving the station when they noticed two men behind them singing Millwall songs. One of the men then attacked the victim and punched him in the face, and then proceeded to attack a second person. As staff went to the aid of the injured men they were threatened with violence. Both injured men sustained cuts and bruising in what the investigating officer DS Krishan Appannah described as a frightening outburst of violence.

On Saturday 16 April 2016, Sunderland fans travelled away to Norwich, and a number of 'Black Cats' fans were involved in pushing and punching a rival fan, who received injuries, in an incident that apparently started off as 'banter'.

The semi-finals of the Scottish Cup took place at Hampden Park during the weekend of 16 and 17 April 2016. BTP Chief Inspector David Marshall co-ordinated operations on the rail network and indicated that people who had been the subject of football banning orders during the preceding two years had been contacted and reminded of the conditions of the order. Officers were deployed wearing body-worn video cameras, and alcohol restrictions put in place on many ScotRail services, both before and after the games taking places on the Saturday and Sunday. To add to the pressure on policing, the Scottish Grand National took place at Ayr Racecourse on Saturday 16 April 2016 with large numbers of people in attendance.

At 5.15 p.m. on Saturday 16 April 2016, a smoke bomb was discharged at Paisley St James station, shortly after the St Mirren versus Morton SPFL match. The suspect, aged about eighteen, set the pyrotechnic off just as a train arrived on the platform and DC Marc Francey said, 'The platform was extremely busy with people waiting for the train and the dangers and potential circumstances of such a stupid act cannot be underestimated.'

On the same day the spectre of trouble from rugby fans raised its head again after a fight took place on a train between Clapham Junction and Sanderstead. The disturbance took place at 11.30 p.m. and involved a number of people, two of whom jumped off the train at East Croydon before running up the platform and getting back on to resume the fight.

BTP officers investigating the fight said that it was possible that two of the men, who were captured on CCTV, were returning from watching a Saracens versus Harlequins rugby match at Wembley earlier in the day. Two men subsequently contacted the police and they were interviewed in connection with the incident.

On Saturday 23 April 2016 Liverpool played Newcastle at home in a Premier League match. What was described as a large group of men travelled on the 18.42 train service from Darlington to Newcastle and, during the journey, they engaged in racist and abusive language, which resulted in a member of the travelling public texting BTP's 61016 non-emergency number to complain. Although police met the train at Newcastle station the group had apparently already left the service; complaints were made that fans were drunk, that someone had pulled an emergency cord, and in one case a fan had even tried to gain access to the train driver's cab.

On Saturday 30 April 2016, Wolverhampton supporters travelled away to Nottingham Forest. A knife was later found on a train transporting Wolves fans, although no certainty could be attached as to whom it belonged.

On Saturday 7 May 2016, the police response to a handful of St Johnstone fans, who were travelling by train to Motherwell, came under fire. Images were captured and displayed on social media of the group of ten or so fans, in their teens, who were surrounded by more than twenty police officers on a platform at Airbles railway station. The editor of St Johnstone fan forum WeArePerth said online, 'Football fans are the most over policed group in Scotland ...' The BTP denied being heavy-handed.

On Tuesday 10 May 2016 West Ham played at home to Manchester United; BTP reported an incident wherein a West Ham fan tried to jump the barriers at a station. After being prevented from doing so, he punched one officer and then head-butted another. On Friday 13 May 2016 a group of men, who were believed to be football supporters, engaged in disorderly and homophobic behaviour following the SPFL play-off match between Falkirk and Hibs. A group of about ten male youths boarded the 22.00 Edinburgh Waverley–Queen Street service at Falkirk High station, and were reported to be shouting and singing offensive songs, as well as drinking alcohol on board the train, which arrived in Glasgow just before 11.15 p.m. They were believed to be Falkirk fans, and their behaviour forced other passengers to change carriages.

In a separate incident a short time later, a group of five men, who were believed to be Hibs supporters, shouted homophobic chants as they waited at Falkirk High station for the 22.30 service to Edinburgh Waverley. PCs Patrick Moran and Fiona MacAulay appealed for witnesses to come forward in relation to both incidents.

On 14/15 May the final Premier League games took place together with the play-off semi-finals. The celebrated era of mainline steam football specials made a comeback on 15 May 2016 when Bulleid Pacific No. 34046 *Braunton*, running as No. 34052 *Lord Dowding*, hauled a train of Crystal Palace supporters from South London to Southampton for the club's final League match of the season. It is thought to have been the first time that steam had piloted a football special on the mainline since Britannia No. 70013 *Oliver Cromwell* was chartered between Carlisle and Blackpool on Boxing Day 1967. An added twist to the May 15 run was that Palace manager Alan Pardew and team travelled back with supporters, who completely filled the £216-per-head train, which included the match ticket and food. The special was the brainchild of multi-millionaire businessman Jeremy Hosking, owner of the Southern 4-6-2, and also a co-owner of the South London club.

On Thursday 19 May 2016 Walsall played Barnsley at Bescot Stadium. A group of Walsall fans were abusive towards train staff, and also caused criminal damage to the train. On Saturday 21 May 2016 at 9.45 p.m., a thirty-seven-year-old Rangers FC fan was approached by two men on platform 3 at Haymarket station. One of the men proceeded to punch him in the face, causing him to fall to the floor, where he was knocked unconscious. He was later taken to hospital for treatment, where he was detained in a stable condition. The second man present was described as wearing a black tartan shirt and a Hibernian FC scarf. CCTV images were released, and a twenty-three-old man was subsequently arrested and made the subject of a report to the Procurator Fiscal.

BTP announced that they would be out in force for the Yorkshire play-off finals at Wembley between Hull and Sheffield Wednesday, with Temporary Superintendent David Oram making an appeal for fans to be on their best behaviour on Saturday 28 May 2016. A dry train policy was put in place for some services returning north after the game, and some officers were assigned to work with body-worn cameras.

Following a further Freedom of Information request by the *Birmingham Mail*, the BTP revealed that at least sixty-seven incidents involving fans of either Aston Villa, Birmingham City, West Bromwich Albion, Wolverhampton or Walsall were logged by the force during the course of the season. At least twenty-six of them had occurred since the figures were previously explored in November 2015. The figures included a case where an Aston Villa fan reportedly took a woman's handbag, sifted through it, took out some foodstuff, and then handed it back.

Further afield, three instances were recorded by BTP of fans indecently exposing themselves. In one case a Newport fan reportedly exposed his genitals to a female member of staff and masturbated, while another individual in a group tried to kiss her. In another case a Northampton fan exposed himself to an elderly woman after being encouraged to do so by a group of drunken fans.

Twenty-three incidents across the force area were classified as assault occasioning actual bodily harm. In one of these incidents, a Millwall fan head-butted a staff member for supposedly not telling him where the toilets were, and an offence was recorded whereby two men, believed to be Arsenal fans, verbally abused and then assaulted a man for speaking Arabic. Eleven incidents were recorded of assaults on police officers. In one of those cases a group of ten Leeds supporters refused to show their train tickets on the day of an away game to Queens Park Rangers, which resulted in one them pushing a police officer three times when he intervened. There were also thirty-six cases of common assault, four incidents of grievous bodily harm, and one more serious offence of wounding.

Significantly, there were six cases of fans 'sexually touching' female train passengers. These cases included an Arsenal fan grabbing a woman's buttocks and groin over her clothing. In another, a Sheffield United fan touched a woman's legs with his foot, and a Grimsby fan groped a woman from behind while alighting from a train.

As previously mentioned, the use of pyrotechnics was more in evidence, with twenty-one incidents reported, including an Everton fan throwing a flare from a train onto the platform and a Brighton fan setting off a smoke grenade.

Leeds fans featured prominently in the figures, as did Newcastle fans, with BTP recording twenty-eight instances relating to that club.

BTP regularly dealt with reports of fans dancing on tables, jumping on seats, sometimes actually lying in overhead lockers, engaging in obscene and abusive chants, and routinely acting in an anti-social manner while under the influence of alcohol.

Commenting on the West Midlands-related figures in response to a newspaper article, 'WC' said,

It's the same all over the country it's not just the Midlands go to London and you see the same thing. In terms of the amount of supporters in football it's a very small minority that behave in this way. And the police don't help the situation with their bad man hailing and heavy handedness on the supporters that are not even involved.

On Wednesday 6 July 2016, hundreds of football fans travelled to Pontypridd town centre to watch the Wales versus Portugal football match in the fan zone. It was being played in France as part of the Euro football championship. After the game a large number of fans arrived at Pontypridd station and a number of them started fighting. Widespread disorder occurred, and train services were disrupted as families with children got swept up by the violence and rail staff were threatened as they tried to contain the situation. The British Transport Police later released CCTV stills of twelve men that they wanted to trace in connection with the incident.

Dan Taylor is the Transport Focus policy lead on security and participates in the Railway Football Forum, sponsored by the Rail Development Group. In September 2016 he commented,

I am aware we do receive complaints from passengers whose journeys have been impacted by travelling fans; typically they relate to the anti-social behaviour of groups as opposed to organised hooliganism or the type of crime you'd associate with such groups. The impact of the anti-social behaviour on passengers and staff, and the challenge it poses to the industry, is however hugely significant.

My understanding, albeit based on limited personal experience, is that the relatively lower level anti-social behaviour is now much more of a problem than the organised violence witnessed on the railways in the 80s. I am aware, having worked with BTP on the RRF forum, that while they tend to publish the overall number of football-related crimes on the railway, they tend not to release any data about which teams are most commonly involved in order not to encourage other groups as seeing those figures as a challenge.

2

DISORDER ON THE STREETS AND AT STADIUMS, 2015/2016

Having highlighted the challenges being faced by the British Transport Police in terms of football-related disorder on the rail network, this chapter now seeks to describe some of the same challenges being faced by Home Office forces, and the parallel 'hooligan' activity taking place in and around UK streets and stadiums during the same period in 2015/2016.

On Sunday 5 April 2015 police made twenty-six arrests of men and boys aged between fifteen-years and fifty-one years in relation to a game at Sunderland's Stadium of Light with Newcastle. The match was won by Sunderland 1-0 during the Wear-Tyne derby. Offences included assault, affray, threatening behaviour, going onto the playing area, and being drunk and disorderly. Two Sunderland men were charged with breaching football banning orders. Four men were detained after being caught on CCTV cameras at the ground committing criminal damage and throwing missiles. Three of them were identified damaging chairs, and one of them was seen throwing coins from his pocket at Sunderland fans sitting below. Five of the arrests related to men entering the playing field at the end of the game.

On Saturday 11 April 2015 Wolverhampton Wanderers played Birmingham City at St Andrew's in a game that the home side won with a score of 2-1. Following the game, clashes took place between rival fans, and West Midlands Police made four arrests as they struggled to keep the two sides apart. Two people were taken to hospital with head injuries. Much of the disorder took place at a traditional 'flashpoint' at Watery Lane Middleway Island as opposing fans mingled, prompting police dogs to be deployed. A large group of fans were kettled within a cordon outside Selfridges in Birmingham city centre as police sought to contain them.

Commenting on media reports, 'JJ' said, 'Blues fans were following a man with a black coat and a beard taking orders', while 'MB' said, 'in Digbeth Street where we were attacked by 40–50 Zulu members which came out of the Connaught bar…' A post-incident investigation was mounted, which initially led to twelve addresses being raided and at least three further arrests for affray being made. As a result of examining CCTV coverage, the police initially released stills of eleven people that they wanted to speak to in connection with the violence, with a further six pictures released later, resulting in fifteen people being interviewed by police.

Three complaints were made against police officers, including one claim that a fourteen-year-old boy had been assaulted; policing tactics attracted criticism as fans questioned the decision to allow both sets of fans to leave the stadium at the same time. Defending police action, Chief Superintendent James Andronov said, 'It is rare these days to hold back supporters – it's not been done at this fixture for several years as evidence suggests that to do so often increases tension and the prospect of trouble.'

On Tuesday 12 May 2015, Manchester United and Manchester City's Under-21 teams played at Old Trafford in a game that United won 4-0. During the course of the match minor disturbances took place inside the ground, and three arrests were made, although they were later released without charge.

One thirteen-year-old was detained for pitch encroachment, while a fifteen-year-old and nineteen-year-old were detained outside on suspicion of assault.

On Saturday 30 May 2015, with a 5.30 p.m. kick-off, the FA Cup final took place at Wembley between Aston Villa and Arsenal, a game that the Gunners won with a score of 4-0. During the course of the game, fighting involving Villa fans was observed on the terraces. Prior to the match a young man wearing a Villa club shirt, with an Aston Villa scarf covering the lower part of his face, appeared on a social media site brandishing a knife, above a caption, 'Ready to draw Arsenal blood #AVFC'.

On Tuesday 14 July 2015, Plymouth Argyle played their first pre-season friendly away against Elburton Villa at their Haye Road ground. During the course of the game a green flare was set off behind one of the goals.

On Tuesday 4 August 2015, Thamesmead Town FC, based in Bayliss Avenue, South London, played Clapton, who are based in Forest Gate, East London. Officers present at the game witnessed missiles being thrown followed by some disorder. Clapton supporters claimed that they had been threatened earlier in the week by a far-right group because of the multicultural make-up of their fans, and anti-racist stance. As they arrived in one group at the ground at about 8.10 p.m., they were immediately bombarded with glasses, bottles, bricks, and even a fire extinguisher. Someone was alleged to have shouted, 'We hate niggers', as a confrontation developed. Officers later detained forty Clapton fans on a bus as enquiries were made, and two people were treated for head injuries.

On Saturday 8 August 2015, more than a dozen males clashed in the city centre in Stirling following a home match between Stirling Albion and Clyde, who won the match 1-0. Mobile phone footage was captured of two rival groups taunting each other before they started punching and kicking each other in Baker Street, Stirling. Two men wearing clothing associated with that worn by Clyde fans were shown among the group. In one particular scene a man ran round a car and punched another in the head, causing him to fall to the ground. As the mayhem continued horrified shoppers looked on, and motorists who had been forced to stop their vehicles due to the fighting sounded their horns. In an illustration of just how powerful social media has become, when the footage was uploaded to Facebook it was viewed 240,000 times.

On Friday 14 August 2015 Notts County played at home at the Meadow Lane Stadium to Mansfield in a match that Mansfield won 2-0 as their fans chanted 'Yellows' before an 11,000-strong crowd. At one point a group of Mansfield fans approached a large metal gate from the outside of the ground, to confront Notts County fans inside on the nearby terraces. As they goaded each other with chanting and the traditional 'come on' signs, a single steward attempted to keep the gate closed as it was shaken violently on several occasions. Eventually a number of police officers arrived outside to move on the Mansfield fans, who included a number of middle-aged men. The events were posted on social media and some very typical comments were posted, with 'AW' saying, 'I bet if the gates actually fell down all the people acting tough on the other side of it would have shit themselves.' 'DB' said, 'It's standing your ground, every football fan knows that.'

On Tuesday 18 August 2015, towards the end of a game between Ramsbottom United and Buxton, a brawl developed on the pitch that lasted for five minutes and involved players and coaches from both teams. It was later described in a match report as 'handbags at dawn'.

On Saturday 29 August 2015 Bury playcd at home to Oldham in a game that finished in a 1-1 draw at Gigg Lane. As two sets of fans goaded each other on part of the terracing, police officers and stewards were deployed in one section of the Oldham crowd to maintain order. Part of the crowd reacted to a person being removed by stewards from the terraces and at least two arrests were made, as officers were obliged to draw batons to keep fans at bay as chants of 'Wankers' rang out and 'We are Oldham we'll do what we want.'

Some of the scenes were captured on a mobile phone and were uploaded onto YouTube. They attracted a comment from an Oldham fan 'MST', who prided himself on his hooligan pseudonym:

> Bury beckoning makes me laugh. They rang us one year to say they were in a certain pub which we happened to be about thirty yards away from when they rang. We told them we were outside and when we steamed the pub they had all run out of the back of the back. Pub was full of ¾ pints. Oh how we laughed at how shit Bury were.

Also on Saturday 29 August 2015 Lincoln City played at home at the Sincil Bank Stadium with Grimsby Town in a match that finished in a 1-1 draw.

In a game that is classed as the Lincolnshire derby, a large police presence was put into place to keep the two sets of supporters apart. A minor disturbance was reported at about 1 p.m. on

Wigford Way, while, during the match, police and stewards had to deal with a disturbance in one of the terraces as fans chanted 'Who are ya' at each other.

On Saturday 12 September 2015 Lincoln again played at home to Boreham Wood in a game that Lincoln won 3-1. At 5.30 p.m., following the end of the game, several police cars were directed to the High Street in Lincoln, following a disturbance outside The Shakespeare Pub during which missiles were thrown, traffic was brought to a standstill, and children who witnessed the fighting were left terrified. Three men were arrested for public order offences; they were aged fifty-three, twenty-four and twenty-seven, all from Borehamwood in Hertfordshire. Three people were reported to have been injured, although none seriously.

The incident was filmed and uploaded on YouTube, with the allegation that around thirty Boreham Wood fans had carried out an attack during which at least one person was punched and kicked to the ground. 'DR' commented, '12 of us went outside so they didn't trash the pub. We all took a beating but we all stood our ground, respect to the few – p.s. if you want to prove yourself put down the weapons and fight like men', while 'IK' said, 'Fair play to Lincoln fronted it got a hiding and didn't write a statement on the bwood boys who got pinched respect Borehamwood fan.'

Also on Saturday 12 September 2015 Birmingham City played at home to Bristol City. The Bristol City Supporters Club and Trust subsequently claimed that fifty-one fans, who had been drinking at the Square Peg pub in Birmingham city centre, were rounded up before the game and taken back to New Street station. A Section 35 dispersal order was allegedly issued by police and the group were put back on trains to Bristol. In an unusual legal precedent this group later launched an action to sue the West Midlands Police for claims of 'false imprisonment' and breach of Article 5 of the European Convention of Human Rights, which states that everyone has the right to liberty and security of person.

On Saturday 19 September 2015, the futility and tribal nature of some of the ritual confrontations were demonstrated when Plymouth Argyle played at home to Bristol Rovers in a game that finished in a 1-1 draw. During the course of the day, skirmishes involving scores of fans took place in a park in Plymouth as vastly outnumbered police officers tried to keep them apart. As one Bristol fan, who appeared to be in his forties, filmed the disturbances, he could be heard constantly shouting 'Come on then. Come on,' towards the opposition, as well as 'Fucking quality', while complaining that the opposition had come for a row and then run off. He attracted a response on YouTube from BH, 'Would love to know what that hillbilly cunt saying fucking brilliant or fucking quality finds so exciting. Looks like a bunch of grandads from Rovers come across a few 13 year-olds from Plymouth ...'

On Tuesday 22 September 2015 Birmingham City played Aston Villa at Villa Park in an evening Capital One Cup tie, which Villa won 1-0. In the days leading up to the match, Offender Management Teams, working with the West Midlands Police Football Unit, visited known troublemakers in an effort to warn them off. Before the game, at about 6 p.m., there was trouble at the Manor Tavern in Portland Street, Aston, when windows were smashed and one person received a minor head injury. Eleven persons were arrested in connection with this incident, on suspicion of violent disorder, and later bailed pending further enquiries. A total of twenty-eight people were arrested throughout the evening for a variety of offences.

On Wednesday 23 September 2015, Arsenal played Tottenham Hotspur at White Hart Lane in a game that Arsenal won 2-1. Before the game, mounted police officers, with batons drawn, assisted public order officers in keeping large crowds of rival fans apart in what can only be described as a very hostile environment. Following the win, some Arsenal fans ripped up hoardings at the ground and smashed seats as they celebrated at the final whistle. Somewhat bizarrely, the signs were thrown down towards the lower tier, where other Arsenal supporters were located. Police officers, some with batons drawn, moved in to quell the disorder. Outside the ground there were clashes between rival fans, and ten arrests were made by police for a variety of offences, including criminal damage.

Also on Wednesday 23 September 2015, Crystal Palace played at Selhurst Park with Charlton Athletic, a game that Palace won 4-1. Disorder took place both inside and outside the ground, which saw bottles thrown and flares set off around children and families.

A number of clashes took place when the whistle was blown for full time. Scuffles also broke out between rival fans travelling home from Norwood Junction after the match. The Metropolitan Police mounted a large-scale operation to investigate allegations of violent disorder and, after arresting twenty-three men, they released still pictures of a further thirteen men for whom they were looking.

During the course of the post-incident investigation, police raided homes in Greenwich, Plumstead, Welling, Lewisham, Tower Hamlets, and Rochester. One of the arrests related to an allegation that a man had attempted to punch the Crystal Palace mascot Kayla, an American bald eagle, during the course of the game.

On Saturday 3 October 2015 Port Vale played Sheffield United in a game that Sheffield ultimately won 1-0. During the match a flare was thrown onto the pitch as a number of fans goaded each other. A number of violent incidents occurred outside Vale Park after the game, as rival fans left the ground. Around fifteen men were seen punching and kicking each other in the Co-op car park and were separated by parking attendants, while large numbers of fans attempted to confront each other in Hamil Road, where police had to form cordons to keep them apart. One female police officer suffered a broken ankle during the fighting, and was taken to hospital, while another was hit in the face by a piece of flying concrete thrown by supporters, and suffered cuts. One man was arrested on suspicion of affray.

Also on 3 October 201,5 Peterborough United played Millwall at home in a game that Peterborough won 5-3. At about 4.10 p.m., while the game was underway in the ABAX Stadium, a fight involving up to thirty people took place in nearby Oundle Road, which police determined was football related. Bottles were thrown and two people were injured, although not seriously. Police made seven arrests on suspicion of violent disorder, with six of the men coming from the London area and one from Peterborough. Police later released still images of two other men, believed to be Millwall fans, who they wanted to trace in connection with the incident.

Again on Saturday 3 October 2015, Hearts played at home to Kilmarnock and, at about 3 p.m., a fight occurred in McLeod Street, near to Tynecastle Stadium in Edinburgh. More than twenty people were reported to have been involved in the fighting and one twenty-one-year-old man from Kilmarnock was arrested at the time. As a result of enquiries by Police Scotland's Football Coordination Unit, a further fourteen males, aged between fourteen and twenty-eight years, were later arrested.

On Tuesday 6 October 2015, Oxford played at home at the Kassam Stadium to Swindon in a Johnstone's Paint Trophy match. Swindon eventually lost the match 2-0. Prior to the evening game, Swindon Town fans clashed with police in Botley Road outside the One Bar, as glasses, red smoke flares, and firecrackers were thrown and officers abused. Four men from Swindon, all of whom were in their forties, were arrested for alcohol-related and public order offences, as officers, some of whom were mounted, struggled with an extremely aggressive crowd near to the railway station. Another man was arrested for being drunk and disorderly in Didcot. Inside, and around the ground, both sets of fans confronted each other and police put cordons in place outside to separate supporters, who shouted abuse at each other with such chants as, 'Oxford United we fuckin' hate you. We are the red and white army. Wanky Wanky Oxford.' A large number of fans were also prevented from attending the match, due to their behaviour, and were escorted out of the city.

On Saturday 17 October 2015 Arbroath played Montrose in a local derby, which descended into violence. Flares were thrown on at least five occasions after fighting in and around Gayfield Park Stadium, Arbroath, with five arrests in total being made.

On Wednesday 21 October 2015 Manchester City played at home to Sevilla in a Champions League game, which City subsequently won 2-1. Prior to the match, a group of Polish Slask Wroclaw fans, some of whom were masked, attacked Spanish Sevilla fans at Sinclairs Oyster Bar in Exchange Square, Manchester. In a determined and violent attack, chairs and tables were thrown, together with glasses and even a bicycle. The attack was said to be retribution for a clash between both sets of fans in Spain before a Europa League tie in 2013. Police subsequently made five arrests.

On Saturday 24 October 2015 Queens Park Rangers played at home to MK Dons, at Loftus Road, in a match that QPR won 3-0. Seven arrests were made, six of which were for causing an affray, after fighting broke out in the away section of the crowd. One person was taken to hospital with facial injuries.

On Sunday 25 October 2015 ten people were arrested during, and immediately after, the Wear-Tyne derby game between Sunderland and Newcastle at the Stadium of Light. Most of the offences were alcohol related, although one man was arrested in possession of a flare, and another was arrested for throwing a missile at the playing area. The vast majority of the 50,000 fans in attendance were, however, congratulated by police on their good behaviour during a game won by Sunderland 3-0.

On Sunday 1 November 2015, Hibernian played Rangers in a game that Hibs won 2-1. Prior to the match, at 12.20 p.m., an incident occurred in Easter Road, Edinburgh, when a thirty-four-year-old Hibs fan became involved in a stand-off with the occupants of a Rangers supporters bus. He alleged that one of those on board had spat on his ten-year-old son as the vehicle stopped next to them and the doors were opened. Together with a friend, he then tried to stop the vehicle driving on by standing in front of it, as a can was thrown by someone and a bottle was thrown from the vehicle.

After the incident the Hibs fan had to close his Twitter account down after online abuse, with such threats posted as, 'This guy should have had his throat slit at birth.' Refering to the game itself, on a social media forum 'SB' commented about a problem that still troubles Scottish football in particular:

> I am writing to highlight the issue of sectarianism among Glasgow football supporters ... A glance at the footage will confirm that in the opening three minutes at Easter Road the Rangers supporters were almost unanimously singing 'The Sash'. A few minutes later in the first half they were almost unanimously singing a banned song about Bobby Sands, to the tune the Fields of Athenry ...

'PB1' commented on the same forum about his experiences after the match:

> I went down to St Claire Street then had to go back up Easter Road to get to the bank. I had to wade through Rangers fans and, along with several others, including kids, was subjected to downright bigotry. Shouting at people in the street that they are 'fenian', 'taig',

'tarrier', 'bead rattler', etc. is inexcusable. Add to that the Sikh father and children in Hibs scarves ahead of me who were called 'pakis' and 'terrorists' and you see the ignorance you are dealing with.

On Friday 6 November 2015, Nottinghamshire police reported making seven arrests at the match between Nottingham Forest and Derby and during subsequent disorder in the East Stand car park afterwards. Three men went onto the pitch at the City Stadium as smoke bombs were let off after their 1-0 win against Derby County. In a separate incident a fan appeared to confront one of the Derby players during the pitch invasion.

On Saturday 7 November 2015, Crewe Alexandra played Eastleigh, at home, at Gresty Road in a match that Crewe lost 0-1. At the end of the game a disturbance took place involving a small number of Crewe fans and stewards after the Railwaymen crashed out of the FA Cup to a non-League side. Five minutes from the end, fans were lining up at the barriers and, at the final whistle, a number of them started to confront stewards. One of the supporters was held down on the pitch until the arrival of police officers, who escorted him away while chants of 'Shitty stewards fuck off. Get a proper job' rang out.

In what was later to be described as 'one of the worst football-related incidents of violence experienced in Cheshire', a steward was assaulted and others were confronted in the stands. Shortly afterwards fighting broke out between supporters in Gresty Road. CCTV evidence was seized and police were able to identify ten males as being involved, all of whom were arrested and charged with violent disorder. All of the defendants subsequently pleaded guilty and three of them received six-month prison sentences, as well as six-year football banning orders.

Again on 7 November 2015, two Worcester City football fans were arrested for being drunk and disorderly as they got off a coach in Sheffield for an FA Cup game against Sheffield United. Three other men were arrested for public order offences and possession of Class A drugs after disturbances inside the Bramall Lane Stadium. On the same date Huddersfield Town played at home to Leeds and, after the match, a group of fans smashed up a town-centre taxi office, GT Taxis, in Lord Street, as a group of Leeds fans waited for a minibus. A group of up to thirty Huddersfield supporters gathered outside, baiting the Leeds fans, before a wooden stool was used to smash windows, and glasses were thrown, showering people with glass. Two Huddersfield fans were arrested.

On Sunday 8 November 2015, Tottenham Hotspur visited Arsenal at the Emirates Stadium in a match that ended in a 1-1 draw. In what was seen as a revenge act for the incident in September, wherein Arsenal fans ripped up hoardings at Spurs ground, the toilets at the stadium were trashed, causing thousands of pounds worth of damage, and pictures were posted on Twitter captioned 'We bite twice as hard.' During the game itself a supporter threw an object at Mesut Ozil, one of the Arsenal players, as eight arrests were made for public order offences, throwing missiles, possession of drugs and assault.

On Saturday 21 November 2015 Stevenage played at home to Luton in a game that finished in a 0-0 draw. Tempers flared between rival fans during the game, and a line of police officers were deployed to the Luton supporters' end. One of Luton's players was sent off after eighty-six minutes. Immediately afterwards a small group of Luton Hatters fans in the Austin Stand ran over to the East Terrace home section, where they clashed, and police had to intervene. One Luton fan jumped over advertising hoardings and started throwing punches before police were able to restore order.

Also on Saturday 21 November 2015, Plymouth Argyle played at Home Park against Exeter during the Devon derby, in a game that Exeter won 2-1. Prior to the game, police officers shadowed known groups of troublemakers in Plymouth city centre. At half time, about sixty police officers were sent into the Lyndhurst Stand to deal with disorder, which broke out when one of the home fans set off a flare. As club stewards went into the crowd to try and apprehend the individual, they were attacked by a group. Bottles were thrown at police officers, with five suffering from minor injuries as a result of being punched or hit by missiles. Ten people were ejected from the stadium as a result of those incidents, with a further seven as a result of other incidents. Six people were arrested.

'SS9' commented in response to a media article afterwards: 'At half time I went to get a coffee but ended up being sprayed with beer from someone throwing cans of beer around. I managed to get near to the toilets when the flares went off which was quite scary ...' After the match some Plymouth fans threw firecrackers at police horses and police dogs, as up to 100 police officers maintained control.

On Sunday 22 November 2015 West Ham played Tottenham Hotspur in a game that Spurs won with a score of 4-1. At 3 p.m., a large group of West Ham fans were being escorted by police near to the club shop outside White Hart Lane, when a number of them tried to attack a Spurs fan. Police officers were obliged to draw batons as mounted officers held fans back. In a separate incident a thirty-five-year-old West Ham supporter was hospitalised after being stabbed in the stomach and, during the course of the game, fans exchanged what were described as vicious chants, some of which were anti-Semitic. 'N' commented on an online newspaper article: 'The whole atmosphere seems to be going back to the bad old days', while 'AIG' said, 'The dark side has never gone totally away in football, certainly in the lower leagues. It's as bad as fighting for religion isn't it?'

On Thursday 26 November 2015 Celtic played at home to the Dutch side Ajax, who subsequently beat Celtic with a score of 2-1. Intelligence had been received to the effect that Ajax fans were planning confrontations in Glasgow ahead of the match, and Dutch officers were on hand to support local police. The clubs had history with each other and, specifically in 2013, trouble took place in Amsterdam when Celtic fans were attacked. Before the match a group of some forty Ajax fans tried to storm two bars near to Celtic Park. Around an hour before kick-off, efforts were made to enter the Hielan Jessie Bar, followed by a similar incident at The Hoops Bar. A picture was widely circulated on social media of a Celtic fan with blood on his face and a cut above his eye. The injured person 'GD' commented, 'That's me in the picture, nothing hurt except my pride … mostly a terrible picture. From what I heard at the hospital 2 guy's weren't as lucky but they should be okay …' Police later escorted three hundred chanting Ajax fans to the ground. One arrest was made before the game, two during it, and one afterwards for minor public order offences.

On Sunday 13 December 2015, St Johnstone played at home at McDiarmid Park to Celtic in a game that Celtic won 3-0. During the course of the game, police intervened on the terraces when fans held up a banner that said, 'Police everywhere, Justice nowhere'. The banner was removed.

At 2 p.m. on Saturday 26 December 2015, a large disturbance took place in Abbey Gate in Colchester, shortly before a football match between Colchester United and Southend United. Nine people were subsequently arrested on suspicion of violent disorder.

On Monday 28 December 2015, Portsmouth played Luton at home and racist chanting was reported. A twenty-nine-year-old man was subsequently arrested and received an official caution.

On Saturday 9 January 2016, Manchester United played at home to Sheffield United at Old Trafford, in a game that Manchester United won 1-0. More than 8,500 Sheffield United supporters, known as the Blades, visited Manchester, and a police helicopter was deployed to monitor crowd movements. At about 2 p.m., a group of about 100 Sheffield United fans entered the Sawyers Arms in Deansgate. Initially they were good humoured, but fans then began standing on chairs and chanting; at about 3 p.m., a flare was set off inside, which filled the premises with purple smoke. By the time that the police arrived they had all left. Shortly afterwards, police vans flooded into the Ancoats area as groups of fans traded kicks and punches. Dozens of officers were deployed in the George Leigh Street area. One fifty-three-year-old man was arrested to prevent a breach of the peace, but then released.

Also on 9 January 2016, Bolton played at Eastleigh at the Silverlake Stadium in a game that finished in a 1-1 draw. During the course of the match, a lone fifty-one-year-old fan ran onto the pitch and got as far as the penalty area of the Bolton goal before he fell in the mud. He was then escorted off the pitch and arrested. Somewhat unusually, his excuse was that he had done it to try and win his partner back, who had 'dumped' him days before, by appearing on *Match of the Day* on television. He was later fined by the courts after admitting going onto the playing area.

On Saturday 16 January 2016 Aston Villa played at home to Leicester in a match that concluded in a 1-1 draw. At 4.15 p.m., ahead of the kick-off, a confrontation took place involving youth hooligan groups from both clubs in Price Street, near to The Bull pub in Birmingham city centre, which was closed at the time. Police came across a group of fans throwing bricks and bottles as they fought, and arrested fifteen youths aged between sixteen and twenty-one years, eight of whom were Villa fans and seven of whom were from Leicester.

Another five were arrested, aged sixteen to seventeen years, after they were found hiding in the nearby Weaman Street National car park.

Also on Saturday 16 January 2016, Hearts played at home to Motherwell at the Tynecastle Stadium in Edinburgh. Hearts eventually won the game with a score of 6-0. Before the match, a group of up to twenty fans from both clubs became involved in a fight in McLeoud Street. Officers from Police Scotland's Football Co-Ordination Unit, operating under the banner of Operation Rebound, subsequently arrested eight Motherwell fans, aged between fifteen to fifty-one years. Another eight Hearts fans were also arrested and charged in connection with the disturbance.

On Saturday 23 January 2016 Portsmouth played at home to Oxford. Police were called to a number of incidents in Fratton involving both sets of fans. At around 1.45 p.m., officers attended at the Red White and Blue pub in Fawcett Road, following a report of a disturbance; a volatile group were then escorted along Goldsmith Avenue by officers with dogs. Likewise, officers had to separate fans after the match in the same area. During the game, one arrest was made inside the ground for criminal damage to a seat. Commenting on a local media article, 'CJ' said,

> Very disheartening, and for some people very frightening also. Major public disorder has largely been eradicated from football, but it still lurks ready to break out, because it still lurks in a somewhat brutalist British society at large ... I was in a pub ... it kicked off, glasses and furniture flying, and several fist and foot connections ... Fortunately for us all the plod were on hand and able to quell the disorder very quickly ...

Portsmouth lost the game with a score of 0-1.

Also on Saturday 23 January 2016, West Ham played at home to Manchester City in a game that finished in a 2-2 draw. At full time, fans from both sides became involved in a confrontation, forcing large numbers of stewards to step in and separate the two groups. City fans in the 3,000 capacity away end in the Sir Trevor Brooking Stand appeared to exchange insults with Hammers fans sat nearest to the visitors, and some briefly clashed before the situation was brought under control.

On Wednesday 27 January 2016, Manchester City played Everton at the Etihad Stadium in a Capital One Cup semi-final tie, which City won 3-1. During the course of the game, an Everton fan in the home section of the ground was attacked by a number of fans and, as he was kicked and punched, cheers and shouts of 'you Scouse bastard' were heard. He was eventually led away by two stewards, but not before he sustained further blows. After the match, police with batons drawn had to rush to separate fans outside the ground, and two fans were arrested as bottles and coins were thrown. Four other fans were arrested during the course of the day, and an Everton fan went to hospital with a head injury.

On Saturday 30 January 2016 Hull played Bury in a game, which they won with a score of 3-1, at Bury's Gigg Lane Stadium. In one corner of the ground, bad-tempered exchanges were captured on video between both sets of fans with chants circulating of 'Yorkshire, Yorkshire', 'We are the mighty Bury' 'Balmy Army' and 'Sheep Shaggers', which culminated in flares being thrown as police and stewards contained the fans.

On Tuesday 2 February 2016 Millwall played away at Oxford, and bottles and stones were thrown at Thames Valley Police horses both before and after the game, injuring two of them. Eight men were arrested at the time for offences ranging from affray, possession of an offensive weapon, criminal damage, and assault. Following serious violence, the police also set up a post-incident investigation team, codenamed Operation Brazil, to identify further suspects involved in the disorder in and around the Kassam Stadium during a game that Millwall won 1-0. They later released six images of men, who were all sat in the Millwall end, in relation to an affray that occurred inside the ground during the half-time interval, when a number of stewards were also attacked.

On Saturday 6 February 2016, Southend United played at home to Colchester in a match that the home team won with a score of 3-0. During the game, a lone supporter from the Southend terraces jumped over a barricade and ran across the pitch, before trading punches with a section of the Colchester fans. He was eventually pulled away by stewards but then was somewhat surprisingly allowed to go back into the crowd, who spilled onto the pitch in apparent support to the sound of chants of 'Who are you.' He even appeared to be congratulated by at least one individual.

The incident was captured on video, and one social media comment from 'EO' said, 'The cunt that ran over needs to be shot, simple.' The pictures have been viewed nearly 200,000 times, which gives a clear illustration of the appetite for this type of material on the internet. More disturbingly, the footage has been 'liked' at least 267 times. During an allegedly bad-tempered game, Colchester fans also tried to get past stewards to confront opposing fans.

On Saturday 20 February 2016, Millwall played at home to Peterborough. After their 3-0 win, a group of Millwall fans attacked police officers in one of the stands, punching and kicking them before the officers managed to extricate themselves. Two men were subsequently arrested for assaulting stewards who were trying to eject someone for breach of ground regulations.

Also on this date, a West Bromwich Albion player was struck in the face during a game at Reading with a coin, which came from a section of the ground housing West Bromwich fans. After the final whistle, the West Bromwich team captain went to applaud fans, who had watched the team defeated 3-1 by Reading, when he was struck and received a cut to his eye. Some of the travelling fans started fighting among themselves, and police with dogs were deployed to the stand they were in to disperse them. A man was arrested in connection with this incident three days later. Earlier on during the second half, a thirty-seven-year-old man from Sandwell in the West Midlands was arrested for a racially aggravated public order offence after a steward was verbally abused and a bottle was thrown at a Reading player.

On Sunday 21 February 2016, Chelsea supporters threw coins at Manchester City players during a game at Stamford Bridge, and one man was arrested for throwing a lighter onto the playing field.

On Saturday 27 February 2016, Birmingham City played away to Queens Park Rangers in London, in a game that they ultimately lost 2-0. At about 2.30 p.m., a large number of Birmingham supporters created a disturbance in Ellerlie Road, near to Loftus Road Stadium. Metropolitan Police officers were required to use batons to restore order, and two police officers were injured, as were a number of supporters. Trouble continued inside the stadium, and missiles were thrown by away fans towards the home end. One QPR player was also struck by a coin. Shortly after the game a home supporter was attacked outside the ground and received a broken nose. Three men were arrested: one for going onto the pitch, one for racially aggravated assault on a police officer, and one for a public order offence.

Also on 27 February 2016, Bolton played at the Macron Stadium with Burnley, in a match that saw Burnley win 2-1. A twenty-seven-year-old was arrested after entering an area adjacent to the playing area and was also charged with assaulting a police officer. The charge of assault was subsequently dismissed, but he was fined for the pitch offence. The magistrates declined to make a football banning order because they took the view that there were no reasonable grounds to believe that making a banning order would help to prevent violence or disorder in connection with any regulated football matches.

Again on the same date, the FA announced that they were investigating yet another allegation of a missile being thrown at a player during the Stoke versus Aston Villa game.

On Saturday 5 March 2016, a large policing operation was put in place for the so-called Cotton Mills derby match, wherein Burnley played at home to Blackburn in a game that Burnley won 1-0. There has been a 'healthy' rivalry between both clubs stretching back many decades. On occasions this has manifested itself in the shape of serious public order incidents.

Also on Saturday 5 March 2016, the North London derby was taking place between Tottenham Hotspur and Arsenal at Spurs White Hart Lane Stadium. The game finished in a 2-2 draw. Ahead of the game, mounted police officers and officers in public order dress struggled to keep fans apart as volleys of beer cans were thrown at horses and blue smoke bombs were let off. As chants of 'Who are they' rang out, some serious aggression was displayed by one group of Tottenham fans, who were seen attacking a small group of Arsenal supporters. As punches were thrown and barriers pushed aside, one elderly man fell to the floor and had to be assisted to his feet by a woman as the attackers continued, oblivious to the consequences of their actions.

Commenting on one social media site, 'BS1' said, 'The good side. All the pussies who say stuff like the ugly side have ripped the heart out of football since 92. English football is about tribalism, take that out and it may as well be a trip to the fucking ballet.' On the other hand 'CD' said 'A lot of Tottenham fans are bullies. I've been to every away ground with Chelsea and the only stadium I've had a problem with is here. Fifty Tottenham fans having it with four Arsenal blokes, that the Tottenham Way.' Two arrests were made in separate incidents at about 12.30 p.m., prior to the kick-off, and one man was featured prominently in pictures in the newspapers with blood streaming all over his face from a head wound.

On Saturday 12 March 2016, Swindon Town played Millwall in a game that finished in a 2-2 draw at the County Ground. Police officers from Wiltshire and the Metropolitan Police lined the streets following the game, as cordons were put in place to keep both sets of fans apart, with crowds of them baying at each other as Millwall fans were escorted back to the railway station. Three arrests were made for minor offences, as a large police presence prevented serious disorder.

On Thursday 17 March 2016 Liverpool played Manchester United at Old Trafford in a Europa League round, which ended in a 1-1 draw. Both sets of supporters were involved in violent clashes inside the ground, and police and stewards were forced to step in during the closing minutes after a small group of Liverpool fans gained access to the upper tier of the East Stand, which contained home supporters, and unveiled an LFC banner, as punches were exchanged and seats thrown. At least one child was caught up in the fighting and was injured after being hit by a plastic seat from the stand. As the fighting was taking place, a number of Liverpool fans in the lower tier chanted, 'Munich' – a reference to the 1958 disaster. Greater Manchester Police arrested four Liverpool fans and a Manchester United fan after the game on suspicion of affray, criminal damage to a minibus window, and being drunk and disorderly.

Prior to the match, fans travelling into Manchester from Liverpool found a sheet tied to a bridge over the M602 in Salford, which read 'murderers' and the date of the Hillsborough disaster. The banner was removed by police and two people were later charged with offences in relation to the banner. Inside the ground, some United supporters chanted about Hillsborough. In contrast, inside the ground before kick-off, a banner was unfurled in the away end bearing the words, 'Hang the Roma 4' – a reference to United supporters convicted in 2007 of fighting with police in Italy, who subsequently had their jail sentences cut on appeal. A Liverpool fan who set off a red flare was arrested and given a caution. Police later revealed images of nine individuals they wished to speak to in relation to the disturbances.

On Saturday 19 March 2016, Chelsea played West Ham at Stamford Bridge, finishing in a 2-2 draw. After the game, mounted officers, with batons drawn, were deployed as skirmishes took place between the two sets of fans. Thousands made their way through the streets, with many chants of 'You're fucking shit' ringing in the air.

Also on Saturday 19 March 2016, a large fight took place outside The Major Oak pub in Pelham Street, Nottingham, between Nottingham Forest and Notts County fans after both teams had lost in separate games that day. No one was seriously injured.

Following a post-incident investigation, eleven Forest supporters were arrested, together with six County fans, at various addresses, and police released pictures of two more individuals for which they were looking. Their ages ranged from nineteen to twenty-eight years, and they were all charged with causing an affray. One aspect of the investigation was to establish whether it was a pre-arranged fight.

On Sunday 20 March 2016, Newcastle United played at home to Sunderland in a major Tyne-Wear local derby. Sunderland fans were escorted by police from Newcastle Central station to St James' Park as minor scuffles took place near to the ground. Hundreds of officers, some in full public order gear, were deployed along the route as twenty arrests were made for offences that included being drunk and disorderly, breach of the peace, throwing missiles, being drunk in a football ground, assault and obstructing the police. One man who ran onto the pitch was among those detained.

After the game, which finished in a 1-1 draw, police cordons, including mounted officers and dog units, kept departing fans apart, although at one stage a smoke bomb was thrown at police lines, some fans threw coins, and a brief skirmish was broken up in St James' Boulevard.

Also on Sunday 20 March 2016, Manchester City played Manchester United in a match that saw United win with a score of 1-0. Police reported minor incidents of disorder and fighting between supporters around City's Etihad Stadium before kick-off and after the final whistle; eleven men were arrested. Inside the ground there were reports of coins and bottles being thrown, as police and stewards formed cordons to keep dozens of fans who were goading each other apart.

One man was arrested for allegedly assaulting a police officer, with other arrests for drunkenness, affray, possession of controlled drugs with intent to supply, criminal damage and public order offences.

On Thursday 7 April 2016 Coventry United played at Sphinx Drive with Nuneaton Griff in a game that Coventry won 3-2. As the final whistle blew, up to twenty Coventry United supporters ran onto the pitch and a couple of punches were thrown at the Griff centre-half. One fan was alleged to have been waving a flag pole, as players, supporters, and coaching staff all became embroiled in a mass brawl. A senior official at one of the clubs sought to minimise the disturbance by saying, 'It was a bit of handbags, there was a bit of pushing and shoving, and a bit of language.'

David Deakin, BBC Coventry and Warwickshire non-League correspondent was at the match and said afterwards, 'Somebody could have been seriously hurt but thankfully nobody was. To see that is very scary. In the Premier League there would be stewards and police, you don't have that at this level.' After his match report, David Deakin received abuse on social media.

On Saturday 16 April 2016 Mansfield Town played at home to Notts County in a Football League division two match. Mansfield ultimately won the game with a score of 5-0. A seventy-three-year-old county councillor, John Wilmott, told local media that he feared for his life as he was trampled on, kicked in the back, and thrown onto a concrete floor when a group of up to eighty Notts County fans surged towards the pitch. Stewards trying to establish control were met with torrents of abuse in the North Stand at the One Call Stadium. Three people were arrested: one for trying to enter the pitch, one found to be in possession of a flare, and one for being drunk and disorderly. Two of them later received three-year football banning orders. Officials at the ground counted the costs further after the toilet block was vandalised. Local police subsequently noted the emergence of a new 'hooligan youth group' that were trying to establish themselves.

On Sunday 17 April 2016, a number of incidents took place in and around Hampden Park and Glasgow city centre during the Scottish Cup semi-final between Rangers and Celtic, which Rangers eventually won 5-4 on penalties. Eighteen arrests were made as police investigated incidents relating to the use of flares and smoke bombs, and offensive singing of a sectarian nature, as well as the display of offensive banners. Trouble was also reported as fans returning from the semi-final clashed at Belfast City airport, and there were reports of sectarian abuse on an incoming flight. One Celtic fan was said to have received an injury to his eye after being attacked by a group of Rangers fans on arrival.

On Saturday 23 April 2016 Millwall played away at Bury in a game that Millwall eventually won 3-1. Police officers escorted a group of Millwall fans from the Metrolink to the ground and, after dealing with some disorder on the car park outside the Millwall, fans were taken into the Gigg Lane entrance. As a group of about 100 away supporters approached the South Stand, which was packed with Bury supporters, determined efforts were made by dozens of both sets of supporters to break through some metal gates in an effort to confront each other. One Bury fan hurled a large temporary barrier at the Millwall fans, while on the pitch stewards had to deal with one fan who ran on to the pitch before the match. Missiles were thrown. It took a couple of minutes for the police to enter the ground before eventually breaking up the violence. Two fans were subsequently arrested for conduct likely to cause a breach of the peace but were released without charge after being removed from the ground.

Millwall fans were kept inside the ground at the end of the game to allow Bury fans to disperse. Afterwards it was disclosed that the costs of providing 125 police officers, plus eight mounted officers, had come to £20,000. Local police advised the media that they were intending to visit local schools to advise youngsters against the notion of getting involved with hooliganism, after it was disclosed that they were aware of an emerging group of some forty risk fans, some as young as fourteen, who styled themselves as the 'Bury Firm'.

Commenting on YouTube, 'CP' said, 'Self-proclaimed hooligans are not only disgusting thugs who plague this country but also thoroughly stupid. I really hope the police are watching this and identify some of the criminals in the video...' 'R' – I am thirty and

I am not a degenerate criminal with shit for brains like you.' 'RJ' replied, 'Fuck off old wanker'.

Also on Saturday 23 April 2016, Manchester United played Everton in an FA Cup semi-final at Wembley. Before the game, in a widely circulated video clip, two men were shown fighting in the car park of a service station, which was believed to be at Cannock Services on the M6 in Staffordshire. As one man, thought to have been an Everton supporter, appeared to fall unconscious to the floor following a punch to the head from another individual, yet another fan threw a blue smoke bomb at his attacker, as the fighting escalated and bottles were thrown. Despite being knocked unconscious, the injured fan apparently later continued onto the match. Police at Wembley reported making a total of fourteen arrests for a variety of minor offences during the course of the match, which United won 2-1.

On Saturday 30 April 2016 there was a full-scale pitch invasion at the end of a match between Millwall and Oldham, which saw Millwall secure a place in the League One play-offs. While on the face of it the incursion appeared to be generally good-natured, the stewards on duty were clearly overwhelmed by the situation.

On Saturday 7 May 2016, Middlesbrough achieved promotion out of the Champions League and supporters gathered in the town's Centre Square to celebrate. In a video that was later viewed online 250,000 times, fans were shown throwing bottles up in the air, with people ducking out of the way to avoid flying objects. The following day the square was left covered in broken bottles, empty beer cans and vomit.

On Tuesday 10 May 2016 a highly charged game took place at Upton Park between West Ham United and Manchester United. It was West Ham's final game at their home stadium, which they won with a score of 3-2. Outside the ground before the game, the coach carrying the Manchester United team got stuck in congestion in Green Street, and some coach windows were smashed as bottles and missiles were thrown at it by several dozen fans gathered outside a local pub. During the disturbances, one member of the public and four police officers sustained minor injuries but no arrests were made.

On Saturday 21 May 2016, the Scottish Cup final ended with scenes of disorder after Hibernian beat Rangers at Hampden Park, following which the Scottish Football Association announced an enquiry. Thousands of fans spilled onto the pitch after Hibs scored a late goal in injury time to finish the game at 3-2, with parts of the pitch being ripped up and goalposts broken. Fans from both sides squared up to each other and punches were exchanged. Mounted police officers formed a line across the pitch to control fans, the first time that horses had been used on a pitch at a Scottish Cup final since 1980. As soon as the disorder began, Police Scotland and the stadium management initiated a crisis liaison group in an effort to bring the situation under control.

Rangers players, including Rob Kiernan, Andy Halliday, Jason Holt, Lee Wallace and Dean Shiels, and some of the back-room staff complained of being attacked on the pitch, and there were reports of up to forty people being injured during the fighting. Rangers goalkeeper Wes Foderingham was said to have been goaded and intimidated by several fans. The match had previously been graded as a Category C Increased Risk match.

Police Scotland set up a post-incident investigation team at Helen Street police office in Glasgow and, shortly afterwards, made an appeal for fans to come forward with photographic or film material that would help to identify offenders. They also announced that eleven arrests had been made for minor offences, with more expected, as eight images were released to the press. Social media went into overdrive as some Rangers fans identified a Hibs fan from Edinburgh who they claimed had assaulted Wallace, and violent retribution was threatened. Further images were released by the media, and one video purported to show a Rangers fan grabbing hold of a Hibs youngster, aged no more than twelve years, and trying to drag him across the pitch, before someone else came along and punched the older man, prompting him to release his hold on the boy. In another picture a Rangers fan can be seen lying on the ground, being hit by Hibs fans.

On Sunday 29 May 2016, Millwall faced Barnsley in the Football League One play-off final at Wembley Stadium in a game that Barnsley won with a score of 3-1. As the third goal was scored, Millwall fans in one of the top tiers tried to force their way into a seating area occupied by Barnsley fans. A few succeeded in breaking through police lines at about 4.35 p.m.; scuffles broke out as punches were thrown and objects were hurled onto Barnsley fans in the tier below. A number of Barnsley fans, including young children, were forced to flee from the fighting. At one stage Millwall fans also started hurling coins at Barnsley players on the pitch.

The Metropolitan Police made fifteen arrests outside the stadium, before and after the match, for public order offences, but confirmed that no arrests had been made at that stage in relation to the disturbances inside. Police later released stills of twelve people that they wanted to trace in connection with the disorder and the criminal damage wherein seats had been ripped up and thrown as missiles. The pictures represented a mixture of fans from both clubs. After the game an online petition was raised in an effort to get Millwall fans banned from travelling to away games, which, in the aftermath of the disturbances, attracted an initial 1,800 signatures. The power of the media and social media was demonstrated when one online article covering the trouble attracted 479 comments and was shared 6,600 times.

On Thursday 16 June 2016 a twenty-nine-year-old football fan was assaulted by a group of people in The Britannia pub in Newcastle-under-Lyme, Staffordshire, after the European Championship match between England and Wales in France. He went home to remove his bloodstained clothing before leaving the house again with the intention of visiting another pub. Prior to leaving, however, he armed himself with an axe and a lump hammer for self-defence. Police intercepted him when he was spotted and he later received a suspended prison sentence.

* * *

It is a matter of record that visual footage of the vast majority of the incidents described in this chapter can be freely obtained on the internet. They are routinely viewed and commented upon by many thousands of people. While it is a fact that it is not unusual to find comments from viewers complaining about the behaviour of a minority of fans, by far the overwhelming majority comment as if they were either spectators or alleged participants in some form of imaginary gladiator-esque contest.

3

SECTARIANISM AND RACIST ELEMENTS

The anti-sectarianism group Nil by Mouth describes sectarianism as follows: 'This word is used to describe a sect, or section within an established group, but most commonly it's used with regard to groups with a particular religious or political basis.'

In the UK, much of it takes place in Scotland, particularly when Glasgow Rangers and Glasgow Celtic play each other in local derby games. The word 'sectarianism' is very often used in Scotland today in association with divisions within a religion, particularly with reference to Christianity and the rift that can exist between Catholics and Protestants. Sectarianism can also be found within other religions. Scotland used to be a Catholic country but, after Protestant and Scottish reformations, it adopted the Presbyterian system (Church of Scotland) as its state religion.

As society becomes increasingly secular, the term is often also used to describe a type of social identity that relates to things other than religious belief. People automatically associate the problem with Glasgow Rangers and Glasgow Celtic football clubs. Rangers are supported predominantly by the Protestant community and Celtic by the Catholic community. The majority of Rangers and Celtic supporters do not get involved in sectarianism, but the minority that do tend to grab the headlines.

It can also extend to the two Edinburgh clubs as well, namely Hibernian and Hearts. Hibernian is perceived as being a Catholic club, while Heart of Midlothian is perceived as a Protestant club.

Similar allegiances are associated with Dundee and Dundee United. In England, Liverpool and Everton are perceived as Protestant and Catholic respectively.

Queen's Park in Glasgow was the first football club ever to be established in Scotland, in 1867; it is also the oldest club outside of England and Wales. This club was associated with the Young Men's Christian Association (YMCA). A lot of other clubs associated themselves with the local church. The Catholic Young Men's Society supported the founding of the Edinburgh club Hibernian.

Celtic FC was founded by a Catholic priest, from the large Irish immigrant population living in Glasgow. There was a lot of prejudice between the Catholics and the Protestants; however, it was recognised that football fixtures could be seen as a way of breaking down these prejudices.

Celtic FC take their name from the shared Celtic heritage of the Scottish and Irish communities. The first strip used by Celtic displayed a Celtic cross emblem. Hibernian dropped their Irish harp emblem; however, both clubs still play in green strips. The very colour of these strips can provoke sectarianism at matches. It is not the colour itself, but rather its associations that can lead to sectarianism behaviour. In Northern Ireland and the Republic of Ireland, colours can still be a very emotive issue, particularly in politics. The colours of Celtic and Hibernian were actually imported from Ireland.

Over the years, links with religious organisations have lapsed. Celtic introduced an open policy of recruiting players from all religious denominations, while remaining proud of its roots. On match days the Irish tricolour is still flown, which gives the impression that it is a Catholic Irish club. At the Rangers Ibrox stadium, the Union Flag and Ulster banner were often displayed. On the other hand, Rangers had a Protestant-only recruitment policy and saw itself as a 'Scots Protestant club', until nearly the end of the twentieth century.

Both Celtic and Rangers have supporters from all religious denominations, and the two clubs have supporters drawn from the city's Muslim community as well. A study a few years ago showed that 74 per cent of Celtic supporters identified themselves as Catholic, while only 10 per cent identified themselves as

Protestant. The figure for Rangers was 2 per cent Catholic and 65 per cent Protestant.

Most of the sectarianism violence is associated with the Old Firm Celtic versus Rangers local derby games. Over the years there have been calls for both the clubs to take measures to combat sectarianism within their respective clubs. Glasgow City Council has also taken measures against street vendors to try to prevent them from trading goods, such as flags, that might provoke sectarian violence. The clubs have also created education programmes to combat the problem.

Celtic's charter now aims for the organisation to be an inclusive organisation that is open to all regardless of age, sex, race, religion or disability. They have made it perfectly clear that sectarianism in any form will not be tolerated. Meanwhile, Rangers commenced a plan that included making public address announcements at every home game condemning racism and sectarianism. They made it clear that they would take disciplinary action against fans, players and staff whose sectarian and racist behaviour brought the club into disrepute. The club acknowledged that it would be difficult to enforce on the stands; however, they sent strong messages that sectarianism was not acceptable.

The two clubs have also worked alongside the Scottish government, church groups, pressure groups such as the anti-sectarianism pressure group Nil by Mouth, schools and community organisations to clamp down on sectarian songs, inflammatory flag-waving, and troublesome supporters. Police Scotland and British Transport Police have used increased levels of policing, intelligence and surveillance to crack down on sectarian acts.

The two clubs share a deep and intense history of rivalry on the football pitch with stories, which often stir up emotions, stretching back decades. One such event is described in Desmond Morris's book *The Soccer Tribe* as follows:

In the inter-war period there was a dramatic death at Ibrox Park during a Rangers-Celtic confrontation. John Thompson, Celtic's young goalkeeper saved his last goal by diving courageously at the feet of the Rangers centre-forward. He managed to deflect the ball but took the attacker's kick full in the face. Sensing a victory now that the enemy goalkeeper was injured, some of the Rangers fans began to cheer, but their team's captain, realising the severity of the injury, ran to the noisy crowd and with outstretched arms made a dramatic appeal for silence. The young keeper was near to death but, as he was being stretchered from the ground, he made one last movement, struggling to raise his body up and gaze back down the field to where his goalmouth now stood empty. It was as if, even while dying, he could not rid himself of the deeply ingrained anxiety of leaving his goal unprotected.

In the 1970s sectarian hatred between the two clubs was often stirred up by songs and chants on both sides. The troubles in Northern Ireland influenced the chants, with some Celtic fans supporting the Provisional IRA and some Rangers fans applauding the actions of Loyalist groups.

Maurice 'Mo' Johnston, a Roman Catholic, was signed by Rangers in 1989 in what was their first major Roman Catholic signing. The signing of Johnston made him the highest-profile Catholic to sign for the club since the First World War. After the signing of Johnston, Catholic players from overseas became commonplace at Rangers. The first Catholic player to be a captain of the club was Lorenzo Amoruso, who took the captaincy in 1999. Although the majority of Celtic fans are Catholic, some of the key figures in the club's history, Jock Stein, Kenny Dalglish, and Danny McGrain, have come from a Protestant background.

In 1992 the British Transport Police launched a major rail safety campaign aimed at children throughout England, Wales and Scotland. One of the central characters was a cartoon character called 'Bobby Ranger', who was dressed in blue. Because of the sectarianism in Scotland, particularly in the Glasgow area, where Glasgow Rangers play in blue, the character was not used for fear of upsetting the religious divides.

It is not only football grounds that have witnessed crowd trouble between Celtic and Rangers, with senseless violence on the streets away from the grounds. In 1995 Mark Scott was stabbed to death for wearing a Celtic shirt as he walked past a pub full of Rangers fans. Five years later, in 2000, several of his friends helped set up the organisation Nil by Mouth.

In 1995 Paul Gascoigne, who was then playing for Rangers, landed himself in trouble in a pre-season Old Firm friendly game as he mimicked playing the flute, infuriating many Celtic supporters who saw the act as a loyalist symbol. Following his actions, Gascoigne claimed he was completely unaware of the significance of his actions but was disciplined by the Scottish FA.

A leading QC was caught on video singing the sectarian song 'Billy Boys' after the Rangers versus Celtic 1996 Scottish Cup Final. He resigned his position as vice-chairman of Rangers, and The Faculty of Advocates fined him £3,500.

In 2002 the mutual animosity was outlined when some Celtic fans began flying Palestinian flags, and some Rangers supporters responded by waving Israeli flags. Also in 2002, Celtic made an unprecedented appeal to a vocal minority of its supporters to stop chanting IRA slogans during games.

Albion Rovers from the North Lanarkshire town of Coatbridge in Scotland, who have no history of sectarianism, was one of the first clubs in 2003 to sign up to the UEFA ten-point plan to tackle racism and sectarianism in Scottish football. The plan has been taken from their website:

> Consequently in line with this commitment it is our intention to adopt the following Plan of Action:
> 1. Albion Rovers Football Club will not tolerate racism, sectarianism, racist abuse or language within its Stadium or environs.
> 2. Albion Rovers Football Club will make public address announcements condemning racism/sectarian chanting at matches.
> 3. It is a condition for Season Ticket holders that they do not take part in racist or sectarian abuse. Any contravention of this will result in the Season Ticket being withdrawn and the holder banned from the Stadium.
> 4. Albion Rovers Football Club will not allow the sale of racist literature or any articles of a sectarian nature inside and around the Stadium.
> 5. Albion Rovers Football Club will take disciplinary action against any player who engages in racial or sectarian abuse.

6. Albion Rovers Football Club agree to contact other Clubs to inform them of their policy on racism and sectarianism.
7. Stewards and Police at all home matches will deal swiftly with any supporter guilty of such abuse. Any such supporter will either be detained by the Police or removed from the Stadium and banned.
8. Albion Rovers Football Club undertakes to remove any racist or sectarian graffiti from the Stadium.
9. Albion Rovers Football Club is an equal opportunities organisation in relation to employment and service provision.
10. Albion Rovers Football Club will work with all other groups and agencies as appropriate to develop pro-active programmes and make progress to raise awareness of campaigning to eliminate racial abuse, discrimination and sectarianism.

In August 2003 Rangers launched its Pride over Prejudice campaign to promote social inclusion, which urged fans to wear the traditional Rangers colours of blue, and avoid offensive songs, banners and salutes. This involved publishing the 'Blue Guide', known as the 'Wee Blue Book'. This book contained a list of acceptable songs and over 50,000 supporters received it.

However research by the Scottish Crown Office in 2006 suggested that football was unlikely to be the main source of sectarianism in Glasgow. An audit in 2006 of religiously aggravated crimes in Scotland between January 2004 and June 2005 found that 33 per cent of these were related to football. Given that 57 per cent of religiously aggravated crimes in Scotland happened in Glasgow, at the very most approximately half of religiously aggravated crimes in Glasgow could have been football related in this period.

In July 2006, following a UEFA fine for the Ibrox club in respect of 'discriminatory chanting', Rangers chairman David Murray said the consequences for the club of fans continuing to sing sectarian songs would be grave. In August 2006, during an Old Firm derby Celtic goalkeeper Artur Boruc, who is Polish, received a caution for crossing himself. This act brought the issue of sectarianism in Scotland back into sharp focus.

In January 2007 British Transport Police officers began patrolling the fifteen stations of Glasgow's Subway system. PC John McCrone from the Subway's Neighbourhood Policing Team said, 'Even small numbers of fans on a Subway train can be very intimidating and having a high profile police presence is very important to people's safety ... We police the system very positively and there is definitely no room for sectarian abuse.'

In February 2010, Chief Superintendent Ellie Bird was appointed area commander for the Scottish area of the British Transport Police. Shortly after her appointment she conducted an interview with the *News of the World*, in which she made her views clear on the issue of sectarianism and hooliganism in football within Scotland. 'Sectarianism is wrong,' she said. 'It is something I will not stand for. This common hatred, this animosity against people, is something I will never allow. There is zero tolerance of football hooliganism, make no mistake.'

In 2009 and early 2010 there were sectarianism and hooliganism incidents on the railway, including Aberdeen fans singing racist songs, Celtic fans on a train chanting sectarian abuse, and Hibernian fans intimidating passengers and urinating in a train corridor. In 2009, sixty-two arrests were made for football-related disorder in Scotland. Following these, and other incidents, the Scottish area of the British Transport Police signed a series of formal information sharing protocols with football clubs in Scotland. The protocols were designed to be a valuable asset to the British Transport Police for sharing information with clubs of individuals who came to notice, and to allow the free flow of information. 'It means that all parties are able to share mutually beneficial information about individual's travelling,' said Chief Superintendent Bird. 'We have to protect the whole transport network and Scotland, in terms of its transport, has a great policing reputation.'

The supporters who travelled by train throughout Scotland were warned that, if they became involved in anti-social behaviour or disorder anywhere on Scotland's rail network, including the Glasgow Subway, which serves Glasgow Rangers Ibrox stadium, then details would be passed on to their club. This action was designed to make sure that the fans were punished accordingly, such as with the confiscation of season tickets and the use of football banning orders.

Dundee from the Scottish League Division was one was one of the clubs to sign up to the scheme. A spokesman for the club said, 'The vast majority of football supporters are well behaved and enjoy the football experience without causing trouble or anti-social behaviour. Dundee FC supports any initiative that promotes a safe and comfortable environment and the club will take punitive action against any supporter notified to us via this arrangement.'

Chief Superintendent Bird promised no mercy for those who brought violence and fear to passengers: 'Unfortunately there is a small minority who can tarnish a reputation. Sectarianism has been described as Scotland's shame; it's reprehensible and inexcusable. We will work tirelessly alongside our partners in law and the Procurator Fiscal to prosecute the culprits.'

Celtic staff and fans were sent suspected explosive devices and bullets in 2011. These events showed clearly that anti-Irish Catholic bigotry still existed. Also in 2011, as the Old Firm met twice during a matter of weeks, disturbances led to 229 arrests during the first game in February, with sixteen persons being arrested within Celtic Park for alleged offences of a sectarian nature. In the second match, on the pitch thirteen yellow cards and three red cards were issued, while off the pitch thirty-four persons were arrested inside the stadium for sectarian, racial, and breach of the peace offences.

In 2012 an Independent Advisory Group was tasked with looking into the issues, on the basis that clubs were continually failing to address the problems and that sanctions were urgently needed. The Independent Advisory Group, headed by the Belfast-based academic Duncan Morrow, released its final report in 2015. It stated that football authorities and clubs must face sanctions for failing to address sectarian behaviour within football in Scotland. It stated that there appeared to be a reluctance on the part of clubs to 'act against the remnants of sectarianism' within the game and gave backing for support for the introduction of strict liability, where clubs could ultimately be deducted points, or have parts of their ground closed in the event of sectarian violence by the fans.

In the report it was acknowledged that sectarianism was a much wider social issue but, in an effort to stamp the problem out, no major effort could achieve success without the cooperation of the fans, the football authorities and the clubs, especially Rangers and Celtic. A raft of recommendations were made in the report for the government, councils, police, educational institutions, churches and parading organisations to act upon. The report also called for a better understanding of 'polite, educated forms of sectarianism' within Scottish professional life, as well as a new perspective on the history of Scotland.

A section of the report dealing with football stated that sanctions were urgently needed and the authors stated that their introduction would not simply be a step towards tackling sectarianism, but also an important step towards clubs and their fans taking responsibility for their actions as others had to do elsewhere in society. It claimed sectarianism in Scotland tended to fuse politics, football-club allegiance and national identity, with religion often far from the most prominent element. It was pointed out that sports teams with links to the Irish community existed in England, although this was not as marked as in Scotland.

In 2015 the Scottish government commissioned a social attitudes survey into sectarianism in the country. Almost nine out of every ten Scots believed that football was a cause of sectarianism in the country. More than half of those who responded stated that football was the main factor. Overall, almost 90 per cent said that they believed that sectarianism was a problem in Scotland. Some 69 per cent said that it was a problem mainly in Glasgow and the west of Scotland, while 79 per cent thought that Orange Order marches contributed to sectarianism. Just 13 per cent thought it was the main factor. In all, 1,500 people were surveyed and 54 per cent thought that Catholics experienced at least some prejudice, with 41 per cent saying that they thought the same about Protestants. People taking part in the survey believed that football clubs, along with other organisations, were well placed to tackle sectarianism.

Nil by Mouth welcomed the research, and renewed its call for Scottish football to implement the recommendations of the Sectarianism Advisory Group and to introduce a 'strict liability', the UEFA standard for tackling offensive behaviour at games, which had already been adopted by the English FA.

On Monday 28 December 2015 the banned 'Billy Boys' song made an unwelcome return when Rangers hosted Hibernian at Ibrox in a Championship League match. Another illicit song, making mention of Hibernian's manager, was clearly audible. 'Billy Boys' reared its head again during the Ladbrokes Championship clash at Ibrox, while another illicit song making mention of Easter Road boss Alan Stubbs was also heard. Rangers officials were said to have been disappointed to see what they described as a minority of supporters taking part in 'inappropriate singing'. They cooperated fully with Police Scotland to identify the offenders.

On Sunday 21 February 2016 Rangers went to Dumfries for a Scottish Championship match against Queen of the South; at the game banners were unfurled that said, among other things, 'Axe the Act' and 'Fans Not Criminals'. An eighteen-year-old man was arrested for public order offences while the banner was being removed from advertising hoardings by stewards and police as being in contravention of ground rules. Some witnesses claimed that he had refused to give up the banner to police.

Police said afterwards that the teenage Rangers supporter was arrested for public order offences in a Scots stadium after a banner protesting against a controversial anti-bigotry law was removed from him for covering an advert. The 'Axe the Act' banner was created to protest against a law designed to help stamp out sectarian abuse at football matches, known as the Offensive Behaviour at Football and Threatening Communications (Scotland) Act 2012. Three other arrests were made during the course of the game.

Afterwards, the Rangers fans group Union Bears complained about the actions of the police and one supporter 'MC' commented to the media, 'I was standing behind the lad and the police sergeant walked from the by-line and tried to snatch it from him. He was a strong lad who never let it go and was then set about by three more policemen, one policewoman, and a steward. Still he held on standing up for his rights well done wee man!' Yet another fan described the man being dragged out of the ground with both arms twisted up his back.

The Scottish Government pushed through the Act in the aftermath of the Old Firm 'shame game' in 2011, with the legislation enacted in January 2012. The Act provides police and prosecutors with powers to tackle sectarian songs and abuse at and around football matches, as well as threats posted on the internet or through the mail, with punishments ranging from a maximum of five years imprisonment and an unlimited fine. An umbrella group 'Fans against Criminalisation' was formed to challenge the need for the Act and to complain about a loss of civil liberties.

On Wednesday 17 August 2016, dozens of Palestinian flags were displayed during Celtic's 5-2 win over the Israeli side Hapoel Beer-Sheva in the first leg of a Champions League play-off. UEFA rules prohibit the use of 'gestures, words, objects, or any other means to transmit any message that is not fit for a sports event, particularly messages that are of a political, ideological, religious, offensive, or provocative nature.' Many Celtic fans traditionally identify with left-wing causes, and include the Palestinian struggle. One Scottish historian Tom Devine commented that he believed it was something to do with Irish Catholics in Scotland feeling over the course of several generations that they had been treated as second-class citizens in Scotland.

Celtic were fined two years ago for displaying a Palestinian flag during a Champions League qualifier against KR Reykjavik of Iceland and have been punished eight times in five seasons for supporter misconduct.

Jon Lighton retired in 2014 as an inspector in the West Midlands Police, with thirty years' service. However, as a child, he was brought up in Coatbridge and then Greenock, which was down the Clyde from Glasgow. He recalls:

Greenock was an industrial town. There was a film made once called *Sweet Sixteen*, which was about drug dealing there. The Scottish accents were so strong that they had to put subtitles in it. My father Richard was a vicar in an Elim Pentecostal church. It wasn't a Protestant church although I do recall, on one occasion, an Orange Order march calling at the church for some reason. My local football club was Greenock Morton Capilow Park and I used to go to some of the matches. There was always tension in the air at any of the games and growing up I became fully aware of the problems of sectarianism in the community. This was brought into sharp focus for me years later when I made an official visit to Belfast as a police officer, and the first question I was asked when I got in a police car at the airport was whether I was a Catholic or a Protestant.

John Wallace was a police officer in Scotland before his retirement, and he recalls an unusual by-product of the Old Firm games: 'I worked in and around the Glasgow city area before I retired and one significant aspect of the Old Firm fixture is a pronounced rise in domestic violence irrespective of the game itself, something that we have tried to tackle.'

Sectarianism is by its very nature a deeply complex issue and, as the recollections below clearly illustrate, an issue that may take generations to solve completely.

Bill McNeish is now sixty-six years of age and for more than sixty of those years he has been a Glasgow Rangers fan, albeit from a distance. He recalls:

When I was fifteen I left Scotland and later joined the Royal Air Force. Fifteen years after that I moved to Birmingham. I know of a lot of Scots who have moved around the country and become supporters of local clubs – but not me, I have always remained a Rangers fan.

My father was an Irish Protestant and, after serving in the British Army, he settled in Glasgow in the mid-1930s. On my grandmother's side we think that some of her relatives came from southern Ireland but, thus far, we have not been able to follow the family tree completely. I have no idea which team my dad supported but, in the late 1950s, we were living in Ayr and had some neighbours who were very strong Glasgow Rangers fans. During this period I went to see my first Rangers versus Celtic match. It was a Cup final at Hampden Park and finished up as a 0-0 draw. Some of the players were playing for Scotland the following week and the talk was that they had saved themselves to avoid injury.

I can remember coming out of the ground after the match and as a five- or six-year-old suddenly becoming caught up in the swirl of the crowd and in danger of losing my footing. Suddenly someone spun me round and literally yanked me out of the mass of people to safety.

In those days the most common form of dissent among the fans was displayed by the throwing of bottles onto the pitch. The problem was that they were all made of glass then and so, if they fell short, people got injured. Both Rangers and Celtic football clubs were started with the best of intentions against a backcloth of political and religious divide. A lot of people came over from Belfast and from southern Ireland, looking for work in the shipyards. There is a long history of tension between Catholics and Protestants in Ireland as a whole, and historically many Catholics believe that the Protestants were used by the British to exercise control over them.

Celtic is focused in the east of Glasgow, with their stadium at Parkhead, and Rangers in the west, near to the Ibrox Stadium, located on the south side of the River Clyde, and the Govan shipyard. Both teams became top-level rivals and at an international level in the 1960s both clubs enjoyed great success. They were, and still are, both really well supported. The difference between the two clubs in my view, though, is quite simple. Celtic is an Irish club based in Scotland, whereas Rangers is a British club based in Scotland. Celtic flies the Irish tricolour flag at their ground while Rangers fly the Union flag. This is where the wedge between them exists.

People say that children are 'not born racist' but some things become inbred and instilled within families as views and information are passed on from mother and father to daughter and son, and from grandparents to grandchildren. If you want to antagonise someone from Southern Ireland you need only to refer to their flag as being green, white and orange, whereas they prefer to refer to it as being green, white and gold. Green is said to be the south, white is the border, and gold is Northern Ireland. Any reference to orange provokes thoughts relating to the Loyalist Orange Order, which doesn't go down well with the Catholic community.

Likewise the songs adopted by both clubs provoke extreme reactions. 'The Sash My Father Wore' has been adopted by Rangers and originates from Ulster, commemorating the victory of King William III in the Williamite War in Ireland in 1690. It is popular with Protestant loyalists and refers to battles at Derry,

Above: British Transport Police officers, outside Arsenal tube station, 1980s. (Tony Thompson)

Below: Happy New Year to the 'railway fuz', 1969, being ejected from a football special. (BTP History Group & PARK – Cartoonist)

Above: French riot police in action, 11 June 2016, at the Old Port in Marseille. (David Deakin – BBC)

Below: French riot police in action, 11 June 2016, at the Old Port in Marseille. (David Deakin – BBC)

Above: Co–author Michael Layton with Simon Pinchbeck. (Michael Layton)

Below: BTP training photo (1990) depicting the so-called 'Bobble Hat Brigade' of travelling supporters. (Tony Thompson)

Above: Co-Author Michael Layton with Mark 'Snarka' Whitehouse. (Michael Layton)

Below: Fans surrounded by stewards at Cardiff versus WBA game, 2013. (Mark Whitehouse)

Above: England fans in Trinidad and Tobago, 2008. (Mark Whitehouse)

Below: Cleethorpes – Grimsby *v.* Sheffield United, 23 July 2016. (Duncan Young)

Above: Cleethorpes – Grimsby *v.* Sheffield United, 23 July 2016. (Duncan Young)

Left: Monitoring football traffic at Wembley Park station in 2014. (British Transport Police Media Centre)

Above: Policing football fans at Kings Cross railway station in October 2008. (British Transport Police Media Centre)

Below: Flag relating to 'The Junior Business Boys' – the youth group of Birmingham City's 'Zulu Warriors' hooligan group (1987).

Zulu Warriors.

Pride of the MIDLANDS

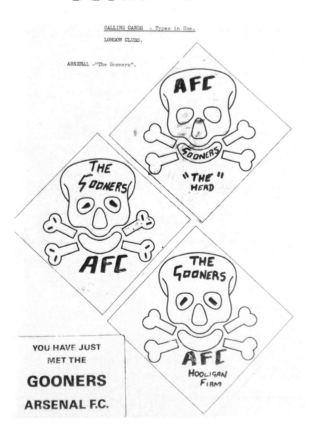

CALLING CARDS - Types in Use.

LONDON CLUBS.

ARSENAL -"The Gooners".

Above: 'Calling Card' for Birmingham City's 'Zulu Warriors' hooligan group (adhesive label type), used to stick on victims of assault (1987).

Left: 'Calling Card' for Arsenal's 'Gooners' hooligan group (1987).

Aughrim, Enniskillen, and the Boyne. Another one they have adopted is 'Derry's Walls', which refers specifically to the siege of Londonderry in the same period. In relation to Celtic, they have adopted 'The Fields of Athenry', which alludes to the Great Irish Famine in 1845–1850 when 15,000 Irish famine victims emigrated to Glasgow. Another one sung by Celtic fans is 'ooh ahh up the Ra', which is described as an Irish rebel song by some. The reference to 'Ra' means the Irish Republican Army.

The strange thing is that, when people sing 'The Fields Of Athenry' at Rugby Union games, nobody says anything but, in the context of what have become known as the 'Old Firm' games between Celtic and Rangers, it is an entirely different matter. There is also a 'New Firm', which is Hibs, who wear green and white, and are supported by Catholics, and Hearts who have a Protestant following.

Bill's son Sean was a police officer for eleven years in London and the West Midlands but, like his father, he is a life-long supporter of Glasgow Rangers:

I can't say that I have ever seen a lot of problems but you can feel the atmosphere at the Old Firm games. About six years ago I went to a game at Parkhead. Some of the pubs around the ground had signs up saying 'no colours' to be worn, while others were clearly designated for specific supporters. I have been in Rangers pubs before and you will always see pictures of the Queen on the wall.

On the day of this particular match, I met a mate in Glasgow and took a taxi from Glasgow Central to a pub near the ground. I was wearing a red British Lions top but, when we walked in, everything else was a sea of green and white. We were in a Celtic pub. Irish music was playing and everyone was singing. It was a moment in time that I will always remember as dozens of pairs of eyes stared at us. I went to the toilet and my mate thought I was going to get done over as three men walked in behind me. Relieved to still be in one piece, we left and outside approached a police officer for directions. He couldn't believe that we had been into that particular pub and told us to stick close to him to make our way to the ground.

Football always brings out the passion in people but also amusing moments as well. I remember one match where Rangers had already won the league but were playing a game with Celtic, which we lost 2-1. To show that they didn't care, at some point loads of Rangers fans sat down and started reading newspapers in their seats in the stands.

I've seen ejections at grounds but not personally witnessed major disturbances. I have, however, been told that domestic violence is a big issue on Old Firm days.

There have been many stories over the years where players have been threatened for one reason or another. Everyone remembers the 'Gazza' incident where he pretended to play a flute after scoring, which was interpreted by many as a reference to Orange Order bands playing flutes. Celtic fans went spare. Likewise Mo Johnston received threats when he went on to sign for Rangers, having previously been a Celtic player.

Bill McNeish recalls one final story:

My wife comes from St Neots and her friend is married to an Irish Catholic. On a Sunday we would sometimes go down and have a few pints in a local Irish pub. It had a big lounge with a bar at the back and on one occasion I could hear people singing 'The Shepherd Boy' song, which is another popular Irish ballad.

The guy I was with kept encouraging me to sing a song so finally, after a couple of pints, he persuaded me and I did a pretty good rendition of 'The Sash', at which point two men burst into the room from the bar, demanding to know what was going on with 'murder in their eyes'. It was a frightening moment and it took us a couple of minutes to smooth things over and to calm the two men down. This is the reaction that one song provoked.

After a number of years of being in the lower divisions of the Scottish League, Glasgow Rangers finally found themselves promoted to the Scottish Premier League for the 2016/17 season.

On Saturday 10 September 2016, the first Old Firm derby in Glasgow for four years was played at Celtic Park, when the two old rivals met in a match that saw Celtic beat Rangers 5-1. There was extensive vandalism, costing tens of thousands of pounds, to a toilet block in the away section of the ground, which was occupied by Rangers fans. There was significant damage to the ceiling, while toilet seats were ripped off and cubicle doors pulled off their hinges. A small number of supporters from both sides, who were clearly intent on causing trouble, were intercepted by police in the Gallowgate area and contained.

Herald Scotland reported the following:

> There was also repeated chants in support of loyalist paramilitary groups the UVF and UDA by a hard-core group of Rangers supporters who stood facing the ground for more than an hour right up to kick-off. Other chants aimed at Celtic fans from their Rangers rivals included one of 'paedo' and 'Jimmy Saville is one of your own' by groups carrying flags bearing the Red Hand of Ulster, as well as the Union flag.
>
> However there was loud pro-IRA chanting and singing from sections of Celtic supporters close to the Celtic Park stadium and in nearby pubs.

Inside the ground effigies of Rangers fans were hung from the stands, and pictures of the sex dolls, with their hands tied behind their backs as if they had been executed, appeared on social media following the game. One was wearing a Rangers scarf and the other an orange sash, with nooses around their necks. They had been hung from a banner that read, 'This is it boys this is war'. A twenty-seven-year-old man was subsequently arrested by Police Scotland in connection with this specific incident.

During the match a huge banner was put on display in the Celtic end that read, 'Know your place hun scum' and sectarian chants relating to the IRA and the song 'Billy Boys' were heard. Police Scotland, however, said that the overwhelming majority of supporters had been well-behaved. One twenty-two-year-old man was arrested for an alcohol-related offence inside the ground.

At 16.30, on the same day, three teenage girls, who were wearing Celtic tops, were travelling on a ScotRail service following their team's victory over Rangers. When the train stopped at the West Dunbartonshire station Kilpatrick, two men on the station platform shouted sectarian abuse at them. One of them boarded the train and spat at one of the girls. The two men are now being sought by the BTP in connection with the incident.

Just hours after the Old Firm derby Rangers striker Kenny Miller, who has played for both halves of the Old Firm, and his wife Laura went to Da Luciano, a fashionable Italian restaurant in Bothwell, Lanarkshire. Trouble flared, involving up to twenty people, when Miller was subjected to a torrent of abuse. During the fracas Laura's hair was grabbed, and she was slapped in the face, causing a scratch to her forehead and a black eye. It is reported that she lost a pair of earrings worth a five-figure sum. The prolonged fracas then spilled into the restaurant's car park. The police were called but, on arrival, it was all over. CCTV evidence was examined and, after everything had died down, a male was seen coming back armed with a lock-knife. Enquiries by Police Scotland continue.

On Sunday 25 September 2016, Aberdeen played Rangers in a Scottish Championship league match at Aberdeen's Pittodrie Stadium. The anthem of Aberdeen fans is 'Stand Free', which some claim sets them apart from religious and racist bigotry. More than 20,000 fans were expected at Pittodrie, with thousands more watching in licensed premises and their homes in North East Scotland and Glasgow.

During the match a number of disturbances took place, with chairs being launched from the Rangers end and pyrotechnics being set off. A twenty-five-year-old male from Aberdeen was charged with being in possession of a pyrotechnic, with a twenty-two-year-old male from Glasgow charged for offensive behaviour within a football stadium. Police also investigated damage to the Rangers team coach during the early hours of Sunday morning while it was parked at their hotel in the Deeside area.

Turning now to England, teams such as Arsenal, Leeds United, Everton and Manchester United have a very strong tradition of representing the Irish communities in their area although, unlike many clubs in Scotland, they were not formed on the basis of representing the Irish community. Consequently, sectarianism has not been a real problem in England. Due to the West Midlands having the largest Irish population in the United Kingdom, Aston Villa has a large Irish following and has featured many Irish players.

Both Everton and Liverpool have roots in a Methodist church but Everton has always been associated with Roman Catholics and has featured a number of Irish International players in the 1950s. Liverpool was formed by a prominent Orangeman, but this did not deter Liverpool people from a Catholic background from supporting the team. Footballer Wayne Rooney, who is of Irish descent, played for Everton in his early years.

None of these clubs have witnessed sectarian violence on the scale that Rangers and Celtic have. Very little of interest has been written about sectarianism in English, or indeed Welsh, football.

However, much has been written about racism in football, which can be described as 'the abuse of players, officials and fans because of their skin colour, nationality, or ethnicity'. Some may be targeted because of their association with an opposing team. There have been occasions of individuals being targeted by their own fans.

Initiatives have been launched by the Commission for Racial Equality, the Football Supporters' Association, and the Professional Footballers' Association in a bid to encourage more people from ethnic minorities to attend matches. The world's first black professional football was Arthur Wharton, who was born in the Gold Coast, which is today known as Ghana. He played as the goalkeeper for Darlington. Other early non-white footballers include Walter Tull, who was born in Folkestone on 23 April 1888 and was of mixed heritage. He died on 23 April 1918. Hong Y Soo was of mixed Chinese and English heritage, born in Buxton on 12 April 1914 and died 25 January 1991. He was the first player of Chinese origin to play in the Football League.

William Ralph Dean, more commonly known as 'Dixie Dean', was born on 22 January 1907 in Birkenhead, Cheshire, and was a dark-skinned centre-forward who played for Everton, among other clubs and England. Dean's family on both sides originated from Chester. His grandfather Ralph Brett was a train driver and, on occasions, drove the Royal Train during the reign of George V. Dean was a committed Everton supporter, thanks to his father William Senior, who took him to a match during the 1914/15 title-winning season.

Dean attended Laird Street School, which was in the street where he was born. He felt that he never had any formal education.

He said, 'My only lesson was football'. When he turned eleven, although he had never been in trouble, he attended the Albert Memorial Industrial School in Birkenhead, which was a borstal school, this being due to the footballing facilities on offer. He was happy to stay at the school due to the lack of space at his family home. He falsely told the other pupils that he had been caught stealing, as he wanted to be 'one of the boys'.

He left school at fourteen and went to work for the railway as an apprentice fitter. His father also worked on the railway as a train driver. Dean then took a night job so that he could concentrate on his first love – namely football. The sons of Dean's manager at the railway were directors of New Brighton AFC and they were interested in signing him; however, he was not interested. He signed for a local team, Pensby United, and at the club he was spotted by a scout for Tranmere Rovers.

Dean, it is said, acquired his nickname in his youth because of his dark complexion and hair, which bore a resemblance to people from the Southern United States. In Dean's obituary, after his death on 1 March 1980, it was suggested that his nickname was taken from a Dixie song that was popular during Dean's childhood. He was the subject of racist comments. On one occasion, as he left the pitch at half time during a match in London in the 1930s, he reportedly punched an offender for racist remarks, before disappearing into the players' tunnel. No action was taken against him by the authorities. A nearby police officer was alleged to have told the victim that he had deserved his punishment.

Clyde Best, who was black and from Bermuda, played for West Ham United in the 1960s alongside Ade Coker, who was from Nigeria. They were subjected to monkey chants and had bananas thrown at them during West Ham's games. The actions of the fans were blamed by Best on the influence of the National Front, who stood on the terraces.

Racism in the 1980s England football games was rampant. Paul Canoville, a black British player, was abused by his own Chelsea fans when he warmed up before making his debut. Garth Crooks, also a black British player, was the subject of regular racist chants and banners from opposing fans during his time at Tottenham Hotspur. When he made his debut for West Bromwich

Albion at Newcastle United, Cyrille Regis, who was of French Guianese origin, was the subject of several monkey chants from the Newcastle United fans. Upon his call up to the England squad, he was sent a bullet in the post. During a match against Everton, Liverpool player John Barnes was pictured back-heeling a banana off the pitch. The Everton fans also chanted racist chant at him.

'Show Racism the Red Card' is an anti-racism charity established in Newcastle, North Tyneside, in 1996. A £50 donation from the then Newcastle goalkeeper, Shaka Hislop, a black English player, was used to harness the high profile nature of footballers as anti-racist role models to educate against racism throughout society in the United Kingdom. Offices were established in England, Scotland and Wales, as well as in other countries.

The charity was founded by a man called Ged Grebby, who was an active member in Youth against Racism in Europe, which sent educational packs to schools. Shaka Hislop got hold of a copy of a magazine, and then pledged £50 and urged more donations after becoming the subject of racist behaviour, which he described in the following terms, 'I was putting petrol in my car at the garage and these kids started shouting racist abuse. Then after a bit one of them realised who I was and told his friends. Then they came over looking for autographs. That really hurt.' The charity has given individual awards to a number of people, including high-profile football stars, for their work against racism in football and society.

In April 1998, during a game at Villa Park, Aston Villa striker Stan Collymore accused Liverpool defender Steve Harkness of racist behaviour. While live on air on ITV on 21 April 2004, Ron Atkinson, a former football manager turned commentator, was alleged to have made an abusive and offensive racist remark about a black Chelsea player, Marcel Desailly from Accra, Ghana. At the time of the remark he believed that the microphone was switched off. The transmission in the UK had finished, but his comments were broadcast to various countries in the Middle East. He subsequently resigned from this role, and later from his job as a columnist for *The Guardian*.

Millwall had the dubious pleasure of being the first club to be charged by the Football Association over racist behaviour by their fans in 2004. The fans aimed a torrent of racial abuse at Liverpool player Djimi Traoré, who was French. The Football Association also charged Newcastle player Emre Belőzoğlu, a Turkish player, with 'using racially aggravated and or insulting words' on 13 January 2007 after an incident during the football match with Everton at Goodison Park on 30 December 2006, but he was later cleared. On 16 February 2007 Belőzoğlu was again accused of more racist behaviour, this time during the match with Bolton Wanderers and involving El Hadji Diouf from Dakar, Senegal. On 1 March 2007, Diouf withdrew the accusations he had made.

It was announced on 6 March 2007 that the Metropolitan Police were investigating West Ham fans for apparent anti-Semitic chants before the match with Tottenham Hotspur two days previously after a video of the chants appeared on the internet.

Kelvin Jack, of Trinidadian origin and a goalkeeper for Gillingham, was racially abused by a Rotherham fan on 7 April 2007 during a game between Rotherham United and Gillingham. A fan was banned for life from the club on 13 April 2007.

Avram Grant, an Israeli, was appointed manager of Chelsea Football Club in September 2007. He became the target of ant-Semitic taunts from some of the Chelsea fans. His father was a Polish survivor of the Nazi Holocaust. He even received death threats and anti-Semitic post.

Mido, an Egyptian who played for Middlesbrough, was in November 2008 subjected to Islamophobic chanting from a small number of Newcastle fans. On previous occasions, he had been the subject of similar chants from Newcastle, Southampton and West Ham fans.

On 22 September 2009 at the Britannia Stadium, Stoke-on-Trent, during a match between Stoke City and Blackpool, Jason Euell, a black British Blackpool player, was racially abused while sat on the substitutes' bench by a Stoke fan, who was arrested by the police. The fan later received a banning order for life. The Blackpool manager said,

> We are human beings and Jason is a footballer, the colour of his skin shouldn't matter. It was disgusting. The stewards believed what Jason said, got the bloke out and I hope he is banned for life.

He is an absolute disgrace of a human being. I thought those days had gone. Jason was just sat in the dugout at the time. I saw his reaction and I had to calm him down. It's absolutely disgraceful.

Euell, who received an official apology from Stoke, later said,

It did hurt. I felt I had to stand up for all colours and creeds and show that we won't accept it. I'm proud that I made a stand. It was a shock to hear what came out of the guy's mouth. Racism in football is not dead and buried but it's still a shock to hear that kind of thing in close proximity. There were people near the idiot who didn't agree with it, but there were others who turned a blind eye, which is disappointing.

Following this incident, Tottenham Hotspur manager Harry Redknapp called for fans who racially abused players to be imprisoned. The comedian David Baddiel launched an initiative in April 2011 to tackle anti-Semitism in football, which was backed by several high-profile players.

Two supporters of Chesterfield were arrested before the start of a game against Torquay in April 2011 for racially abusing a young black Torquay player, who was taking part in the pre-match entertainment. They were subsequently banned from watching football or from the venues of any Chesterfield matches for three years.

On 15 October 2011, Liverpool's Luis Suárez, who originates from Uruguay, was accused of racially abusing Manchester United's Patrice Evra, who originates from Dakar, Senegal. Following the incident, the FA began an enquiry into the incident and announced that they would be charging Suárez. Liverpool meanwhile announced support for their player. On 20 December 2011, after a seven-day hearing, the FA fined Suárez £40,000 and banned him for eight matches for racially abusing Evra. Suárez claimed that the term he used was in fact a term of endearment in his native South American country, but this was not accepted by the FA.

Following being charged with two counts of racial abuse at a match against Barnet, also on the 15 October 2011, Aldershot Town striker Danny Hylton was given an eight-match ban and fined £1,000. He was also warned about his future conduct.

During a match on 23 October 2011 between Queens Park Rangers and Chelsea, QPR's Anton Ferdinand, a black British player, was alleged to have been subjected to racial abuse by the Chelsea captain John Terry, who was said to have used offensive and abusive words towards him. This allegation was disputed by Terry.

Subsequently, on 1 November 2011, the Metropolitan Police began a formal investigation into the allegations. In January 2012 death threats were made to Ferdinand and he also received a bullet through the post. Following the investigation, Terry appeared at Westminster Magistrates' Court on 1 February 2012, charged with a racially aggravated public order offence, to which he pleaded 'not guilty'. At a subsequent four-day trial, which began on 9 July that year, he was acquitted. After the trial, Terry was charged by the FA with 'using abusive and/or insulting words and/or behaviour, which also included a reference to colour and/or race' towards Ferdinand, contrary to the FA rules.

In September 2012 Terry was found guilty after a four-day trial. He was fined £220,000 and banned for four games. Ashley Cole, Terry's teammate, gave evidence in his defence. Ferdinand's brother Rio later made some disparaging racial remarks via Twitter about Ashley Cole. In August 2012 Rio Ferdinand was fined £45,000 for his remarks.

On Monday 12 March 2012, during a Premier League match between Arsenal and Newcastle United at the Emirates Stadium, the Sky Sports cameras caught a twenty-nine-year old Arsenal fan committing a racially aggravated public order offence, as he abused Newcastle's Cheick Tioté, who was of Ivorian descent. The fan was arrested.

Gillingham played Crawley Town in a league match on Tuesday 20 March 2012. In the fifty-third minute Dean Howell, a black British player who played for Crawley Town, reported to the assistant referee a racist altercation with a fan in the Gordon Road Stand. The exchange between Howell and the fan was overheard by a steward, but enquiries at that point failed identify the suspect.

On 15 April 2012, during an FA Cup semi-final when Chelsea played Tottenham Hotspur, racial abuse was directed at Chelsea player Didier Drogba and a man from Isleworth, London, was banned for life from Stamford Bridge and given a three-year banning order from matches in the UK and abroad. He was arrested after other fans reported him to a Wembley steward. Chelsea FC condemned the fan's action and praised the fans who reported him. The incident also saw a number of other persons being banned from Chelsea games for using racial and abusive language.

On 6 October 2012 a thirteen-year-old boy from the London area racially abused Bolton forward Marvin Sordell, an England Under-21 International, during a game between Millwall and Bolton Wanderers at the New Den. Millwall's reaction to the incident was to exclude the teenager from the ground for 'the foreseeable future' but did not go as far as imposing a lifetime ban on him. Instead he was offered a place on a club educational programme in the hope that the club could change his outlook on equality, racism and life. The boy wrote a letter of apology to Sordell, which was accepted. The FA fully supported Millwall's actions.

A police investigation took place following the Manchester United versus Chelsea fourth-round League Cup game on 31 October 2012, when a twenty-eight-year old fan was pictured making a monkey gesture towards United striker Danny Welbeck after he lost possession of the ball.

On 10 November 2012 six Millwall fans were arrested after unfurling a racist banner of abuse aimed at Marvin Sordell during their home game against Derby County, which Millwall won 2-1. The offending banner was quickly removed by Millwall staff.

In October 2013, while travelling on a train returning from a game against Fulham, a number of fans started singing songs glorifying Gary Dobson in relation to the racially motivated murderer of Stephen Lawrence. Six supporters of Charlton Athletic were subsequently sent to prison after having been found guilty of racially aggravated fear of violence.

At a match in March 2014, two Wolverhampton Wanderers players, Carl Ikeme and George Elokobi, claimed that they were racially abused by Walsall fans at a game at Walsall's ground, although no action was taken against the club.

Malcolm 'Malky' Mackay, and Iain Moody, who was sporting director of Crystal Palace, were in August 2014 accused of sending each other racist, sexist and homophobic text messages. Moody left his job and Mackay apologised for the texts. He was defended by the League Managers' Association, claiming that the texts were merely 'banter' for which they later apologised. Mackay later denied being racist, sexist or homophobic.

Liverpool player Mario Balotelli was subject to racist abuse on Twitter in September 2014, following his tweet mocking Manchester United. Balotelli made comments about their 5-3 defeat to Leicester City. He was said to have been the target of more than 8,000 abusive posts between that time and March 2015, of which more than 4,000 of these were said to be racist in nature.

In February 2015 Chelsea fans were involved in a racist incident on the Paris Metro when they refused to let a black passenger on to a train. The incident was captured on film and received international television coverage. Following a police investigation a number of people were made the subject of football banning orders in the UK.

On Saturday 12 December 2015 Derby County played away at Brighton and Hove Albion in a game that finished 2-2. During the course of the match an allegation was made that a Derby supporter, standing with a child, racially abused a Brighton player by calling him a 'black bastard'.

On Monday 28 December 2015 Sheffield United played at home at Bramall Lane with Bradford City in a game that Sheffield won 3-1. During the course of the match a section of the Sheffield United supporters started chanting 'You're just a town full of ISIS' at Bradford fans. 'JF' commented in one media article, 'Racist chanting by a very small section of home fans which was quickly stopped by stewards. This very small section was about 50–100 people in a crowd of nearly 25,000 people – 20,000 of which were home fans and all of whom were also disgusted by the racist chanting,' while 'SEH' sought to justify it by saying, 'Banter. It's banter. Get a grip. It's good to chant to wind the other lot up.' During the game there was also a report of a coin being thrown at a Sheffield United player by a Bradford fan after one of the goals was scored. Sheffield United later handed out their own banning orders to a number of fans.

Following a pre-season friendly match on Saturday 23 July 2016 between Bradford City and Burnley, Burnley FC issued an apology to Bradford after one of their supporters was ejected following an alleged racist incident against an unidentified Bradford player. The player claimed that he had been repeatedly racially abused. Player Andre Gray slammed the fans actions on Twitter, calling them 'ignorant prats'. No arrests were made. The supporter concerned denied the allegations but other witnesses backed up the complaints of the player involved.

Scotland has also suffered from incidents of racism. Andrew Watson was the first black football player to represent Scotland. In the book *Race, Sport and British Society*, there is a reference stating that there was racial abuse of Glasgow player Paul Wilson, who was born in Bangalore, India, by the supporters of neighbouring rivals Rangers in the 1970s. Black players in Scotland were regularly greeted with bananas being thrown at them from the crowd, while a barrage of monkey chants was aimed at them, notably at Mark Walters of Rangers and Paul Elliott of Celtic.

On 2 January 1988 Rangers were in an Old Firm derby with Celtic when Rangers winger Mark Walters made his debut at Celtic Park. Celtic won the match 2-0 and Walters was subjected to racist abuse from the opposing Celtic fans. They were caught on camera chanting like monkeys, throwing fruit, mostly bananas, onto the pitch and dressing in monkey costumes. It was reported that Rangers used 'implicit racism' on the same day by singing a racist song. The Scottish FA remained silent about the episode, but Celtic football club denounced it.

Mark Walters stated that he had experienced worse racial abuse in Edinburgh against Hearts. Rangers actually banned some of their own season-ticket holders following the racial abuse aimed at Walters. A reporter from *The Scotsman* newspaper wrote, 'It is depressing to think that enforcement as much as enlightenment might account for Walters being the only black footballer in this country to have had any bananas thrown at them.'

Lorenzo Amoruso, who in 1999 was captain for Rangers, had to make a public apology to Borussia Dortmund's Nigerian striker Victor Ikpeda after making racist comments about him during a match in December 1999. Ranger's fans in March 2003 were accused of racially abusing French player Bobo Balde and Mohammed Sylla from Bouake, Côte d'Ivoire, during a match. In May 2004 some Rangers fans were condemned for their racism by player Marvin Andrews from Trinidad and Tobago. The then manager of Celtic, Martin O'Neill, suggested in November 2004 that Neil Lennon, originally from Northern Ireland, was the subject of chants of a 'racial and sectarian manner'. St Johnstone's Jason Scotland was the target of racist taunts by a few Motherwell fans during a 2007 Scottish Cup tie between the two clubs. The chairman of Motherwell later issued an apology on behalf of the club.

Maurice Edu, a black American player for Rangers, stated that he was racially abused by some Rangers fans while leaving Ibrox after a UEFA Champions League match against Romanian club Unirea Urziceni, in which Rangers were defeated in October 2009. Edu later wrote on Twitter, 'Not sure what hurt me more the result or being racially abused by a couple of our own fans as I'm getting in my car.'

In June 2009 the 'Famine Song' was ruled by three Scottish judges to be racist because it targeted people of Irish origin. The chairman of the Scottish Football Association suggested that the song caused embarrassment for Scottish football and that it should be stamped out. The Scottish Football Association stated that it was determined to contribute to the eradication of offensive songs from Scottish football. A Rangers fan was found guilty of a breach of the peace (aggravated by religious and racial prejudice) in November 2008 for singing the 'Famine Song' during a game against Kilmarnock. Reports circulated in February 2009 after an Old Firm game at Celtic Park game wherein Rangers fans had sung the 'Famine Song', and the song was also sung at a Rangers game by their fans in March 2011.

In an Old Firm match at Celtic Park in February 2011, a Celtic supporter was caught mocking black Rangers player El Hadji Diouf with monkey noises and gestures as he was about to take a corner kick.

The then manager of Celtic Neil Lennon received an explosive device in the post in April 2011. This was described as being due to anti-Catholic and anti-Irish racism. Suspected explosive devices were sent to a number of high-profile Celtic supporters at the same time. The then leader of the Scottish Conservative Party Annabel Goldie MSP described the incidents as 'racism and sectarianism', while at Hearts' Tynecastle stadium an attempted assault was made on Neil Lennon. Following this a motion against anti-Irish racism was lodged in the Scottish parliament.

At the end of November 2011 the British Transport Police picked up an award at the Scottish Policing Awards for tackling sectarian-related football violence on Scotland's railways.

Celtic player Aleksander Tonev, a Bulgarian, received a seven-match ban for racially abusing an opponent in October 2014.

* * *

As an additional note, it was announced in August 2016 that Howard Gayle, who was born in Toxteth, Liverpool, and was the first black footballer to play for Liverpool in 1977, had turned down an MBE. He stated that his ancestors would be 'turning in their graves after how the Empire and Colonialism had enslaved them', should he have had accepted.

The honour would have been in recognition of his work with the anti-discrimination charity Show Racism the Red Card.

* * *

On 21 September 2016 the BBC's Victoria Derbyshire programme discussed the findings of a report by the organisation Stonewall, which highlighted a rise in homophobic behaviour in football. Research had shown that some 72 per cent of supporters in the UK had witnessed homophobic behaviour in the preceding five years. It was pointed out that there are currently no openly gay football players in Premier League football. While it was stressed that this type of behaviour came from a small, but vocal, minority of fans, concerns were raised that 22 per cent of young fans just saw this as banter, while one in five fans aged between eighteen and twenty-four said that they would be embarrassed if their favourite player turned out to be gay.

One person who responded during the course of the programme said that 'Everyone gets abuse … Not everyone is PC'. Examples of good practice were highlighted, however, such as that being conducted by Arsenal's Gay Gooners group, and the use of the Kick it Out app, which allows fans to report any type of discrimination.

4

HOOLIGANS ON TOUR

Organised football hooligan groups in the UK have a well-documented history of following their own teams abroad, or coming together under the banner of their national team. This chapter deals with some of the incidents that have occurred during the 2015/16 period, as well as looking back at some of the milestone historical football events and using them as a means of comparison. It is clear that, during the course of some of the incidents described, on occasions these groups are not the main protagonists, but the reality is that the reputation of English hooligans makes English fans in general a target for those looking to enhance their own warped credentials.

Richard Shakespeare, from a Midlands force, trailed the thugs for fifteen years and has described it in the following terms: 'I would describe it as a cat and mouse game. We're the cats – and I've never yet seen a mouse eat a cat. You follow the intelligence as it is occurring – normally by the minute – and just follow your nose, follow your instinct. It's like a hunt.' What follows are his personal recollections of the 1998 World Cup finals in France:

On Saturday 13 June 1998 most of the team flew to Marseilles, the host city for England's first game against Tunisia. No sooner had we landed than we were out on the streets helping French police to deal with disorder in the Old Port, where several hundred English fans were drinking. Four arrests were made after bottles were thrown, but the disorder was described as minor.

On Sunday 14 June 1998 a large group of English fans massed at a waterfront bar called O'Malley's. Some then left the pub and tried to burn an Irish flag, before chanting 'No surrender to the IRA', following which threats were made to the police. A 40-yard no-man's land opened up between police in riot-gear and England fans. We found the attitude of the French police, who simply stood their ground, firing teargas when the hooligans got too close, a little hard to understand. There was little attempt to disperse the fans or to make arrests. Still, it gave us plenty of chances to video the ensuing riot with handheld cameras. After two hours, the police moved forward, banging their shields like Zulus, and dispersed the crowds of supporters.

Elsewhere, on the other side of the harbour, English fans fought with local Arab youths and local football hooligans. One fan trapped down a side street had his throat cut.

During that weekend a lot of people were walking around bloodstained. A lot of trouble was caused by what the French police referred to as 'French Arabs'. On one occasion I was actually walking with another officer in plain clothes down a back street when we were also confronted by a local, who was holding a machete in a threating manner. Instinctively we both just shouted loudly at him and told him in no uncertain terms to 'eff off' and thankfully he turned on his heels and did just that.

On Monday 15 June 1998 the undercover police team reviewed the video material that we had and, after filming this sort of stuff for fifteen years, it was probably the best evidence I've ever seen. The material was later used to convict the ringleaders and we literally started looking for these people everywhere we went in France.

Inside the Stade Velodrome that day, the teams watched the crowds, filming some faces with handheld cameras and trying to pick out people who had been involved in the earlier disorder. A valuable source of information was the flags revealing the names of home towns and clubs.

Some skirmishes occurred later as England scored the first of two goals that gave them victory and a number of people were injured by missiles at a big screen on the beach.

On Tuesday 16 June 1998 the team took a pause for breath. Putting things into perspective, however, there were probably

10,000 to 15,000 English fans in the stadium. At the height of the disturbances on the 14th there were only 300 involved, of which perhaps half were actively trying to orchestrate disorder. During this period, quite by accident, we came across one of the hooligans who had been captured on video while we were in Montpellier, and we had him arrested by the local police.

On Sunday 21 June 1998 the team had moved to Toulouse and we worked with a number of plain-clothes French police officers, who were deployed as an arrest team. It was to be a day not of arrests, however, but of fight prevention. In one particular incident three local Arab youths tried to provoke a group of England fans in the main square, which was full of cafés. One of the three brandished a large stick as a confrontation developed, but we managed to get French police there quickly and they arrested the local youth and diffused the situation. We actually got a round of applause from the England fans.

We spent the day trying to keep the lid on things and, at one stage, we were even asked to mediate with some fans that were standing drinking and blocking the roads. It was a difficult situation and not what we were there for but we did our best.

On Thursday 25 June 1998 I found myself in Lille, a busy city with a Channel Tunnel terminal. The information we had was that this location was likely to attract the heaviest hooligan groups from the UK, as it was the easiest location to reach for the first-round matches. Thousands were expected, many of whom would be without tickets. In one Lille bar, which was packed with English supporters, we spotted two supporters who were classed as Category C targets, which meant that, if their convictions were serious enough, we could get them thrown out of the country. The problem was that they were in the middle of a packed bar and we didn't want to start a riot.

The French police wanted to go straight in but we persuaded them to wait. After two hours they came out in a group of six. We had already established that one of the two could be kicked out but, as they were identical twins, we finished up taking both back to the police station. Over the next twenty-four hours, Lille became the focus of some of the most formidable English football hooligans, who were totally streetwise and hardened fighters.

By the end of the night about fifty arrests had been made, but thankfully there was no serious disorder.

On Friday 26 June 1998 we split up, some going to Lens some twenty miles away, some monitoring the railway station at Lille, while we set up an observation post in Lille city centre, equipped with binoculars and video. In one small bar we spotted hooligans from Wolverhampton and Huddersfield, a German who had been seen quite a few times with the English, and some Chelsea fans. Tension was in the air as fans tried to pick fights with the police, and several minor altercations took place.

At some stage we were spotted in our observations point and the fans started to wave and make less than complimentary gestures. It was time to leave.

In one instance we were able to direct French police towards a fan we had previously spotted throwing bottles at police in Marseilles. To be more precise, it was a box of bottles. We had a video still of him and spotted him in Toulouse, but he saw us first and ran off. His luck ran out in Lens and, after going to a small skirmish outside Lens stadium, we saw him again and had him arrested. He was from Fulham and was later jailed for four months as a result of our video evidence.

The power of video filming is unbelievable and, together with another colleague, I was once able to stop a fight by standing 'back to back' and filming both sides at the same time. It stopped them long enough in their tracks until the cavalry arrived. This was at a game between Cardiff and Wrexham at Cardiff Arms Park.

On Tuesday 30 June 1998 we were waiting at Saint-Étienne police station for several hours when a well-known Huddersfield Town hooligan was brought in, in handcuffs. He actually started to take the mickey out of us for our dress sense, proudly showing off his Burberry and Stone Island tops. On this date England lost to Argentina and that was it – the end of a dream and, apart from a few minor skirmishes in the ground and the town afterwards, it was all over.

This operation was the end of an era for me and, shortly after returning to the UK, I transferred to other duties in another force, doing a totally different job. If I am honest, I missed it, and perhaps I still do. I enjoyed the challenge of being part of the effort to tackle football hooliganism. Perhaps I even became addicted to it!

On Tuesday 21 July 2015 Leeds United played a friendly game with Eintracht Frankfurt in Salzburg. Approximately 450 Leeds fans travelled to Austria, while about 300 fans travelled from Frankfurt. Riot police with dogs were forced to break up fighting on the pitch at full time as about 100 Frankfurt fans, some wearing balaclavas, confronted Leeds fans. Fifty Frankfurt fans stormed the stadium entrance and injured two security staff on duty. A Leeds fan and a police officer were treated for injuries at the scene and seven people, including three Leeds fans and two police officers, later received hospital treatment. Seventeen Frankfurt fans were arrested, as were eight Leeds fans, one of whom was arrested for throwing a bench at police officers. Clashes occurred later in Eugendorf town centre and police officers deployed pepper spray to break them up.

On Friday 24 July 2015 200 Derby County fans attended a friendly game in Holland with FC Utrecht at their training ground. Riot police were called in after disturbances threatened to break out over an argument about taking a flag down. Police made fifteen arrests, none of whom were Derby fans.

On Thursday 6 August 2015 riot police, with batons drawn and supported by horses, were deployed in Arnhem town square ahead of a Europa League match between Southampton and Vitesse Arnhem. Bottles and chairs were thrown, as both sets of fans, plus fans from another club, Feyenoord, clashed in the Korenmarkt, which resulted in fifty Dutch fans being arrested and three English fans. More than seventy arrests were made in total, before and after the match, seven of whom were Southampton 'Saints' fans, four of whom were arrested on suspicion of 'public violence and harassment of a police officer'. One officer suffered minor injuries.

On Wednesday 26 August 2015 dozens of football fans were arrested following Manchester United's 4-0 Champions League play-off victory away to Club Brugge. In what was believed to have been an arranged fight, a number of Brugge's hooligan element attacked the Charlie Rockets pub in the centre of the city, where a number of United fans, who had travelled without tickets, had gathered to watch the match on television.

As police moved in, twenty-five Manchester United fans were arrested, twenty-three of whom were later released without charge.

Fifteen Brugge fans were arrested. At the stadium twenty-five Manchester United fans were detained, some of whom were held for not being in possession of a ticket, which is a criminal offence in Belgium. Seventeen fans were arrested on suspicion of breaching the peace, as plain clothes police spotters from Greater Manchester Police supported local police. One fan was arrested after running onto the pitch at the Jan Breydel Stadium.

On Tuesday 20 October 2015 UEFA charged Dynamo Kiev with racist behaviour and crowd disturbances after a video circulated showing four black Chelsea fans being punched and kicked in the stands. The incident took place at the NSK Olimpiysky Stadium in Kiev and, prior to the match, another group of about thirty Chelsea fans were ambushed as they left the Shato Brewery just off Independence Square in Kiev. Several fans suffered cuts and bruises, and one required hospital treatment in what was believed to have been a pre-planned attack by youths wearing balaclavas.

On Thursday 22 October 2015, Tottenham Hotspur was due to play away to Belgian side Anderlecht in the Europa League group stages. Tottenham sold all of its 1,300 ticket allocation for the match. The two clubs had a history of trouble between them; in 1984 a Spurs fan was shot dead before the club played the UEFA Cup final first leg in Brussels.

At around midnight, the night before the game, about fifty Tottenham fans were drinking in the BarBQ bar, near to the main station, when they were attacked by up to 100 Anderlecht fans. The fighting, which went on for some twenty minutes, spilt out into the streets, as a window was smashed, beer glasses were thrown, and tables and chairs broken, in what was strongly believed to have been a pre-meditated attack. When police arrived, Tottenham fans complained that they were unfairly treated as the aggressors. Two Spurs fans were treated for minor injuries.

On Tuesday 3 November 2015 Sevilla played at home to Manchester City in a Champions League clash. More than 2,000 fans travelled to support Manchester City, and 1,000 police officers were deployed to keep order. The night before, Manchester City fans were drinking at O'Neill's Irish Pub in Seville when a group of up to fifty people, with their faces covered, who claimed to be Sevilla fans, launched an attack. Armed with batons and shouting 'hooligans, hooligans', the gang smashed windows and doors, and threw chairs and tables as fighting erupted. Outside cars were damaged and a number of people were left injured; the gang made good their escape before police arrived. There were no arrests.

On Thursday 7 April 2016 Borussia Dortmund played Liverpool at the Signal Iduna Park Stadium in a Europa League clash, which finished in a 1-1 draw. Both clubs faced a UEFA investigation following the game, as stairways were blocked and Liverpool fans set off fireworks after their opponents scored the opening goal.

On Wednesday 18 May 2016, the UEFA Europa League final took place at St Jakob-Park in Basel, Switzerland, between Liverpool and Sevilla, in a match that Liverpool subsequently lost with a score of 3-1. There was a crowd attendance of 34,429, while the ground itself had a capacity of only 35,000. Fifteen minutes before the game started, clashes took place inside the ground between up to fifty Liverpool and Sevilla fans, as punches were exchanged. Plastic bottles were hurled on the concourse behind one of the goals, where the bulk of the Spanish fans were sat. The club had not managed to sell all of its ticket allocation and, as such, half of their allocated area was occupied by Liverpool fans. With no segregation in place, stewards struggled to separate the protagonists, some of whom were booed at by other supporters for their behaviour.

There was some suggestion that the fighting had started after Sevilla fans wearing t-shirts with the word 'Ultra' on had commenced booing as the Liverpool fans started singing, 'You'll Never Walk Alone'. There was further aggression when Liverpool scored in the first half of the game, but no further problems after the Spanish team scored three times in the second half, although riot police were obliged to stand guard in the stands to avoid a repetition.

It was estimated that half a million fans would travel during the course of the European Championships, with England having a ticket allocation of 10,720 for the opening game with Russia on 11 June 2016 in Marseilles. During a similar game in the France '98 World Cup, nearly 500 fans were involved in violent clashes. A further 6,080 tickets for the game with Wales on 16 June 2016, in Lens, were made available, and 6,720 tickets for the match with Slovakia four days later.

On 5 June 2016, the British Transport Police set up an operation at St Pancras International, Ebbsfleet International, and Ashford International railway stations to monitor the movement of fans travelling to France, under the codename Operation Novella. BTP search dog Buster was one of the resources deployed at St Pancras on 6 June 2016, in addition to armed officers, and Eurostar applied a restricted alcohol policy on some trains.

Two arrests of England fans took place the night before, following disturbances in Marseilles, but no incidents were reported by BTP as fans travelled in large numbers on Eurostar services. Some of these were escorted by officers, who reported that there had been a great rapport with travelling fans.

On Thursday 9 June 2016 one England fan received a head injury after being hit across the face with a wooden chair. During the weekend commencing Friday 10 June 2016 serious disturbances took place in Marseilles involving local French fans and England and Russian supporters; television screens were filled with images of supporters fighting as French police responded with teargas and, in at least one case, a water-cannon, in an effort to disperse them.

During the course of the violence on the Friday night, one fan from Huddersfield was actually thrown into the harbour at about 6.20 p.m., after being beaten, as England fans sang songs about the IRA and German bombers being shot down. The fan was photographed swimming back to safety sporting a black eye. Over that weekend period it was estimated that 25,000 England fans and 10,000 Russian fans were in the city.

On Saturday 11 June 2016 Marseilles Old Port area, near to the Queen Victoria and O'Malley's pubs, was described as a 'war-zone' in some media reports, and two English fans were left fighting for their lives in hospital, as twenty-nine others were treated for injuries. At about 2 p.m., four Brighton and Hove Albion supporters were among a group of about a dozen English fans who became involved in a confrontation with Russian fans in the main square.

They were observed by British police officers, who were working as spotters, engaging in disorder and were caught on camera throwing street furniture at the Russians before confronting the undercover officer filming the incident, while in the background a French waitress shouted for them to stop. All four were subsequently made the subject of five-year football banning orders, after appearing at court in the UK, and a fifth fan from the same group got a three-year banning order.

There was evidence of Russian Ultra fans engaging in organised attacks on English fans, despite the presence of more than 1,000 police officers in the Old Harbour, the Fanzone area, and at the ground. One man suffered a heart attack as he was repeatedly kicked in the head, and another was left critically ill after he was hit with an iron bar, as orchestrated attacks took place at about 3 p.m. by about 150 highly organised Russians. Social media once again went into overdrive, as opposing fans posted pictures of their 'victories' on Facebook, YouTube and Twitter.

David Deakin was a BBC reporter for five years, and is a life-long Birmingham City supporter. This is his eye-witness account:

It was meant to be a holiday as well and six of us, five men and one woman, flew to Turin first, hired a minibus, stopped off at Nice and Monaco, and had an absolutely great time. On the Friday before the England game, we sat in an apartment in Aix-en-Provence looking at social media and the news channel, and we could see that it was kicking off in Marseilles on a larger scale than on the Thursday. We watched the France versus Romania opening game on television and discussed what to do next day. We didn't want to get caught up in an area of trouble so we agreed to avoid the Old Port area, where the majority of England fans were congregating.

We got up bright and early, ready to go, and drove the forty minutes into Marseilles in the minibus. As we got closer to the centre, the atmosphere inside the vehicle changed. Our surroundings suddenly felt quite intimidating and we could actually feel the mood change in the group. We found an underground car park to put the minivan, which was mistake number one. As we walked out of the car park, a metal barrier banged shut behind us as we walked into a square, which was occupied by 200–300 local people. You could hear a pin drop as people started staring at us and then some started shouting in French in a very menacing manner. The looks of detestation in the eyes of these people was obvious and on impulse we needed to make a decision as to where to go. What did we do? – We headed to the Old Port on the basis that there would be safety in numbers. We needed to get away.

When we arrived at the Old Port area we found a brilliant atmosphere. There must have been at least 5,000 people there in the bars, dancing and singing. It was a festival atmosphere that you would expect from a European championship. People were mixing with Russian fans without any problems. One Russian fan was actually chatting to me and we were having a laugh because, for some strange reason, he had an Aston Villa tattoo and he was laughing at my BCFC tattoo on my lower left leg. It was bizarre.

We started to relax and felt that we were among like-minded people. We moved to a small pizzeria to get some food and I did a radio report on how good the atmosphere was and that everyone was behaving themselves. Although it wasn't a working trip I was still utilised to do some reports. I had no sooner come off air than about forty-five seconds later we became aware of teargas being thrown towards England fans on the opposite side of the square. The fans didn't appear to be doing anything but, after the teargas, there were clashes with fans with bottles and chairs being thrown opposite the harbour.

We carried on eating but we could hear bottles smashing and then there was a bit of a roar. It was apparent that some form of attack was going on, which is when I made mistake number two. Being a journalist I thought I would have a good chance of getting a photograph so I left my friends and walked up a side street at the side of the pizzeria. After all, it was my job!

Half-way up the side street, England fans were retreating towards me as I walked up towards them. I took my phone out to take a picture and then as I looked up I was suddenly aware that there was nothing in front of me. It was empty.

I couldn't understand what was going on and then suddenly a man appeared at the top of the side-street. He was wearing black trainers, a black T-shirt, black trousers, and a black balaclava. He pushed what looked like a gum-shield into his mouth and sort of punched his chest and shouted 'Russia'. At this point I heard a roar and between eighty to 100 men dressed in a similar 'uniform' came around the corner.

My legs went to jelly. It was a real sense of fear that I have never felt before.

I turned around and thought, 'I need to get out,' but it was like a pincer movement with more Russians coming from behind me. I was in the middle with nowhere to go. I wanted to run but I was in just 5 feet of space on my own.

A guy wearing a balaclava appeared in front of me. He was holding a large knife, which was at least 12 inches long with a wooden handle.

He stood staring at me from 2 feet away with his arm stretched straight out in front of him holding the knife. The sheer size of these men – I wouldn't have stood a chance.

He suddenly swung the knife towards me but, as he did so, an England fan, one of a group of about thirty in the narrow side street by then, got pushed into the space between me and the Russian, and this guy finished up getting slashed across the face.

The Russians waded in, going for everyone. They didn't care. The England fan went down. There was a gap and I just started running back out towards the harbour. At the bottom of the side street, another England fan was on the deck with yet another Russian just laying into him. I ran at the Russian and used him as a hurdle to jump over him. That was probably mistake number three because, as I leapt over him, he hit me with the bottom half of an umbrella pole and caught the bottom half of my foot.

I just about managed to keep my balance as another Russian caught me with a punch in the ribs, as I literally fell out into the area next to the pizzeria. As I hit the floor my friends came out and grabbed me, and off we ran as a group towards where the bulk of the England fans were.

There must have been at least 150 police officers there but you could see some of them just standing next to people fighting. I watched the police deploy teargas about three times in the square and each time England fans had to go up side streets to get away from it and guess what – the Russians were there ready to attack them.

At one point I must have been about 40 feet from the teargas. I can tell you it stings. I felt really disorientated. It was like a scene from a fiction film, where bombs go off and one person is looking around looking entirely vacant. That's how I felt until I started to calm down.

My ticket was in the Russian end of the ground and, after the trouble, I said that I wouldn't go to the match but amazingly a guy who I didn't even know gave me a ticket in the area in which my friends were.

Kevin Miles, chief executive of the Football Supporters' Federation, commented in the press on the difference in policing styles:

The English police don't police football in the same style and there's a good reason for that. They've learned from experience that there are much more effective ways of policing a football crowd. I don't think the policing style that we've seen is particularly suited to de-escalating situations. It contains and it can disperse, but it doesn't de-escalate the situation.

David Deakin went on, 'We had a horrible walk to the stadium because of fear of ambush.'

Further disturbances took place at the city's Stade Velodrome and at the end of the game between England and Russia, as Russian fans broke through a sterile area and again attacked English fans.

David Deakin concludes,

At the final whistle the Russian fans charged across the terraces in the area that I would have been in. When we left the ground we came across another group of about eight Russian fans, big guys dressed in black t-shirts. They started making gun gestures with their fingers and shouting 'Princess Diana' – more bizarre behaviour as they tried to goad us.

It was a two-mile walk back to the minivan. We actually took a guy from Castle Bromwich back with us who had lost his bag. You weren't allowed to take bags inside the stadium and he had left his in one of the dedicated kiosks but, when he tried to recover it after the match, there was no queuing system and they were simply throwing bags out to people. Needless to say he couldn't find his and we wanted to help him out, so we took him with us back to Turin to get a flight home. All he was worried about was what his wife was going to say!

In conclusion, I think that the England fans were targeted and ambushed deliberately in an effort to gain notoriety. I would never follow England away again. I phoned my dad and my girlfriend after the fight in Marseilles to tell them that I was okay. I heard the pain and fear in their voices. It was supposed to be a holiday. I felt guilty that they had to hear the fear in my voice. It's put me off for life.

Mark 'Snarka' Whitehouse was also in Marseilles that day and talks about both it and some of his previous experiences travelling with England supporters:

I am a committed England supporter and travel to most of the away games as part of the England Supporters Travel Club. I've been going to England games all over the world since 2002, and have some great memories of being away with lads from all parts of the country. I've been to places like Brazil, Russia, South Africa, and even went to Trinidad and Tobago for a friendly game. I vividly remember a police officer in Malmo in Sweden, who was literally 7 feet tall, offering to tie up some of our flags for us above a bar we were sat outside. On another occasion my wife actually moved house while I was away without me knowing and I finished up going home to a different address! It was and still is a big part of my life.

I'd say in all that time that the violence I have seen has been orchestrated by supporters from other countries trying to make a name for themselves by attacking England fans because of our reputation. That's not to say of course that there are some English fans that do look for trouble.

For example, I was in Croatia, possibly in 2006, and we were at a bar in Zagreb when one of their so-called 'Bad Blue Boys' approached us and asked us if we wanted to have a fight. We were all older guys and told him that we were just there for a beer. Eventually him and a few of his mates just sat down with us and had a chat, although I do know that some England fans were attacked on a tram later on. We were also attacked in Ukraine, and in fact in most of the Eastern European countries they were up for a fight.

I was at the European Championships in Marseilles on 11 June 2016. We got there the day before and, on the day, I was in the Old Port area but not in the main square. I was with some friends, about twenty-four of us, from Portsmouth, Oxford, West

Bromwich Albion, Millwall and the Villa. We were all sat outside a bar just to the side of the harbour area, and I remember suddenly hearing a funny rumble and then a chant going up. We stood up to see what was going on and saw about sixty people all dressed in black. It was Russian supporters basically running through the square, hitting anyone in their path. This included women and children. It was sickening and totally indiscriminate.

Some of the lads in my group were big lads and no one came near us. People were running back and forth, with some of the older English fans trying to have a go back, but then the police started firing teargas and people were running around all over the place.

It's only a rumour but what I heard from one fan was that some of the Russians had come in on a train and had been searched by the police but nothing had been found on them. The suggestion was that someone else had put a load of gear in some lockers beforehand and, once they had been searched, they went off and got tooled up with weapons, gloves and gum-shields.

I'd had one previous experience of Russian hooligans before, in 2007, I think it was, when some of them attacked a hotel in Moscow, where English fans were staying. Unfortunately for them the hotel had hundreds of English fans staying in it and they were well outnumbered.

On Monday 13 June 2016 BTP officers were posted to St Pancras to take witness statements from returning fans who may have witnessed some of the disturbances.

On Tuesday 14 June 2016, the then Home Secretary Theresa May announced the deployment of more British public-order-trained police officers to assist French police, as well as the deployment of additional British Transport Police, to provide support on local suburban French rail services from Lille, to stations in the vicinity of matches.

Acting Assistant Chief Constable Alun Thomas commented,

To ensure that they have a safe and enjoyable journey, British Transport Police have been accompanying Euro 2016 fans since the beginning of the tournament. The response from fans, as well as our partners in the French authorities, has been extremely positive, and this engaging and reassuring presence will continue. In addition to the patrols on Eurostar trains, officers will now extend their patrols on French rail services in order to support fans ...

On Wednesday 15 June 2016, teargas was used by police as violence erupted in Lille, with flares and bangers being lit as officers charged at chanting fans; thirty-six arrests were made. Earlier in the day a small group of Russian fans threw a flare at England fans, who responded by charging at them. The police responded with teargas as fans covered their faces, some holding t-shirts across their mouths as the teargas took hold. Some fans defied a drinking ban in the streets in the evening and climbed street signs as British police officers urged England fans to behave.

Late in the evening, some 250 English fans came together just as French fans were taking to the streets after the end of a game with Albania. French police formed a cordon between the two sets of fans, as bottles and fireworks were thrown. Officers charged at chanting fans as teargas was sprayed and, in one case, an England fan was sprayed with pepper spray as he ran towards them. Away from the main square, another group of England fans were contained in the Café Oz as they drank by a cordon of up to ten police vans.

Near the Lille Flanders station, large numbers of England fans chanted at police, 'God save the Queen', 'England Til I Die', and 'Where were you in Marseilles.' Another group by the railway station were penned in after one of the fans lit a flare within the group as they chanted at police. French authorities later confirmed that sixteen people had been treated in hospital following the violence.

Among those arrested were six Russians, who had allegedly been involved in the violence during the previous Saturday. Five others were arrested for drunkenness on a train from London that was stopped before it got to Lille.

After the England versus Wales game on Thursday 16 June 2016, BTP officers escorted both sets of fans on trains between Lens and Lille, and a contingent of BTP officers from Cardiff provided an escort for Welsh fans returning via Paddington, a real tribute to the flexibility and resilience of the officers. The French authorities confirmed that seventeen people had been arrested in Lille on that date, although nationalities were not confirmed.

Nearly 10,000 fans watched the game in the 'fan zone' and then congregated in the bars in the city. Among those arrested were six people who allegedly committed an aggressive act against a member of staff at the 'fan zone', and others who let off a flare near a police officer. David Deakin commented on events in Lille:

> Since returning from France I have seen a video on social media taken in Lille where a group of England fans were in a bar where there were also some women and children. Some of the locals started to attack them and the next thing you hear is Zulu chants as a group of Birmingham City fans confronted them. The local hooligans backed off.

On 17 June 2016 BTP provided eight travelling serials to bring fans back from Lille. On 18 June 2016, BTP reported a quiet day with few fans travelling via St Pancras, although the numbers picked up the following day. On 19 June 2016 BTP reported that a fans' embassy had been opened outside the train station in a 'very wet' Saint-Étienne.

As part of their positive engagement policy the BTP set up a dedicated Twitter account under @BTPEuro2016 and provided updates throughout the tournament. Their choice of language was in stark contrast to some of the policing tactics deployed on the streets of France, with phrases like 'Enjoy, we'll be around if you need us', and 'Come and say hi. Safe journey all.'

On 23 June 2016, UK police announced that they were conducting a post-incident investigation in support of the French police, in relation to the disturbances that took place on 10 and 11 June 2016. They initially circulated pictures of twenty English fans that they wished to identify and stated that, in addition to supporting the French investigation, they would look to apply for football banning orders in the UK, with Detective Superintendent Andy Barnes leading the investigation. The UK Football Policing Unit subsequently released pictures of seventy-two English fans that they wanted to trace in connection with the disorder.

It was confirmed that fourteen England fans had received hospital treatment, including fifty-one-year-old Andrew Bache from

Portsmouth, who suffered a cardiac arrest, extensive brain injuries, and a lung infection after being set upon by Russian supporters wielding iron bars. It later transpired that Chief Brigadier Patrice Martin, of France's elite police force – the CRS, had gone to his aid and, despite coming under attack from a barrage of missiles thrown by the thugs, he managed to give Andrew CPR. For his bravery, Patrice was subsequently honoured with a Ministry of the Interior Medal at a ceremony in Paris, which was also attended by Amber Rudd, the British Home Secretary. Patrice said, 'I'm very proud and honoured'. Mr Bache was understood to be recovering slowly.

A second seriously injured fan, forty-seven-year-old Stewart Gray from Leicester, had been part of a group of English fans in the city centre at about 2.30 p.m.; he was left in a coma, after being found injured near the Rue Forte, Notre Dame, that afternoon. The attacks by 150 Russian supporters were described as being 'hyper rapid, and hyper violent'.

An officer from the UK National Investigation Unit confirmed that forty-one English fans were among the 500 arrested to date during the course of the tournament, most of which were for drugs and drunkenness offences. Six of those fans, aged between twenty and forty-one years, subsequently received prison sentences, ranging from one to three months.

In a joint statement, England and Wales fan groups highlighted the differences in policing styles adopted by the French police saying, 'In Marseilles we saw the police adopt a purely reactive approach, where they did not prevent the hooligan groups from forming up and preparing attacks on English fans, but reacted only after the event. Their subsequent use of teargas was an indiscriminate tactic that impacted on innocent fans at least as much as it did on the attackers.' They also highlighted the fact that a number of fans owed their wellbeing due to the personal intervention of UK officers in extremely difficult circumstances.

Professor Clifford Stott, a public order expert from Keele University, reinforced this by highlighting the difference in policing tactics at Marseilles and those at England's third fixture in Saint-Étienne, where officers patrolled in pairs in the central square, engaging with fans, in an effort to avoid any negative escalation in crowd behaviour. He was quoted in the media as saying, 'That's so important with England fans. They're a difficult bunch, no one is pretending otherwise.'

One twenty-four-year-old from Tipton in the West Midlands was issued with a five-year football banning order after being arrested on his return from Marseilles, having been identified by officers as throwing chairs during the fighting.

On 29 June 2016 the arrest figures were updated when it was confirmed that forty-five England fans, eleven Northern Irish fans, and nine fans from Wales had been arrested, making a total of sixty-five arrests of supporters from the UK in all. The English total was made up of six for assault, fourteen for public order, thirteen for drunkenness, nine for criminal damage, two for drugs, and one for ticket touting. The arrests of Northern Ireland fans related to two for criminal damage, two for public order, one for drunkenness, four for assault, one for ticket touting and one for pitch encroachment. There were some skirmishes involving Northern Ireland fans and Polish fans during the tournament. In respect to the Welsh arrests, five were for drunkenness, two for assault, and two for possession of a flare.

On Monday 27 June 2016 England's bid to progress further in the European Championships came to an end when they were beaten 2-1 by Iceland.

The games, which involved twenty-four teams competing, concluded on 10 July 2016 in a final between the host nation France and Portugal, in a game that Portugal won in extra time with a score of 1-0. Before, during, and after the game, groups of French supporters fought running battles with squads of heavily armed police around the Eiffel Tower and the Champs-Élysées. Teargas and batons were used as they battled with masked youths, as shop windows were smashed and vehicles set on fire. Fifty arrests were made in Paris as trouble broke out in other French towns and cities, including Lyon, where nine people were charged with public order offences.

History will determine whether the competition would be remembered for the footballing skills of the various teams, or the extremity of the behaviour of some of the hooligan fringe groups. In all, 1,000 football 'fans' were arrested during the course of the games, of which 600 were charged, with fifty-six convicted to date.

To put this issue into some form of context, however, the quote of a television presenter at the end of the games perhaps sums it up: 'For every sinner there were a thousand saints'.

Wales made history in 2016 by reaching the Euro 2016 semis in the European Cup. Chris Coleman, the Wales manager, and the Wales team players branded the tens of thousands of fans who travelled to France in June to support the dragons the 'Red Wall'. The French daily newspaper *L'Équipe* described them as magnificent, numerous and noisy, but peaceful. The local police praised the Welsh supporters for their 'exemplary' behaviour throughout the tournament. The Red Wall, as they affectionately became known, was recognised with an 'outstanding contribution' award from UEFA. Icelandic fans, as well as those from Northern and the Republic of Ireland, were also recognised with the award.

In the aftermath of the violence, some English hooligans have boasted about creating a Firm of Firms to take revenge on Russian hooligans at the World Cup in Russia in 2018, with anecdotal talk of hooligan groups from Arsenal, Bradford City, Leeds, West Ham, Chelsea, Aston Villa, Birmingham City, Burnley and Blackburn coming together to form a hooligan alliance for the games.

For their part Russian groups boasted about setting up 'all-female' gangs of hooligans and commented that there would be 'dead Brits' in 2018.

On Saturday 23 July 2016, West Bromwich Albion was due to play a pre-season match against PSV Eindhoven in a game at Arnhem as part of the Fox Sports Cup, hosted by Eredivisie side Vitesse. The game was, however, cancelled on the advice of the Dutch police after they received intelligence to suggest that dozens of PSV fans were planning to travel to the game to confront Vitesse Arnhem fans.

5

FOCUS ON THE FIRMS

We can trace football hooliganism in Great Britain back to the 1880s, when trouble broke out at football matches caused by individuals referred to as 'roughs'. The worst trouble was usually reserved for local derby matches, a trend that continues to this day. The history of organised football violence in the UK has been well documented over the years, from the emergence of gangs in the 1960s through to the height of their activities in the 1970s and '80s, followed by a lengthy period of changing police tactics and some sustained improvements in the general standards of fan behaviour.

Caroline Gall is a BBC journalist and the author of *Zulus – Black, White and Blue* (2005), and *Leeds Service Crew* (2007), as well as playing a key role in the writing of *Sons of Albion* (2009). The books deal with the history of organised football hooligan groups, who affiliated themselves with Birmingham City FC, Leeds United, and West Bromwich Albion, respectively. During the course of her research for the books, Caroline routinely came into contact with members of these groups and recalls the following:

First of all, being a woman massively helped. Other people, some of whom had themselves been involved in hooliganism, were writing about the subject at the time but some of the guys I met in Birmingham and Leeds told me that talking to someone who may have been in another 'firm' didn't really appeal to them. They thought that they would get a fairer hearing from me because I was independent and also because there were very few females who were actively involved in hooliganism. I remember that there were a couple of 'hard-core' females who had hung around with the Leeds group and a girl called Angie, I think it was, who had been close to the Zulus.

Before the books were started, I discussed the scene over the years with the main guys from Leeds and Birmingham. In the case of the Zulus that was Wally and Cuddles, who were well respected as leaders by the others back then. Once they had agreed to get involved, the word was passed down and the others followed suit.

I actually thought that they were all pretty down to earth – they had a sort of 'old school' vibe. In the case of the Zulus they felt they were defending territory – in this case, Birmingham. Many fell into different categories. For some it was just a bit of fun at weekends, which escalated at times. Some lived and breathed it. They loved to tussle with anyone – it was a way of life. And others were doing really well with their own businesses and just mixed it up at the weekends before going back to 'normal' in the week.

I spoke to members of the inner core within all three firms and they all had the same outlook. They wanted to be up front and to tell the truth and, in the main, I think that they did. The only difficulties that arose were when they were talking about incidents that they had both been involved in. For instance, when I spoke to Leeds and Birmingham about fights between them, they gave slightly different versions about some parts and some felt that each had been unfair to the other.

When it came to the other things influencing the scene – the music and fashion – they were big things in their lives. You could see the impact they had. Leeds were into the Indie music, while Blues were more soul and later hip-hop. They were visually different too, and Burberry and Pringle were favourites in Birmingham. Overall, they were mostly young lads feeling part of something, and some of them just plain enjoyed it.

They had their own ethics and always stressed that it was about trying not to get innocent people involved. They just wanted to fight with like-minded people. I remember one story where I think some Leeds fans were fighting with some Portsmouth fans on the terraces in the 1980s. In the middle of all this, a guy was trying to get a woman in a wheelchair out of the way. Someone shouted 'Stop', and the fighting stopped as some of them helped to move her to safety. After this they started fighting again!

Certainly Leeds and Birmingham saw themselves in the top tier of the hooligan groups, along with West Ham, Millwall and Chelsea.

After the Leeds book was published, I had a strange experience; I think it was in 2008, when I was contacted by someone who told me that he was a Millwall hooligan and that they were interested in doing a book. To my knowledge, nobody had written a book on Millwall before, so it sounded like a bit of a coup, but it wasn't long before it started to feel as if something was not right. I communicated with him by phone and email before we met up in London. When we did get together, he mainly spoke about the epic Millwall/Luton clash in 1985 and not much else, which made me a bit suspicious. He was really keen to know how I had done my research on the other books, and I actually started to question who he was and that maybe he wasn't who he claimed to be. I never saw him again after this one meeting and, when I tried the numbers he'd given me about six months later, the lines were dead.

I never felt frightened or intimidated by any of the hooligans I met. I would normally just arrange to meet them in a pub and let them talk while I listened. I had a lot of stories from a lot of people, often on the same events, so it was hard using them all – obviously a lot of people wanted to be in the book, too.

There were lots of characters among the firms. The Zulus were a totally diverse group, which broadened the mix of music that they listened to; it was the same with the West Bromwich group, who were also mixed. It was a whiter group overall in Leeds, however. In the 1970s and 1980s, it was not unusual to hear monkey chants on the terraces and jokes about bananas and, when this happened in front of any black lads in the firms, they'd often be told 'but you're okay'.

One of the Birmingham characters was Errol Parker, who was affectionately known as 'Fat Errol'. He was one of the original members of the Apex gang, which later merged into the Zulu Warriors. Errol was extremely well-known and liked among the Blues, and hundreds turned out for his funeral service in April 2016 after he sadly lost his battle against cancer. A lot of the guys are still around today but the heyday has gone.

As long as there are football teams, there are going to be lads who will stand up for their teams or the firms they belong to. The recent increase in violence at non-League clubs might add another dimension to the problem.

All that said, one has only to do a basic search on the internet to reveal a plethora of websites dedicated to the sharing of visual images relating to incidents of football disorder both in the UK and elsewhere. One such site examined in 2016 had received no less than 29,745 likes.

It would be unhelpful to create a league table of current hooligan groups operating under the cover of football; however, as a result of some of the recent activities described within this book, the co-authors have sought to document the history of some of the groups mentioned within earlier chapters in the form of a short synopsis for each.

For ease of purpose they have been placed purely in alphabetical order and absolutely no meaning should be attached to the order in which they are described.

Arsenal

Arsenal FC was founded in 1886 by a group of workers from the Royal Arsenal in Woolwich and was originally known as Royal Arsenal. In 1893 the name of the club was changed to Woolwich Arsenal. In 1913 it dropped Woolwich from its title when they moved to a new stadium in Islington. Nearby was an Underground station called Gillespie Road, but the club were successful in having the name of the station changed to Arsenal. It is the only station on the London Underground system to be named specifically after a football club.

Every time the late Eric Morecambe coughed on *The Morecambe & Wise Show*, he would always say 'Arsenal', and this would raise a laugh. However, the hooligan elements of Arsenal FC were no laughing matter. The club is known for two hooligan firms, namely 'The Herd' and 'The Gooners' – a spoof name for the official nickname of the 'Gunners'. The Herd firm were made up of white, white Irish, Asian and black British supporters and was mainly active between 1978 and 1999. They still exist today, but tend to remain very low key. They have the distinctive war cry 'E-I-E'. This is believed to mean, 'Every Idiot Enjoys'. Their main rivals in the 1980s, and even today, were West Ham's ICF (Inter City Firm), and other London clubs.

The Herd's two most notorious clashes were in 1988 with Millwall fans at Highbury, in which forty-one Millwall hooligans were arrested after fighting in the stands, and their clash in 2000 with Galatasary fans in Copenhagen's City Hall Square. Four fans ended up being stabbed and eleven were injured during the latter, one with a serious head injury. Fifty-four fans were arrested.

In the 1970s and early 1980s, an English football match was often not pleasant to attend and Arsenal games were no exception. One violent incident is recalled below.

The Gooners were usually made up of 'up and coming' street gangs, mainly consisting of violent skinheads. The usual practice for West Ham fans when visiting Arsenal was to march on to the North Bank, which was the Arsenal stronghold, virtually unopposed. This practice was met with very little resistance from Arsenal's fans. On 2 May 1982, things were very different. The West Ham fans gathered on the North Bank. The Arsenal fans without warning immediately attacked their rivals, kicking and punching them. This disorder quickly spilled onto the terrace, which, when full, could hold up to 20,000 supporters. The Metropolitan Police battled to gain control, while at the same time another West Ham gang had forced their way into the middle of the North Bank and set off a smoke bomb.

Pandemonium broke out, as clouds of thickening smoke billowed across the pitch, just as the game had kicked off. The players had to be led off the pitch, and panicking Arsenal fans stampeded onto the pitch fearing for their safety. This left the West Ham gang slap bang in the middle of Arsenal territory. They were then, arguably, the largest, most vicious gang of football thugs in the country, doing what they did best, bullying and taunting their beaten rivals.

A few of the Arsenal fans, however, had not panicked and they launched a counter-attack; the West Ham fans went on the retreat and were brutally pushed right to the edge of the North Bank.

The police, fearing for the safety of the West Ham fans, surrounded them until the final whistle, when they were escorted out of the ground.

An Arsenal fan was brutally stabbed to death about an hour after the match, when he was surrounded by a gang of West Ham thugs. His killer was never caught. After this violent confrontation, West Ham fans never ventured on to Arsenal's North Bank again. However Arsenal fans in following years were known to have taken liberties on West Ham's manor, something unheard of previously since the old skinhead days of the late 1960s. The Metropolitan Police carried out several undercover operations and many of the main protagonists were arrested.

Aston Villa

The Aston Villa organised hooligans are known as the 'Aston Villa Hardcore', which is often shortened to Villa Hardcore. The 'Villa Youth' relates to the younger element of the group. The Hardcore have been active since 1993, following on from previous Aston Villa hooligan firms such as the Steamers, and C-Crew.

They have been involved in some high-profile hooligan fights in Europe while following Aston Villa and the national England team. It should not be surprising that the Hardcore has clashed a number of times with their fiercest rivals, the Birmingham Zulus, who support Birmingham City.

In September 2002, in what was described as the Battle of Rocky Lane, Aston Villa fans and Birmingham City fans clashed before a game at Villa Park. In October of that year, following a policing operation, officers from the West Midlands Police arrested fifteen people in a series of dawn raids in connection with the serious disorder in Rocky Lane. One member of the Villa Hardcore was jailed for six months for his part in the fight. In 2005, the same person received a twelve-month jail sentence and was banned from attending football matches for ten years – this was for his part in an organised brawl between Villa Hardcore and Chelsea Headhunters, near to London King's Cross station in March 2004. Innocent members of the public, including young children, were caught up in the violence. Five other Villa fans were jailed in 2004.

Some of the hooligans have written or ghost-written books about their exploits. One such book about the various exploits of the Aston Villa hooligan firms, which included details of clashes with Birmingham City Zulus, was due to be launched in Balsall Heath, Birmingham, in November 2006. However, this launch had to be cancelled due to threats that the Zulus would come to the launch and cause trouble. The Zulus were said to have taken exception to the launch of the book and the presence of rivals on what they considered to be 'their territory'.

The Hardcore youth have received their own fair share of publicity for all the wrong reasons. In January 2010, two members of the firm were banned from attending Aston Villa matches on match days, as well as away games. They were also banned from using trains to travel the country and from entering the relevant town centres. They were branded as ringleaders by police and also were made to pay a fine of £500 each in court. Also, later on in that year another known Villa youth hooligan was handed a three-year banning order at Warwick Crown Court while being held on remand after serving a twelve-month prison sentence. He was handed the banning order after troubled flared outside Birmingham City's ground in 2009, after Villa won the game 1-2 with Gabriel Agbonlahor scoring a late winner. Police statistics claim that, after the three leaders of the youth faction of the Hardcore were all banned, reports of violence and potential organised clashes fell by 75 per cent.

In October and December 2010, there was more disorder between Aston Villa and Birmingham City when they played in a League match on 31 October 2010 and in a League Cup match on 1 December, with many fans being arrested. In the first game, there were scenes of violence outside Villa Park, with Villa fans throwing a flare at Birmingham fans leaving Villa Park. There were a small number of arrests, including of a Birmingham City club chef.

In the second of the two games, after Birmingham had beaten Villa 2-1, Birmingham supporters invaded the pitch and confronted the visiting Villa fans. In retaliation, Villa fans ripped out seats and hurled them into the Birmingham supporters. Furthermore, a flare was thrown from the Villa fans section into the Birmingham fans on the pitch. The offending Villa fans were convicted after being picked out on CCTV after the game for offences that included an attack by Villa hooligans on a pub near St Andrew's that was frequented by Birmingham City supporters. There were also flash points before and after the game, and the events were described as a war zone by a supporter who attended the game.

The *Birmingham Mail* on 13 August 2011 published an appeal for information after several Villa fans caused serious damage to a train taking supporters to Birmingham New Street after Villa's friendly match away against Derby County on 3 August. The damage included tray tables being ripped from the backs of seats, seat coverings being damaged and lights being smashed. The damage meant the train had to be taken out of service for twenty-four hours for repairs, at a considerable cost to the train operating company.

Known Villa fans were in action again on 8 January 2013 when they were involved in scuffles with the police and rival supporters in Bradford city centre prior to Villa's League Cup semi-final first leg against Bradford City. It is claimed that a Bradford fan was head-butted by a Villa fan.

Birmingham New Street station was the scene of a clash on the concourse between Rotherham and Villa supporters on 28 August 2013 after the two teams met in the second round of the League Cup at Villa Park. Several Villa fans were arrested for fighting with West Bromwich fans at the Rose Villa Tavern in the Jewellery Quarter of Birmingham on 25 November 2013 before the two teams met in a Premier League match at the ground of West Bromwich Albion, The Hawthorns.

On 28 December 2013, during a match between Villa and Swansea at Villa Park in the Premier League, three Villa hooligans were arrested by West Midlands Police after organised violence, using bottles and sticks, broke out between Villa and Swansea supporters near to the stadium. It is said that innocent onlookers were traumatised by the incident.

Birmingham City

In 1964 a film was made that told the story of 150 British soldiers who defended an outpost during the Anglo-Zulu war of 1879 and successfully held off a force of 4,000 Zulu warriors. The film was based on the Battle of Rorke's Drift, the defence of a supply depot and hospital, by a force of largely sick and wounded soldiers, which followed a crushing victory by the Zulus against the British at the Battle of Isandlwana. The small garrison beat off attacks for more than twelve hours, with the loss of just seventeen men. The Victoria Cross was awarded to eleven of the defenders. Zulu chants, reminiscent of the film, were first heard from Birmingham City fans during a game with Manchester City at a game at Maine Road in 1982.

Many members from different ethnic backgrounds made up the Zulus, in stark contrast to most other hooligan firms that emerged around the same time, which were almost universally white, and contained followers of far-right organisations, including the National Front. Their main rivals are the fans of fellow Birmingham club Aston Villa, on the outskirts of the city.

There have been a number violent clashes before, during and after the local derbies between the two clubs. The Zulus maintain that they are 'defending their city' from invading firms. A gang known as Apex existed before the Zulus, and before that there was the Brew Crew. The Junior Business Boys also operated within Birmingham as part of the Zulus' youth element. As well as Aston Villa, they are known to clash particularly with the supporters of the following clubs: Millwall, Stoke City, Wolverhampton Wanderers, Cardiff and West Ham.

The Leeds Service Crew, supporters of Leeds United, travelled by train to Birmingham and then on to St Andrew's for the final game of the season, which was held in May 1985. Violent disorder broke out between the fans, leaving over 200 injured, including ninety-six policemen. This was the lowest point in English football history. When analysing football's problems, Lord Justice Popplewell described the scenes as 'more like Agincourt than a football match'.

In 1987, one of this book's authors, Michael Layton, was responsible for the day-to-day management of Operation Red Card, an undercover police operation with the aim of addressing the growing levels of violence perpetrated by the Zulu Warriors. This operation is documented in the book *Hunting the Hooligans* by MILO publishers. It resulted in sixty-seven arrests.

Twenty fans were arrested after five police officers were injured in May 1989, when fans invaded the pitch at a match against Crystal Palace at Elmhurst Park. Seven mounted police officers were deployed to clear hundreds of Birmingham fans off the pitch. The game was stopped for twenty-six minutes as the referee took the players off while the police, using batons, failed to separate the fans in one stand.

In May 2002 during the play-off semi-final against Millwall at Millwall's ground, violence erupted after the game. Sergeant Russell Lamb of the Metropolitan Police Service, a veteran of the May Day and Poll Tax riots, described this as the worst violence he had ever experienced.

Following violent clashes on 27 March 2004 in North London, fourteen Birmingham City hooligans received banning orders in 2006. In February 2006 Staffordshire Police came under attack from the Zulus after fighting broke out in Stoke-on-Trent after an FA Cup match between Stoke City and Birmingham City. The trouble began in the Britannia Stadium, when a group of about 200 Birmingham fans tore down fencing separating them from Stoke fans. As fans left the ground, the police faced what a senior police officer described as 'extreme violence' from both Birmingham and Stoke fans.

September 2007 saw five Birmingham hooligans receiving jail sentences of up to eight months, and one given a suspended sentence, for their part in violence at a match the previous month in which a steward lost the sight in one eye. Birmingham City fans had started ripping up seats in the away end and throwing them, as well as coins and a lump of concrete, during a match against Cardiff City at Ninian Park in Cardiff. One missile hit a steward in the face, causing him to lose the sight in his left eye. In a statement to the court, the steward said, 'They paid no regard to the terrified men, women and children around them.' Other stewards were also hit, and families with children fled the ground as the violence broke out. One Birmingham City fan was struck on the head with a £2 coin. He said, 'The behaviour of our fans was appalling.'

In recent years there has been some animosity between Birmingham fans and Manchester United fans and, on one occasion, the manager of Manchester United at the time, Sir Alex

Ferguson, described St Andrew's as the most intimidating place he had ever taken his team.

Blackpool

For obvious reasons Blackpool FC is known as The Seasiders; their supporters are known as The Muckers. They take their name from the word 'mucker', meaning good friend. They have also been known as Benny's Mob, Rammy Arms Crew, and Bisons Riot Squad. Their main rivals are Preston North End, Bolton Wanderers and Burnley.

The problems caused by The Muckers are, by comparison with other Football League clubs, relatively small, but they have a long history of violence. One of the reasons for this is that a feature of Blackpool life is fighting, especially as, in the summer months, groups of young men would visit the town, giving the locals ample opportunity to fight whenever they wanted. 'B', one of the leaders of Benny's Mob, stated that 'Blackpool is full of mobs, especially in the summer'.

During a home game at Bloomfield Road against Bolton Wanderers on 24 August 1974, a seventeen-year-old Blackpool fan, Kevin Olsson, was stabbed to death at the back of the Spion Kop. In August 2009, the thirty-fifth anniversary of his death, Blackpool supporters raised money for a memorial plaque in memory of Kevin. The plaque was unveiled on the front of the North-West Corner, beside the club shop.

The first organised firm, known as the Rammy Arms Crew, began taking their name from the pub they drank in – the Ramsden Arms, opposite Blackpool North station. The Rammys' most famous moment was when they led the England fans' charge into Italians in Turin at the Italy versus England match in 1980.

Even concerts were not immune from football hooligans. During the late 1970s, as punk rock became popular in the UK, football fans would also attend punk rock concerts. In 1978 at a concert in Blackburn King Georges Hall, a Skids concert (incorrectly reported as being The Dickies) was the scene of a near-full-scale riot as a group of about fifty Blackpool Rammy boys clashed with over 250 Blackburn fans, disrupting the concert, before riot police were called in to restore order.

On 6 May 1978, at a concert by The Vibrators, in Preston, a young man from Preston was stabbed to death during clashes between Preston and Blackpool fans. This ushered in a new era of hatred between fans of the two clubs, following the attempts by Blackpool fans to burn down the Town End at Preston's Deepdale Stadium the year before, when two fires were lit during a match between the two clubs.

In 1978 Blackpool was relegated to the third tier of English football for the first time. Around the same time, a new, younger gang appeared, known as Benny's Mob. In August 1980, a group of about 150 of Benny's Mob met up with the Pompey Skins from Portsmouth at Blackpool's coach park. They also clashed with Sheffield United fans in 1982, when a Sheffield fan was stabbed during clashes between fans in the West Paddock at Bloomfield Road, while police were already dealing with an incident in the South Stand involving the Rammy Arms Crew.

However, it was in 1984 that the Blackpool hooligans started to earn their reputation. In March, Rochdale was totally overwhelmed when 3,000 Blackpool fans descended on their Spotland Stadium, when they usually had crowds of about 1,300. A mob of Blackpool fans went on the rampage, causing a trail of havoc. Twenty-one cars were damaged, two parked vehicles overturned and four police cars damaged. The police held the Blackpool fans in the ground after the match. Sixty-four Blackpool fans were arrested and five police officers hurt.

Another gang appeared in this period, known as the BISONS or Bisons Riot Squad (BRS). They allegedly took their name from the noise they made when attacking rivals. They soon earned a reputation for carrying knives, with four people slashed at a game in Brighton. Furthermore, one of the principal Blackpool BISONS members was reported to have taken a gun from one of the younger BISONS gang before they set off for Brighton. It resulted in three fans being banned from every football ground in England, the first time the courts had made such bans.

The Muckers came along in 2005 when a group of twenty-five Blackpool fans, all friends, started to organise The Muckers Firm. They very soon started to earn a reputation in an era wherein CCTV had elsewhere severely restricted hooligan activity.

The rivalry with Preston fans reignited itself on Saturday 2 September 2006 when a mini-riot broke out on Preston station between Blackpool fans returning from their match at Millwall and local fans returning from an England match in Manchester. Bottles, cans and signs were hurled, as the two sets of fans fought each other, and two British Transport Police officers were injured in what the police described as a large-scale disorder.

In November 2007 Blackpool police warned football hooligans not to attend the local derby against Preston North End in Preston on 8 December 2007, as it was alleged that Blackpool fans were planning to infiltrate the home stands at Preston's Deepdale Stadium. The match had already been moved forward to a 12.30 p.m. kick-off at the request of the police, in an attempt to avoid violence, while local pubs were told not to open until 12.00 p.m. and not to serve alcohol until 12.30 p.m., the same time as the kick-off. A huge police operation on match day resulted in 300 police officers being on duty outside the Deepdale Stadium and in Preston city centre. Blackpool fans arriving at Preston station went through airport-style security scanners to check for potential weapons.

Blackpool won the match 1–0, but the day was marred when Blackpool hooligans went on the rampage, smashing windows and ripping seats out of specially chartered buses laid on to transport them from the railway station to Deepdale, causing thousands of pounds worth of damage. Nine people were arrested. Later that same day, a group of about thirty Preston hooligans attacked a pub in Blackpool in revenge, throwing bins and bottles at the pub while innocent staff and customers were inside.

Burnley

Burnley FC has a hooligan element called the Suicide Squad. The membership of eighty to 100 fans is made up of mainly white British youths; it is believed that it was formed in 1983. The title derives from previous behaviour at away games where their fans' involvement in violence against overwhelming odds could be described as suicidal.

The early 1980s was a black period for Burnley, as they fell from the old Division One, where they had played for a number of years, to the fourth division, with the threat of being relegated even further to non-League football. A lot of the original members, who had previous convictions for violence, left, but the void was filled by a new, more menacing group. Considerably younger, they named themselves the Burnley Youth. They would remain associated with the older hooligan group known as the Suicide Squad, but refused to abide by the rules of the game.

The new group was more determined and less affected by the police tactics than their older colleagues. Some members of the Suicide Squad became genuinely concerned that the new members of Burnley Youth were way out of control and were travelling to away matches with weapons.

In November 2002 Operation Fixture, an operation aimed at combating football hooliganism in and around Burnley's Turf Moor Stadium, was set up in a partnership between the football club and the Lancashire Constabulary. The operation was successful, with a number of arrests being made, plus more bans and quicker convictions through the cooperation of the local courts. Racist behaviour was also tackled under this operation. During a Worthington Cup match against Tottenham Hotspur a Burnley fan was arrested for giving a Nazi salute.

A tragic incident occurred in Burnley's town centre when, on 7 December 2002, a Nottingham Forest fan aged just seventeen years was killed during violence between Burnley and Nottingham Forest fans. Two days later, a nineteen-year-old Burnley fan from the so-called Suicide Youth Squad was arrested and charged with murder. He was later sentenced to seven years in youth custody after pleading guilty to manslaughter. He received a ten-year ban from all football matches.

When passing sentence, the trial judge commented that the attack had happened 'for absolutely no reason, other than he supported a different football team and had the temerity to visit a public house the defendant and others believed he should have kept away from' and added that football hooliganism was a 'scourge on the sport', and that the courts should make it clear that anyone involved in violence would face harsh sentences. He was released from prison in 2006 and, within weeks, he was back in court for breaching his football banning order while at Turf Moor and was fined £200.

In July 2007, one of the founding members of the Suicide Squad wrote a book about his exploits with the firm as he was coming to the end of a three-year ban from attending both England and domestic matches. The Lancashire Constabulary then applied for a fresh banning order, with the start of the new season only weeks away. In May 2009, another founder of the Suicide Squad was banned for a further three years from English and Welsh football grounds. The ban followed a steady stream of incidents since an original ban expired in February 2007, including being the central figure in disturbances during games against Stoke City and Sheffield United in the 2008/9 season.

Following the first FA Premier League derby between Blackburn Rovers (Burnley's closet rivals) and Burnley on 18 October 2009, members of the Suicide Squad were in action once more, as they fought violently in the Station public house in the Cherry Tree area of the town. A number were arrested and eventually twelve members of the Suicide Squad received prison sentences totalling thirty-two years, along with lengthy banning orders. The main perpetrator of the violence received the heaviest sentence of five years in prison, along with a ten-year banning order.

The Suicide Squad has also been featured in television documentaries.

Cardiff

The football hooligan element of Cardiff City FC are known as the Cardiff City Soul Crew; they are commonly known as the Soul Crew, who number in the region of between 600 and 800. With this large number of followers, the firm have become one of the biggest and most active football firms in the United Kingdom. The name comes from skinhead hooligans who had an enthusiasm for soul music. It is said that the former host of the television show *Soul Train*, Don Cornelius, gave his blessings to the group in 1986, when a hooligan follower of Cardiff City formed them.

In February 1988 Cardiff City played Reading at Ninian Park in a FA Cup replay. Before the start of the match, eleven suspected members of the Soul Crew were detained by the South Wales Police. At the end of the game, police in riot gear had to be called in to prevent outbreaks of violence.

Following a friendly match between Swindon Town and Cardiff City, on 25 July 2009 a group of eight Cardiff City supporters went to the town centre from a pub near to the railway station for cheaper drinks. They confronted a group of Swindon Town supporters in a pedestrianised area of the town. A ten-minute riot ensued, which was captured on CCTV. One of the fans was seen to push, grapple and punch a Swindon fan, repeatedly. He then punched two Swindon fans, and charged at another group of Swindon fans. Another, who had stripped to his waist and wrapped a belt around his fist, was seen kicking and punching. A third was seen to punch another man and drag an advertising sign along the floor.

At a subsequent court hearing, the eight Cardiff City fans were banned for five years from football matches. Ten Swindon Town fans were given bans ranging from three to five years, as well as community work totalling 2,400 hours, after pleading guilty to affray. The Crown Prosecutor said: 'A number of witnesses made statements explaining their fear and alarm at what was going on, including the police officers who found it a very intimidating situation. Owners of business premises removed all their street furniture and barricaded them inside to protect themselves.' She said that the eight Cardiff fans told interviewing officers afterwards that they were defending themselves.

All eight Cardiff fans pleaded guilty to affray.

Summing up, Judge Euan Ambrose said: 'There were members of the public present; it was a quiet Saturday afternoon in the high summer. For all those present it was a frightening experience.'

Cardiff City's fiercest rivals are Swansea, and the derby matches between the two are regarded as one of the fiercest rivalries in British football. Both clubs are based in Wales but play in the English Football League and have won honours in that league. Cardiff lifted the FA Cup in 1927 and Swansea the Football League Cup in 2013.

Cardiff and Swansea first met in a local derby on 7 September 1912 at Swansea. Over the years they have met in League and Cup matches, along with fixtures in the Welsh Cup. As they are fierce rivals, it goes without saying that, when they meet, trouble is not far away and their matches have been plagued by hooliganism between the two sets of fans. A group of Cardiff fans were chased into the sea by a group of Swansea fans in September 1988. Ever since that incident, Swansea fans mockingly suggest to the Cardiff fans that they should 'swim away'.

Just before Christmas in 1993, a match between the two sides was dubbed The Battle of Ninian Park, as the Swansea fans were placed in the Grandstand. As Cardiff went into the lead, Swansea fans ripped out seats and threw them at the Cardiff supporters, which caused the Cardiff fans to run on to the pitch. The story made the national news, causing shockwaves throughout the nation. The Football Association of Wales was forced to ban away fans from this fixture for several years. This was the first ever fixture in Britain to do so.

Celtic

Glasgow Celtic FC was founded in 1887 by a Catholic priest, with the purpose of alleviating poverty in the East End of Glasgow, where there was a large immigrant Irish population. Throughout the years Celtic have enjoyed great success in the Scottish League, winning League titles and Cup finals, and also in Europe, winning the European Cup. Their first match was played against Glasgow Rangers in May 1888. Their fans have the names of Celtic Soccer Crew, Roman Catholic Casuals, Celtic Baby Crew and the anti-fascist Green Brigade.

Celtic's long-standing and fiercest rivals are their near neighbours, Glasgow Rangers. Over the years the two teams have been dominant in football in Scotland. The clubs have become known as the Old Firm. However, the hatred of each other runs much deeper than football. Religion divides the two clubs. Celtic are from the Catholic part of Glasgow, while Rangers are from the Protestant half.

Bill Rogerson has his own recollections of dealing with Celtic supporters while he was stationed at Crewe as a sergeant in the early 1980s:

> There was a sleeping car train from Glasgow Central to London Euston, which ran via Kilmarnock and Dumfries to Carlisle, and then down the West Coast Main Line to London. It was due into Crewe at around 02.10. Information was received to the effect that the train had left Glasgow with numerous unescorted Celtic fans on board, travelling to the Continent. It went without saying that they had numerous cans of beer and lager, along with bottles of whisky with them. Police had to be called to the train at Kilmarnock, Dumfries, Carlisle and Preston, due to their behaviour and the communication cord being pulled. By the time the train arrived at Crewe it was around two hours late. Fortunately the Celtic fans were all asleep in their drunken stupor. The train continued onto London without further incident.

In 2003 it was estimated that their fan base was around 9 million worldwide, and there are in excess of 160 Celtic supporters' clubs in over twenty countries including Ireland.

On Saturday 25 February 2006 a riot broke out in a public house in the O'Connell Street district of Dublin. It is believed that many Dublin–based hooligans who support Glasgow Celtic had congregated in the city centre, intent on taking advantage of more formal protests being held against the Love Ulster parade. The public house concerned broadcast all Celtic's fixtures. As the violence broke out, a large group was seen exiting the pub wearing Celtic jerseys, even though there was no game on that Saturday. Garda sources believed that, while there was no history of football hooliganism in the Republic on the scale of that day's riots, a relatively small group of Dublin-based football supporters had previously been involved in mini-riots in previous years. The Garda stated that, because the disturbances had been organised by football hooligans, they would have found it almost impossible to detect the plans in advance. It is believed that the hooligans used mobile phones to call and text each other to start the riots.

In December 2013, at a Motherwell versus Celtic match, hooligans, believed to be Celtic's Green Brigade, went on the rampage and, in what could only be described as disturbing scenes, destroyed over 100 seats at Motherwell's Fir Park Ground. The damage was in excess of £10,000. In addition to the damage, one flare and two smoke bombs were lit, with one smoke bomb landing on the pitch. The violence caused an outcry from the Scottish Football Association with demands that fans stop using pyrotechnics before someone was killed. Shortly afterwards, the Green Brigade issued a statement in which they empathically denied it was their members, although they accepted the fact that the violence took place under their banner.

Glasgow Celtic fans make full use of the rail system in Scotland to travel to home and away games. They are closely monitored by the officers from the Scottish Division of the British Transport Police.

Chelsea

The Chelsea FC hooligan firm are known as the Chelsea Headhunters, and are mainly white British. Their closest rivals are with the North London clubs, Arsenal and Tottenham Hotspur. Ever since the 1970 FA Cup final, they have also had a very strong rivalry with Leeds United. More recently they have clashed with Liverpool after meeting in Cup competitions, and also class Manchester United as their rivals.

At a match between Bristol Rovers and Chelsea in 1980, violence broke out between the two sets of supporters. Thirty-five people were taken to hospital as a result of the trouble, which started at Bristol Rovers' ground and spilled out onto the surrounding streets. A large number of Chelsea supporters were seen to throw stones at their opponents. A police officer intervened. He grabbed one supporter by the shoulder in order to arrest him and was punched in the face. A struggle ensued and the police officer found himself on the ground, being kicked and punched by a number of Chelsea fans. A female colleague witnessed what was happening and threw herself on the ground to cover her colleague's face and prevent further injury until reinforcements arrived. Following the disorder, thirty football fans found themselves appearing at Bristol

Magistrates' Court on charges of criminal damage, threatening behaviour and assault on police officers. Two were jailed and fourteen fined a total of £4,850.

On 8 November 1985, a high-profile member of the firm was found guilty of being involved in a violent assault in a pub on Kings Road, Chelsea, after Chelsea had lost a match. For this attack he received life imprisonment, which was cut to three years on appeal. He and other hooligans stormed into the pub, chanting and swearing at the American manager, who was violently assaulted. A second man was arrested for the assault and received four years' imprisonment.

On 13 February 2010 the Chelsea Headhunters clashed with the Cardiff City Soul Crew at the FA Cup fifth round tie at Stamford Bridge, which resulted in several people being injured, including a police officer whose jaw was broken. Twenty-four people were subsequently convicted at Isleworth Crown Court. All received banning orders from all football grounds in England and Wales, ranging from three to eight years. Eighteen of the defendants received prison sentences of up to two years.

When they travelled to Paris, via Belgium to avoid detection, for a UEFA Champions League quarter-final in April 2014 against Paris Saint-Germain, 300 Headhunters took part in pre-planned violence around the city.

Hibernian

Scotland's capital city Edinburgh is home to two Scottish Football League teams, one of which is Hibernian. The hooligans who follow them are known as the Capital City Service (CCS) and have been active since 1984, when the casual hooligan subculture took off in Scotland. They were formed from previous hooligan firms that followed the club. Locally they are more commonly known as the Hibs Casuals, but within football hooligan circles they are known as the Hibs Boys.

In the late 1990s a split in their ranks was caused by a nationwide hooligan firm made up of casuals from different teams. Shortly after their formation, football hooliganism in Scotland began to decline and the activities of the gang diminished. However, at the beginning of the twenty-first century, there was a resurgence in football hooliganism at various clubs in Scotland, and the firms responsible, including the CCS, were closely monitored by police forces including the British Transport Police. Their fiercest rivals are the Aberdeen Soccer Casuals, who follow Aberdeen FC. The Aberdeen Soccer Casuals were seen by some to be one of the leading casual gangs at the time in Scotland. In the formative years of the gang, before one Hibernian versus Aberdeen game in Edinburgh the two sets of hooligans fought on Easter Road. After some violent fighting, the Hibs Capital City Service ran away. One Hibs youth was severely beaten and was in a coma for a week.

At the next Hibs match, which was being played at Tynecastle against another Edinburgh club, Heart of Midlothian (Hearts), the CCS came up against the notorious Gorgie Aggro, the Heart of Midlothian hooligan element. The gang had an informal hierarchy, with no gang leader as such. Instead there was a committee of five individuals who earned the respect of their peers. They took on the task of planning and organising for the gang's hooligan activities at football matches. By the 1990s, this system was replaced by two protagonists, who arranged most fights. Over the years Hearts and sometimes Old Firm fans who lived in Edinburgh were integrated into the mob.

Their tactics were to try an ambush another firm and to strike at them at their weakest point, which was usually in the middle of their mob. Whenever opposing gangs were being escorted by the police, a group of Hibs boys would often make their way to the front of the escort while another group would hang around at the back. The group at the front would act as a decoy and start causing trouble in an attempt to lure all the police officers to rush in and assist their colleagues. This tactic left the rear of the escorted fans open to attack from the Hibs fans positioned there.

On match days, in the days before adequate CCTV coverage, the gang used to meet at a back street public house near to Edinburgh Waverley railway station. The reasoning behind this was that it kept the fans away from the police. They had look-outs positioned within sight of the exits from the railway station to see which route visiting fans would use. After matches the bars near to the railway station were frequently scenes of clashes between opposing fans.

In their formative years, the CCS favoured scheduled rail transport to away matches from either Edinburgh Waverley or Edinburgh Haymarket stations. The railway network provided convenient access to the requisite city or town centre, and from there the CCS would walk to the football stadium, regardless of distance, looking for confrontations with home fans. In order to try and overcome the effective policing of the British Transport Police, and their Scottish counterparts, on match days the CCS travelled earlier to away matches to avoid detection and subsequent police escort. In December 1986 the CCS twice met and caught early trains to their destinations, enabling them to arrive well before 12 noon.

On the first occasion they caught the Grampian police off-guard. However, when they travelled to Dundee a fortnight later, the Tayside Police was alerted to their early arrival. When the authorities became fully aware of their tactics, the hooligans travelling in this manner became easy targets for the police to intercept. They then changed their travel plans, using motor coaches, cars, minibuses and the like, to avoid the police presence at railway stations and city centres.

The CCS even went to the trouble of carrying out pre-match day recces at football grounds in order to plan for their violence. At a game to be played at Ibrox Stadium in Glasgow in the 1980s, they considered smuggling in a set of pyrotechnics. In order to attack Celtic supporters, the following season they travelled to the area surrounding the ground a few days beforehand, to plan their tactics. In 1990 Hibs played a friendly against Millwall in London and the gang even travelled to London beforehand to find out the favoured transport links and pubs used by the Millwall fans.

Leeds

Leeds United is the most sung-about English club but not in a good way. On FanChants.co.uk there are 117 anti-Leeds fans chants, which is more than double that for any other club, with the favourite being 'We all hate Leeds scum.'

The hooligan firm linked to this club are known as the Leeds Service Crew. They were formed in 1974 and named after the then ordinary public service trains that the hooligans would travel on to away matches, rather than the football excursion trains, which were escorted by British Transport Police officers. In that same year police made a total of 273 arrests while policing matches at Leeds United Football ground.

Leeds hooligans have fought with various weapons, such as darts, iron bars, knives and even axes. They have set buses, coaches and chip vans on fire and, in one incident, the driver of a coach had to run for his life. They have caused major damage to pubs, shops and trains. They have even dressed in Ku Klux Klan outfits and made Nazi salutes outside pubs. In a special report on one of the BBC *Six O'Clock News* programmes in 1985, they listed the worst football hooligan gangs creating mayhem across England, and Leeds United fans were among the worst five.

On 28 May 1975 Leeds played Bayern Munich in the European Cup final at the Parc des Princes in Paris, France. The striker Peter Lorimer had a goal disallowed in a game that Bayern Munich won with a score of 2-0. The Leeds fans were already incensed at having two penalties rejected by the French referee when scores of them, in their first high-profile incident, ripped seats from the stands and threw them onto the pitch. Some of the Leeds fans then became involved in fights with the French police as they invaded the pitch. This action resulted in Leeds being banned from European competitions for four years. This was later reduced to two years on appeal. However, it was some seventeen years later before they saw action in Europe again.

The 1982/83 season saw Leeds in the old Second Division of the English Football League, after being relegated from the First Division. Their first game was against Cleethorpes. Some 600 Leeds fans stayed the night before the match and went on a heavy drinking spree, along with looting and fighting.

In October 1982, at the home game at Elland Road against Newcastle United, two Newcastle players were hit by missiles thrown by the Leeds fans. The FA ordered an enquiry into the incident.

In the early 1980s a new hooligan faction, The Very Young Team, came on the scene and quickly rose to prominence. Sadly on the same day as the Bradford City Fire, which killed fifty-five people, in May 1985 a riot at a game between Leeds United and Birmingham City saw an innocent teenage boy crushed to death when a wall collapsed on him.

In January 1987 Leeds were drawn away against non-League Telford United in an FA Cup third-round tie. Due to the club's terrible reputation for hooliganism, Telford United refused to hold the game at their Bucks Head Ground. West Bromwich Albion ended up hosting the game at their Hawthorns Ground.

In the final game of the 1989/90 season, Leeds were drawn away to AFC Bournemouth on 5 May 1990, a scorching hot day on a bank holiday weekend, when Bournemouth was full of holidaymakers. Leeds won this game 1-0, which saw them being promoted back to Division One after eight years in the Second Division. This game was marred by episodes of violence in town-centre pubs and shops, and cigarette machines and other missiles were hurled through shop windows. Petrol tanks on motorbikes were also set on fire. The town centre was also the scene of a series of violent confrontations between the police in riot gear and Leeds fans. A total of 104 people were arrested and twelve police officers were injured.

Improvements in security and the installation of CCTV at grounds have, in common with other firms, largely curtailed the hooligan activities of the Service Crew. Hooliganism does continue at Leeds United but it is now largely away from the stadium.

During a Championship game against Ipswich Town at Elland Road on 28 April 2007, around 200 Leeds fans invaded the pitch, which forced a thirty-minute delay after a late Ipswich equaliser all but sealed the relegation of Leeds to League One. Approximately 100 Leeds supporters ran towards the South East Stand, where the Ipswich supporters were located. At a subsequent court appearance in January 2008, thirteen Leeds United fans were handed football banning orders totalling forty-five years, after they pleaded guilty to affray in connection with the pitch invasion.

In November 2007, Cumbria Police made twenty-one arrests when Leeds and Carlisle fans clashed in Carlisle city centre; this was in spite of the biggest police operation of its kind for thirty years.

In 2008 Leeds supporters found themselves in Northampton, when they clashed with rival supporters hurling rocks, road signs and manhole covers at Northampton supporters. Eighteen men, all supporters of Leeds, were arrested and dealt with by the courts.

Leicester

The hooligan firm that follows Leicester FC is known as the Baby Squad, and members are mainly white British, and number around 100 hard-core members. In August 2000 they were listed as the second most violent group of hooligans.

In November 2001 the Luton Town hooligan firm The MiGs travelled up to Leicester and, on arrival at Leicester station, they were ambushed by the Baby Squad before officers from the British Transport Police could split them up.

They have had several clashes with the Chelsea Headhunters.

February 2008 saw Leicester fans in a running battle, using knives and other weapons, outside a pub in Earlsdon, a suburb of Coventry, when Leicester were due to play Coventry City, some five miles from their Ricoh Stadium. Up to 100 Leicester and Coventry supporters were involved in the violence, in what police described as a pre-arranged fight. Terrified shoppers in the quiet street sought refuge in nearby shops and houses, and even a church, as the violence intensified. One man suffered head injuries, and police confiscated a number of knives. At a subsequent Crown Court hearing all were dealt with, receiving appropriate sentences and banning orders.

On Saturday 30 April 2011 two mass brawls broke out in Doncaster town centre, and it is believed that Leicester and Doncaster supporters were responsible. In the first outbreak of violence, six men were arrested for public order offences. Minor injuries were sustained by the hooligans. In the second incident, another six men were arrested.

Manchester City

Thirty-nine separate chants are frequently directed against Manchester City supporters, of which thirty-two come from Manchester United fans. The football hooligan elements of Manchester City are known as the Guvnors. They have also been known as The Blazing Squad, Cool Cats and Maine Line Service Crew.

Their biggest rivals are with their near neighbours Manchester United, against whom they contest the Manchester derby game. It is interesting to note that, before the Second World War, when travel to away games was rare, many Mancunian football fans regularly watched both teams, even if considering themselves to be the supporters of only one. This practice continued right up until the early 1960s, when travel became much easier and the rivalry intensified.

For some strange reason in the late 1980s, Manchester City fans started a craze of bringing inflatable objects to matches. Initially they were oversized bananas. The reasoning, although disputed, is said to go back to a match with West Bromwich Albion, when chants from fans, which called for the introduction of Imre Varadi as a substitute, mutated to 'Imre Banana'. During the 1988/89 football season, the terraces were packed with supporters waving inflatable bananas. The craze spread to other clubs; Grimsby Town waved inflatable fish, and it reached a peak on 26 December 1988 at the away game with Stoke City, a match that was described as a fancy-dress party.

On 22 September 2001, Sheffield Wednesday played a home game with Manchester City; a number of City fans arrived by train. After the match, as the Manchester City hooligan element made their way back to Sheffield station, there were running battles. At around 10 p.m., there was serious disorder at the railway station, wherein four police officers were injured. The train departed with the hooligans on board but there was continuing trouble throughout the journey back to Manchester.

In early November 2003, Barnet FC met Stalybridge Celtic in an FA Cup first-round tie at Barnet's Underhill Stadium. Disorder broke out at the stadium and nineteen football hooligans were thrown out. The local police made four arrests in the section reserved for away supporters after trouble broke out when around thirty fans claiming to be Manchester City managed to gain access to the game. It is believed that approximately fifty Manchester City fans, including known hooligans, had travelled to the game in addition to the Stalybridge fans. The Manchester City fans also fought among themselves in a two pubs in Barnet. No supporters were injured but one police officer suffered a cracked rib.

Before he signed a record deal, Noel Gallagher used to know some members of Manchester City's Guvnors and was a regular at the old Maine Road ground in his youth. He has been quoted in a national newspaper as saying that he used to regularly wonder if he would get home without injuries after matches. He acknowledged that the grounds he used to frequent were dangerous places, especially at the night games.

Manchester United

There are thirty-four chants that are routinely directed against Manchester United's supporters, of which fifteen originate from Manchester City fans. The hooligan firm who follow Manchester United were known as the Red Army. They were formed in the 1970s. The term nowadays is used to identify the fans in general. They are one of the largest football firms in British football. As the members dress in black clothing, they are also known as Men in Black. There are smaller firms within the Red Army and these are known as Young Munichs, The InterCity Jibbers and the Moston Rats. It is said that the InterCity Jibbers are dedicated to other crimes, in addition to football hooliganism.

In the 1974/75 season Manchester United were relegated to the second division of the English Football League. Mayhem ensued at many of the grounds that the Red Army visited, where they often regularly outnumbered the home team supporters.

On 4 November 2014 Manchester United played their fiercest rivals Manchester City in a local derby at City's Etihad Stadium. City went on to beat Manchester United. About an hour and a half after the game, in a bar near the Etihad Stadium, a group of the Red Army stormed in, throwing bottles and flares at the City fans who were drinking on a terrace at the rear. The City supporters retaliated by running out, throwing chairs and missiles at the United fans. Between seventy and 100 fans from both sides were involved in the savage brawl. One man was injured but refused to go to hospital after being seen by the paramedics, while a number of arrests were made.

At another local derby being played at the Etihad Stadium, fights broke out in the car park between the rival supporters, and gangs of ticketless United fans broke through police lines to gain entry into the ground. The police managed to round up about 150 of them and eject them from the ground. Dozens more United fans managed to get tickets for the home stands and fights broke out in all the four stands. The pitch was also invaded and Rio Ferdinand was hit by a coin. At one point a Manchester United fan even infiltrated a police briefing before being ejected.

Millwall

The hooligan firm associated with Millwall came to notice in the 1970s and 1980s, with a firm known originally as F-Troop, before eventually becoming known as the Millwall Bushwackers. In his book *The Soccer Tribe*, published in 1981, Desmond Morris makes reference to them being described as 'nutters' and 'headbangers' by other fans because of the level of violence that they displayed. The book also contains a quote from an alleged F-Trooper as follows: 'I go to a match for one reason only: the aggro. It's an obsession, I can't give it up. I get so much pleasure when I am having aggro that I nearly wet my pants – it's true. I go all over the country looking for it.'

Millwall quickly gained a reputation as being one of the most notorious hooligan gangs in England. The Football Association have closed Millwall's The Den ground down on five occasions for hooligan behaviour associated with their fans, while the club has been fined on numerous occasions for crowd disorder.

Violence attached to Millwall can be traced back over 100 years. On 17 September 1906 Millwall played an away game with West Ham at the latter's Upton Park. The supporters from both sides were made up of the nearby dock workforce. The Dockers were rivals working for opposing companies who were touting for the same business. From the very first kick of the ball, it appeared that trouble was on the horizon. Millwall had two players sent off. Two players collided with each other, causing considerable excitement among the spectators, and fighting broke out.

In the 1920s, Millwall's ground was closed for two weeks after home supporters threw missiles at the Newport County goalkeeper. He jumped into the crowd to confront them and was knocked unconscious. In 1934 the ground was again closed after disturbances in Bradford Park Avenue. Pitch invasions resulted in another closure in 1947. The club was fined after a referee and linesman were ambushed outside the ground in 1950.

On the evening of 13 March 1985, Luton Town met Millwall at Luton's Kenilworth Road ground in an FA Cup sixth-round match.

Luton was asked by Millwall to make the match all-ticket but this request was ignored. As a result, rival hooligan firms gained access to the stadium. The match became one of the worst, and most widely reported, incidents of football hooliganism. Approximately 20,000 fans packed into the ground, which usually held around 10,000, and Luton beat Millwall 1-0. There were numerous pitch invasions, fighting in the stands, and missile-throwing, with one object striking Luton's goalkeeper.

A total of thirty-one fans were arrested, and many of them were identified as being Chelsea and West Ham supporters. An enquiry by the FA was held, as it was not satisfied that Millwall FC had taken all reasonable precautions in accordance with their rules. The club was fined subsequently fined £75,000, although this was withdrawn on appeal.

In May 2002 Birmingham City beat Millwall in a play-off game at Millwall's ground. Hundreds of the hooligan element attached themselves to Millwall and involved themselves in disorder around the ground. The BBC described the violence as one of the worst cases of civil disorder seen in Britain in recent times. During the savage thuggery that went on, forty-seven police officers and twenty-four police horses were injured.

Newcastle

Newcastle United, who play at St James' Park, Newcastle, have a hooligan firm called the Gremlins. They are mainly white British and number 200–500 individuals. Their fiercest, most bitter rivals are Sunderland. Their allies are the English Border Front (Shrewsbury Town) and the Fine Young Casuals (Oldham Athletic). Whenever local derby games between Newcastle and Sunderland are played, trouble is often not very far away.

Prior to being known as the Gremlins, Newcastle's hooligan firm were called the Newcastle Mainline Express or NME, due to their use of the railway network when travelling to away games. The NME were an extremely active firm during the height of football hooliganism in the 1980s. They caused absolute mayhem wherever they went. At one game with West Ham, they threw a petrol bomb at West Ham fans, who were housed in a corner of St James' Park. This area of ground is commonly referred to as 'fire-bomb corner'.

A derby match in March 2002 saw the Gremlins fighting with Sunderland's Seaburn Casuals at a pre-arranged clash near the North Shields ferry terminal. The violence between the two sets of fans could only be described as some of the worst football-related fighting ever witnessed in the United Kingdom. A number of fans from both sides were arrested and charged with football-related offences. At a subsequent Crown Court appearance, the leaders of the Gremlins and the Seaburn Casuals were both jailed for four years for conspiracy. Twenty-eight other fans were jailed for various terms based on evidence gathered by police, who, during their investigation, examined a number of mobile telephone messages that had been sent on the day of the fighting.

On 2 April 2003 England played Turkey in a UEFA Euro 2004 qualifying match at Sunderland's ground. Around 200 fans of Sunderland and Newcastle began fighting with each other outside the ground. They then attacked the police, pelting them with missiles including cans, bottles and wheel trims. The violence was attributed to a resurgence in the conflict between the Gremlins and the Seaburn Casuals. In total some ninety-five fans from both sides were arrested and charged with a variety of offences.

On 9 January 2005 Newcastle United hosted Coventry City at St James' Park in an FA Cup match. After the match, at around 6 p.m., several men, believed to be the Gremlins, entered a pub in the city centre and attacked the Coventry fans inside. The violence spilled out onto the adjacent street. After being tracked by CCTV, members of the gang were arrested. A full police investigation was carried out. Raids followed, and a total of seven men were arrested and charged with affray.

Oxford

Oxford play at the Kassam Stadium in Oxford. Their rivals are Swindon Town, Reading and, to a lesser extent, Wycombe Wanderers and Luton Town. The hooligan element that follow them are known as the South Midland Hit Squad.

On 27 November 2004, Chester played Oxford in a Coca-Cola League Division Two match. On the day in question, in a Chester city-centre wine bar, a violent brawl erupted between Chester and

Oxford football supporters, which continued in the street. The violence was so bad that members of the public had to seek refuge in nearby shops. This incident was captured on the bar's and city centre's CCTV systems. Several Oxford fans were arrested and subsequently appeared at Warrington Crown Court. Nine Oxford United fans were subsequently given football banning orders for their part in the violence.

In July 2007 two of Oxford United's fans, who were described as organisers by Thames Valley Police, were found guilty at Oxford's Magistrates' Court of causing fear or provoking violence before a game with York City in 2006. On 30 September 2006 they were in a crowd of about eighty men in a street near to the Kassam Stadium, shouting and making threatening gestures at the York fans. The two groups came face-to-face in a confrontation. When police officers arrived on the scene, they found the fans throwing bottles and glasses at each other. After the match, which Oxford won 2-0, police were called to a pub near to the stadium that had been trashed by York fans.

After a four-day trial at Gloucester Crown Court in May 2010, two Oxford FC supporters were found guilty of violent disorder. At the end of the trial, the court learned that one of them had a previous conviction for a similar offence in 1992 and that the second had been given a three-year banning order for public disorder in 2004. The court appearance resulted from a violent brawl that took place in a Cheltenham pub at 5 p.m. on 7 February 2009. A double-decker coachload of Oxford United fans visited the pub in the town centre of Cheltenham when their match against Kettering at Wellingborough had been postponed due to bad weather. They became involved in a violent confrontation when the Oxford fans began gesticulating at Cheltenham Town fans. Furniture, bottles and glasses were thrown across the pub in a terrifying ten-minute brawl, which was described by witnesses as like something from a Wild West film. Over £5,000 of damage was caused by the thugs and the pub lost £8,000 in trade.

Due to Oxford United returning to the Football League in the 2010/2011 season, six Thames Valley police officers, under the command of a detective inspector, became part of a new unit set up to tackle recent hooliganism at Oxford United matches.

Rangers

Glasgow Rangers were founded in March 1872. Their bitter rivals are neighbours Glasgow Celtic. The traditional support of Rangers is largely drawn from the Protestant community, while Celtic's is drawn from the Catholic community. The football hooligan firm who follow Rangers have been known as the Intercity Firm, Her Majesty's Service, Rangers Soccer Babes and Section Red. Clashes with Celtic have historically been extremely violent, with public order offences and assaults, which have led to death on occasions.

Following an incident in the 1979 League Cup final, there is also a bitter rivalry with Aberdeen FC. A Rangers player provoked the fury of the Aberdeen supporters in what they believed was a blatant dive, but nevertheless resulted in the sending off of an Aberdeen player. The following season an Aberdeen player had to be given the kiss of life at Ibrox, during a Rangers home game, after a vicious stamp on his throat. Relations between fans were further soured during a league match on 8 October 1988, when a tackle on a Rangers player resulted in him being seriously injured. The fixtures have been described as 'even more of a powder keg' than the Old Firm games between Rangers and Celtic.

Co-author Bill Rogerson has one hitherto unpublished account of his dealings of Rangers supporters. During the early 1980s he was on night duty as the duty sergeant at Crewe, when he received information that there were a number of unescorted Rangers fans on a train returning from the Continent and travelling from London Euston to Glasgow Central via Dumfries and Kilmarnock. The group of about forty supporters were described as being in high spirits.

During the journey to Crewe the police had to be called to the train at Rugby due to their behaviour. On arrival at Crewe, at around 1.20 a.m., there was a train-crew change. The guard taking the train forward to Carlisle had got wind of the trouble and refused to take the train forward without a police escort. The fans were still very noisy, and Bill and a constable travelled with the train to Carlisle. Before they set off, Bill located a fan who appeared to be the ringleader and told him in no uncertain terms that they would stand no messing and would be dealt with accordingly. The ringleader went back to his fellow supporters, said a few words to them, and they all quietened down.

On Tuesday 28 September 1999 Glasgow Rangers played PSV Eindhoven in the Netherlands in a vital Champions League match. Prior to the game, it was believed that the Rangers Casual fans who were members of the Rangers' notorious Intercity firm were behind organised violence that took place immediately before the match kicked off. Thirty-five Rangers fans were arrested when Dutch police in riot gear broke up a fight between the Rangers and 200 PSV Eindhoven fans outside the Philips Stadium, just as the game kicked off. The violence marred Scotland's international reputation for good behaviour among supporters.

Sheffield United

Sheffield United are known as The Blades. Their closest rivals are Sheffield Wednesday. Their hooligan element call themselves the Blades Business Crew (BBC), which is taken from the club's nickname, and were formed in 1983. They have a following of around 200.

After knocking out a linesman during a Division One game in March 1998 against Portsmouth, a member of the firm received a term of imprisonment. In 2002, during a Division One fixture at Bramhall Lane against West Bromwich Albion, fans of both clubs were involved in fighting outside the ground. The game was eventually abandoned, and the incident was dubbed the Battle of Bramhall Lane.

In 2003, when Sheffield United beat Cardiff City 5-3 in a Division One match, there were numerous outbreaks of violence, including coin throwing, between the two sets of fans; four Cardiff fans were injured. The Blades Business Crew threw missiles at visiting Barnsley fans at Sheffield station in 2011, following the club's relegation from the Championship. British Transport Police officers intervened and arrested supporters. Three men were later convicted of affray.

On 9 December 2013, a group of Sheffield United football supporters caused an unprovoked fracas in Leeds city centre. About 100 were returning in two coaches to Sheffield from an away game in Carlisle, when they decided to stop off in Leeds. At around 8 p.m.

they visited a pub that was popular with Leeds City fans, and began chanting outside. They started smashing the windows of the pub with bottles and glasses. One group remained outside the pub, while two more groups went into the pub and started throwing tables and chairs. During the ensuing fight several people were assaulted, including the landlord. The damage caused was around £3,000 but fortunately no one was seriously injured in the attack. It is believed that the group then moved onto another nearby pub, before boarding coaches and leaving the city. The West Yorkshire Police, in conjunction with their South Yorkshire Police and Cumbria Police colleagues, studied CCTV images in an effort to identify and arrest the culprits. Following enquiries, a number of arrests were made and, in July 2014, four Sheffield United fans were jailed for their part in the violence.

Sunderland

Sunderland has thirty-five chants directed against its supporters, of which twenty-seven derive from Newcastle fans. Sunderland FC is located in the north-east of Sunderland; their hooligan firm are known as the Seaburn Casuals. Their fiercest rivals are Newcastle United.

Bill Rogerson recalls travelling up to Seaburn station, which was adjacent to Sunderland's ground, while escorting Aston Villa fans. For operational purposes, the trains were always routed via longer and little used routes. The return escort consisted of one sergeant and four constables. On departure from Seaburn, the officers were told to make sure that all the window blinds on the carriages were pulled down. The reasoning behind this was that Sunderland fans had a habit of throwing stones and bricks at the returning football trains. Sure enough, a few minutes out of Seaburn, the train came under attack from missile-throwing Sunderland supporters. When the train was clear of the area, it was discovered that the train had sustained a few broken windows and dents to the metal bodywork, but that no one had been injured.

In 2000 the police service released details of how many fans were arrested during the 1999/2000 Football League season. Top of this 'league' was Sunderland, with 223 fans being arrested.

At Newcastle Crown Court, on 12 March 2002, a court heard that, on 18 March 2000, a gang of thirty Sunderland Seaburn Casuals had caught the ferry across the River Tyne from South

Shields for a pre-arranged fight. They were met by a group of some fifty Newcastle supporters, which included members of their gang, the Gremlins. What could only be described as a fierce brawl followed, whereby weapons were used that included bottles, pieces of wood, pool-balls and CS gas. This savage battle between the two sets of thugs lasted for around ten minutes. Not realising that one of their number was lying unconscious on the jetty, with a depressed fracture to the skull, the Sunderland supporters got back on the ferry for South Shields.

As the ferry was departing, Newcastle supporters threw bricks and bottles at the ferry. The Sunderland supporters threw their weapons overboard before the waiting police met them. A total of thirty-five men subsequently appeared in a total of three court hearings, and jail sentences totalling almost fifteen years were handed out for offences of violent disorder and conspiracy to commit violent disorder. The two ringleaders of the gang were jailed for a total of four years each.

In August 2009 Sunderland fans had arranged to meet in Newcastle city centre for a mass fight with Newcastle Gremlins that would coincide with the Sunderland fans arriving back on the train after a friendly match in Edinburgh. About forty troublemakers clashed with police officers who were trying to escort the fans aboard a train home. A number of arrests were made in connection with the trouble.

In January 2013, less than an hour before a game with West Ham at Sunderland, a pre–arranged violent fight broke out in Low Road, Sunderland, between at least twenty Sunderland and West Ham fans.

Tottenham Hotspur

Tottenham are the subject of forty-two separate football chants, of which twenty-five originate from Arsenal supporters.

The North London club has a hooligan element following named the Yids, as well as the Tottenham Massive and Spurs N17. They have a large fan base in the United Kingdom, drawn mainly from the Home Counties, and all over the world. Tottenham Hotspurs, or Spurs as they are more commonly known, have rivalries with several clubs. The fiercest of these are North London rivals Arsenal. They are also rivals with Chelsea and West Ham. The club has a large Jewish following.

The Tottenham Hotspur versus Feyenoord European match in 1974 was ill-tempered, with Tottenham fans rioting and damaging seating in the stadium, throwing them onto the pitch and at each other. On 9 January 2002, Chelsea played Tottenham. Fighting broke out between the hooligan elements of both clubs and outside West Kensington Underground, one man was stabbed. A small group of Tottenham hooligans attacked Chelsea fans at Victoria station. During the game Jimmy Floyd Hasslebank was hit by a coin, while a bottle was thrown at Les Ferdinand.

On 10 February 2002, after a Tottenham versus Chelsea match, both sets of hooligans fought outside Tottenham's White Hart Lane Stadium. The Tottenham fans smashed a coach window as Chelsea left the area, while two men were stabbed and a police officer suffered a broken foot. Coins and missiles were thrown during the game.

On 4 August 2002 at 11 a.m., before a Millwall versus Tottenham match, more than 100 Millwall hooligans travelled to Jamaica Road in Bermondsey for a pre-arranged confrontation with Tottenham's Yid Army. There was vicious fighting between the two sets of fans. Ten minutes before the match finished, the hooligans from both sides left the stadium to continue their brawl. The Tottenham hooligans returned to Bermondsey at around 8.30 p.m. and attacked a pub. During this day, thirty police officers, and three police horses, were injured. A man was taken to hospital with knife wounds.

On 23 August 2009 West Ham played Tottenham Hotspur in a Championship League game at Upton Park. Following the game, which Spurs won 2-1, violence that had been pre-arranged in a pub erupted between the two sets of fans, near to the ground. In all, there were around sixty hooligans fighting each other with bottles and glasses. One fan even ran behind police lines to try and attack a West Ham supporter. After a court hearing in February 2011, the ringleader was jailed for six years for his part in the affray.

At the end of October 2009, a gang of more than twenty Spurs fans emerged from Holloway Underground station and attacked Arsenal fans as they drank in a pub in Holloway to celebrate their

3–0 victory over Spurs. Members of the public saw the gang coming, and managed to lock and barricade the doors before they arrived. The Tottenham fans were not deterred by this course of action, smashing all the windows and throwing missiles at the crowd inside. They also armed themselves with chains, barriers, bins, sticks bits of wood and anything else they could lay their hands on. The two ringleaders later received jail sentences of fifteen months and were banned from attending any football matches for six years.

West Ham

West Ham FC is based in the East End of London. Their hooligan element firm are known as the InterCity Firm and were formed in 1972. The name came from the use of InterCity trains that they made use of to travel to away games. Their members are predominantly white British. They have had books written about them; television documentaries have been made about their activities; and a film was made about them, which made its debut in August 2008. Their fiercest rivals are Millwall's hooligans, the Bushwhackers.

On Tuesday 26 October 2004, fifty hooligans from West Ham's InterCity Firm dressed in designer clothing, hired a coach and travelled to Bournemouth to wreak havoc at a Bournemouth versus Cardiff match, a game in which they were not even involved. At about 7 p.m., the West Ham fans posed as ordinary customers in a pub close to Bournemouth's stadium, where Cardiff fans were enjoying a quiet drink. Right on cue, they started singing their theme song 'I'm Forever Blowing Bubbles' and began fighting. The violence spilled out onto the street, with bricks being thrown. It was absolute pandemonium.

After being struck by a brick, a young Cardiff fan suffered a broken jaw and required hospital treatment. A second Cardiff fan was treated for facial injuries. Fortunately, there were about a dozen police officers on patrol outside the pub, and they were able to control the violence. Two men from London and two from Bournemouth were arrested and charged with public order offences.

In July 2008 West Ham played a friendly match against Columbus Crew, of Ohio, USA, and their hooligan element fought at half time. At least thirty West Ham supporters went to the north-east corner of the stadium where Columbus's most boisterous supporters were based. They fought with 100 Columbus fans. The police and security staff had to intervene. Several people were handcuffed, but only one arrest was made and that was outside the stadium for disorderly conduct.

In the League Cup in 2009, West Ham and Millwall played against each other; this was the first time that the two teams had met together for four years, as they had been in different divisions. Several hundred fans battled with each other, in scenes of massive unrest, on the streets outside the stadium. On several occasions, the pitch was invaded by West Ham supporters, and one Millwall fan came close to death after being stabbed.

In 2009, it became apparent that the internet was becoming responsible for an increase in football violence. Fans officially banned from grounds around the country were using mobile phones and the web to arrange violence at matches, and West Ham fans were no exception. In July 2009, trouble flared at the Millwall cup tie. Shortly after 6 p.m., as fans headed to the ground at Upton Park, fans threw bottles and bricks at each other, as the two sets fought viciously. Three people were taken to hospital after receiving injuries, and one forty-four-year-old man was stabbed in the chest. A number of arrests were made.

On Tuesday 25 August 2009, before, during, and after the Carling Cup match between West Ham and Millwall, there were six hours of confrontation between the two sets of fans, which had been pre-arranged via mobile phones and the internet. One man was stabbed, while thirteen arrests were made. A number of the thugs that were arrested had been subject of football banning orders. During the match, fans invaded the pitch, including one with his young son on his shoulders. Play had to be suspended for safety reasons.

* * *

While the impact that organised hooligan groups can have on the community at large is self-evident, it is also very clear that so-called local derbies occupy a special place in the history of football violence. In addition to those already referred to in this book, the below is yet another specific example.

Chester FC and Wrexham AFC are thirteen miles apart, and the local football cross-border derby matches between the two clubs have always been a flash point for trouble. In fact, open hostility has existed between the two clubs almost since their creation. The original Chester FC was formed in 1885, while Wrexham was formed in 1864 and is the oldest club in Wales. It is the third-oldest professional football club in the world.

In 1983 Wrexham were relegated to the old Fourth Division – the same league as their rivals, Chester – for the first time in six years. At their first meeting there were a series of violent clashes between the two sets of fans when a group of Wrexham supporters infiltrated Chester's old Sealand Stadium by masquerading as Blues fans. A brawl broke out, in which supporters attempted to demolish the wooden barriers that were in place to keep both sets of fans apart.

In 1985, when the two clubs met during an ill-advised friendly, there was a city-wide running battle between the hooligan elements of both clubs. Fighting broke out and very quickly spilled onto the pitch, causing disruption to the game. Police dogs were used to quell the violence. Cheshire Police reinforcements from Crewe had to be called in to assist in the arrest of fans.

In 2014, Chester fans accumulated a number of football banning orders in a single game. They have a hard-core contingent called The 125s. During a minute's silence to commemorate the eighty-year old anniversary of the Gresford Mining Disaster, near Wrexham – a tragedy that caused the deaths of 266 men in Wales – The 125s banged drums, chanted obscenities and generally caused a commotion. Also during the game, this group of Chester hooligans mocked the death of a prominent Wrexham supporter, who passed away after suffering a seizure in 2013.

Over the years, the clubs have been in different leagues and divisions but, for the last four years, they have been in the Vanarama National League. The first meeting of the two teams for the 2016/17 season was fixed for 24 September 2016 at the Racecourse Ground, Wrexham. In an attempt to eradicate the violence both clubs, Cheshire Police and the North Wales Police introduced 'safe travel' restrictions on the fans. This meant that the matches would be all-ticket and that fans could only travel on officially organised coaches in what the police term as 'bubble' matches.

The Wrexham versus Chester derby match duly took place at 12.15 p.m. on the above date. On the day of the match, Chester fans travelled in ten coaches to Wrexham with a police escort, which included the use of a police helicopter. The match, which was watched by 5,058, ended in a goalless draw and passed off without incident; no arrests were made. A local councillor, however, called for the bubble-style policing to be ended for future games. He slammed police for their 'Robocop' style of policing, as they were dressed in riot gear. Criticism also came from the local police and crime commissioner, himself an ex-police inspector from North Wales.

6

THE FIGHT BACK

In the 1980s, the UK government and the police started to take on the hooligans with a variety of new tactics and legislation that were designed to curb their activities. Some of these initiatives were more successful than others but, through trial and error, progress was made.

In late 1985 the Metropolitan Police set up Operation Own Goal, which was an undercover operation designed to infiltrate the hooligan gangs who affiliated themselves to West Ham, Chelsea, Millwall, Crystal Palace, and Arsenal football clubs. It was a ground-breaking initiative that resulted in numerous arrests. However, ultimately, there were allegations that the officers deployed undercover were inexperienced, lacked supervision, and had insufficient knowledge of the standard of evidence required to obtain convictions – this meant that many of the cases were later dropped at court.

In the first case to come to court, nine alleged Chelsea Headhunters were tried and five men were jailed. However, a later case involving a further eight Chelsea fans collapsed and, as it involved some of the same undercover officers, the way was opened for an appeal in the first case. A later trial involving eleven West Ham fans collapsed, and ultimately the decision was taken not to proceed with a further eighty-nine cases.

Chris Hobbs, a retired Metropolitan police officer, recalls some of the changes to police tactics as the fight back against hooliganism gathered pace. He recalls:

A move to Special Branch as a DC saw me gain promotion to sergeant, which meant a return to uniform, albeit a temporary one. This in turn meant a limited return to policing football. Improvements had taken place, however. There was a much more determined effort to segregate rival fans in the ground, with CCTV becoming a valuable weapon within the police's armoury. Problems continued, however, and spread outside those grounds as police struggled to contain the numbers involved.

One game I policed was the visit of Bristol City to local club Brentford. There was but one serial of us, despite the fact that then, as now, Bristol City fans had a formidable hooligan element. [Recent YouTube footage shows Bristol City fans attempting to attack newly relegated Newcastle's supporters outside the ground.] Fighting broke out on the half-way line, where most City supporters were congregated, with the situation being made worse by the fact that there was no Chelsea game that day, meaning that some Chelsea fans had decided to attend Griffin Park.

In the second half, more fighting broke out, this time on the opposite side of the pitch, as Chelsea and City fans clashed. This was also an area where a number of young Brentford supporters were situated and, during a convenient break in play, I ran across the pitch, past startled players, before jumping over the barrier with truncheon drawn, which was vigorously applied.

That incident prompted me to write a report suggesting improvements in policing football. It made a number of suggestions, the first being the sending of spotters to away games. Most of the major clubs now had individual officers who policed home games on a regular basis, meaning that they were thus experienced in policing football and also familiar with their own hooligan elements. It seemed a waste of knowledge not to deploy these officers to away matches to assist the home force. The idea was simply an extension of good 'home beat' policing, with the officers concerned not only being able to offer advice to the host force, but also able to exercise a degree of control over their own supporters. The second strand involved the deployment of undercover officers, which was based on the ease with which I was able to get on nodding and chatting terms with hooligan elements.

I submitted a report via my chief superintendent and then applied for a post in the Met's Training, Planning & Evaluation Department, as I was most definitely not enjoying my time as a shift sergeant other than in those rare opportunities to actually police the streets. I was successful and now had to travel to the Met's training school at Hendon, where the unit was based. My move coincided with two earthquake events in the football world – namely the Bradford fire and Heysel.

The Met decided that it wished to ensure that there would be no repetition at any of its football or other sporting venues in London and, with my interest in football and football crowds, it was decided that I was the man for the job, together with a very capable inspector who had already been awarded a BEM. We began by visiting several football grounds on match days and nights to see best practice, which also included a visit to Liverpool. Merseyside cops took us to the trophy room, and I was able to touch the famous 'This is Anfield' sign above the players' tunnel to the pitch.

As we were working on this, I was informed that the powers that be at New Scotland Yard had viewed my report and liked it. It was decided to conduct a pilot operation at Chelsea, both in terms of spotters and the undercover operation. The idea was that the spotters would also liaise with local police regarding the undercover officers and look out for their welfare as best we could, bearing in mind that we had no mobile phones in those days.

I was nominated to be one Chelsea spotter, and would attend away matches with one of the three Fulham PCs: Tony, Dave and Terry, who policed all Chelsea's home games. This dovetailed perfectly into the training package we were preparing. Our first away game saw us travel to Liverpool and thus began my love affair with the British Transport Police. It was agreed, quite rightly, that we would not police any train unless requested to do so by travelling BTP officers, and would travel in 'half blues', changing into full Met uniform on arrival at our destination.

On a bright Saturday morning, we reported to the BTP at Euston and were ensconced in our own compartment, where the BTP officer who was escorting us ensured we were supplied with coffee and sandwiches. We were welcomed at Lime Street by Merseyside officers, who told us that they'd be bussing Chelsea fans to the ground by a route that would avoid the various favourite ambush points by Liverpool 'scallies'. Once in the ground, we were able to use the CCTV in the control room to point out the pockets of Chelsea hooligans. Merseyside officers of all ranks seemed to welcome our presence and the match passed off without incident.

Another early trip was a mid-week trip to Everton, where the undercover team witnessed a clash away from the ground between the Chelsea Headhunters and Everton fans. We saw the aftermath, as a bloodied Chelsea leader returned to where the Chelsea coaches were parked. Our concern for his welfare was met with the rejoinder that he had been struck with a truncheon 'by one of your lot'.

The season flew by and was eventful. I got to know the Chelsea Headhunters well, and we had an amicable relationship. We were able to refer to the key hooligan 'players' by name, and consequently could exercise a significant amount of control. There were, inevitably, a number of incidents, while others, away from police eyes, were seen by the undercover team. At the season's final away game at Aston Villa, a number of fans came up to thank us for 'looking after them'.

Without going into detail, the detective sergeant in charge of the undercover team and I then submitted a report expressing our concerns regarding future football undercover operations. Senior management had not stuck to the original blueprint and, although arrests had been made of some of the Chelsea Headhunters, I was worried about some aspects of the approach. It was decided to extend the undercover operations to West Ham and Millwall, while all London's top clubs were to utilise spotters. I was seconded to the Met's Public Order Branch for a year, pending my return to Special Branch.

In the meantime, after extensive consultation, we had completed the training package in respect to ground safety. It was at three levels: PC level, supervisor level and senior officer level. All three packages came with a training video, made with the cooperation of Chelsea FC; it featured vivid scenes from Bradford, Heysel and the riot at the Birmingham versus Leeds match, where one spectator died. While we had requests for the package from forces that had assisted us, there was no national roll out.

The next season I was in my element. Every Saturday, and for midweek matches, I would go to NSY, change into uniform, grab a multichannel radio and then head across the road to the London Transport BTP control room, contained within St James's Park station, where I'd pick up a BTP radio. I would then head out solo, by public transport, to the biggest, high-risk game in London.

After the game had finished, and the crowds dispersed, I would frequently head to the Euston/St Pancras area, where there were frequent confrontations as visiting fans returned north or to the Midlands. By this time, a strong working relationship had been built up among the spotters and the BTP officers, especially the dog handlers, who would, like us, anticipate confrontation points. I was not infrequently given a lift by the BTP dog handlers and, with one exception, was generally given a warm welcome by ground commanders and officers on the ground.

I also began producing a weekly newsletter, which recorded events of the weekend. As well as incidents across London, many of which I'd witnessed, I'd also ring football liaison officers of clubs that had hosted games at which there was likely to be trouble. The circulation of this newsletter expanded dramatically from just London spotters to forces across the country, including the BTP. One copy to the Home Office became three, one of which went to the Home Secretary.

The newspaper was written using a humorous, colloquial style; yobs were called yobs, which clearly upset a sour Scottish superintendent who policed Queens Park Rangers. I was summoned to the control room at a game towards the season's end and, in the presence of PCs and sergeants, was asked whether I was the author of this weekly 'rag.' I replied that I was, and he went into one saying that the newsletter was a disgrace and that the use of words such as 'yob' was also a 'disgrace' – all within earshot of the other officers in the control room. He then asked who actually read this rag.

I replied that it was circulated throughout the country, with three copies going to the Home Office, one of which was read by the Home Secretary. I also pointed out that each issue was approved by the Public Order Branch commander before it was circulated. Behind his back, the PCs and sergeants collapsed in silent mirth, with one giving me the thumbs up. I finished with, 'Will there be anything else sir?' before leaving. On Monday, I trotted along to the commander's office, explained what had happened and listened to his reply, which was, 'Don't worry, I'll ring Mr C– in a minute and tell him to f**k off!'

During that season, I obviously encountered more memorable public order situations than you could shake a stick at and submitted two further reports. One suggested the formation of a National Football Intelligence Unit. I presented the idea, together with a resume of current operations, at a meeting of police chiefs at Guildford and was warmly applauded when I finished. I also submitted a report early on that suggested the spotter system be extended to the England team. The commander then knocked it back, but it was later implemented after I was back in Special Branch. I received a phone call at home inviting me travel to Germany as a spotter/advisor. Alas, I was off sick and couldn't travel. I wasn't asked again.

At the end of the season, Scotland played England at Hampden Park. We knew that just about every hooligan group in England intended to turn out for that one. The BTP officers travelling had to take an oath that would enable them to have authority in Scotland. We, as spotters, desperately tried to get up there as well, but the commander declined to approve it.

We found out from our colleagues in Nottingham that England's most notorious hooligan, Forest supporter Paul Scarrott, intended to travel. We managed to get a photograph, which we sent to the BTP officers travelling to Scotland that night who, in turn, handed it to our Glasgow colleagues.

The disorder began in Glasgow in the early hours of the morning, as England fans travelling overnight arrived. There followed some of the worst disorder that Glasgow has seen. Glasgow police, however, found Scarrott, who was targeted by a plain clothes team. They let him lead one charge of England's finest but, after the second, he was jumped on and arrested. England's number one hooligan was sentenced to twelve months in a Scottish prison.

The undercover operations saw Chelsea fans sentenced after the conclusion of Operation Own Goal. Operation Full Time saw further arrests at Chelsea, and also arrests at West Ham and Millwall. While I was back in Special Branch, I was told that the West Ham trial had collapsed. This was followed by other trials, which related to Chelsea and Millwall fans, being terminated, while those convicted after Operation Own Goal were acquitted on appeal. Several acquitted, 'innocent' hooligans went on to write about their exploits as hooligans.

None of the undercover officers were subject to any form of discipline after extensive enquiries, although a couple did suffer stress-related breakdowns. I was summoned to the commander leading the enquiry, who commented; 'You saw this coming didn't you?' Indeed we did. Lots of lessons were learnt regarding undercover operations, while the spotters continue to this day, albeit under a variety of guises. Just about every club, even some that are non-League, has at least one officer dedicated to football, most of whom travel away.

Spotters now travel with England and club sides into Europe.

Notwithstanding the problems that the police faced, officers in Leeds successfully mounted an undercover operation against their football hooligan firm, as did West Midlands Police against Birmingham's Zulu Warriors under the banner of Operation Red Card in 1987. This operation was managed on a day-to-day basis by one of the co-authors, Michael Layton, the story of which has been told in *Hunting the Hooligans*.

In the autumn of 1987, Operation GROWTH was born, which was appropriately termed 'Get Rid Of Wolverhampton's Troublesome Hooligans'. Richard Shakespeare became an undercover officer on this operation; these are some of his recollections:

I was one of eight officers working undercover; we had other staff from the British Transport Police, West Mercia, West Midlands and Staffordshire police forces. In those early days of this type of operation we had to improvise as there were no real guidelines.

We created our own 'legends' so that, when people asked who we were and why we had suddenly just appeared, we had a plausible story. As a youngster I had worked in a fish and chip shop, so my story was that I had been working for ten years in a fish shop in Skegness and had just moved back to Wolverhampton. I was so concerned for my family during the operation that we used to go and do the shopping literally miles away; I used to stay in character just in case I bumped into anyone.

The scariest moment I had on the job was right at the very beginning. We had to go to Hartlepool on a Saturday. Two of us went on a train, and there were about ten other football fans on it, men and women from the 'bobble hat' brigade. The only two scummy-looking guys on there were us. We got off the train at Hartlepool and went looking for the ground with the bobble hats. With the ground in sight, we spotted ten guys across the road from us, who were obviously looking for a bit of sport. One guy came over and asked me the time. It was the classic chestnut to catch your accent. This guy had cuts all over his face and he was literally in my face. I can picture it like it was yesterday!

I tried to fob him off by saying that we weren't looking for trouble and, out of the corner of my eye, I saw a woman with a baby, and another child, walking towards us. I stood back to let them through and this guy did as well. Unfortunately he then just went straight back into my face. Just then, in the distance, I saw some police vans arrive at the ground. I pointed towards them and said, 'Look, coppers!', at which point he punched me on the jaw and ran off. That was my welcome to the job! It did me good though because, although there was a certain loss of pride, it sharpened me up as to what I was going to face. The operation resulted in more than eighty arrests; one of them was the guy who assaulted me. As luck would have it, the attack was witnessed by a local reporter who knew this guy. When the undercover phase was over, he was arrested and I picked him out on an ID parade. To the best of my memory we only lost one case at court.

Bryan Drew OBE, QPM is the retired director of the United Kingdom Football Policing Unit, with extensive expertise in dealing at an operational and strategic level with football-related policing matters, both nationally and internationally.

Bryan recalls:

The 1970s and '80s are often referred to as the decades of football violence. During the late '80s, following the Bradford fire and Heysel disaster, the Home Office and the ACPO Public Order Sub-Committee, then led by Greater Manchester Police Chief Constable James Anderton, began to look at how to develop national and international football policing. The first football specific legislation was introduced during the 1980s, with the Sporting Events (Control of Alcohol) Act 1985 and the Public Order Act 1986.

The genesis of the current football intelligence network/structure in England and Wales was established following serious disorder at the June/July 1988 European Championships in Germany, and after over 300 arrests were made at the end of the season in May 1989. Much of this work was led by the Greater Manchester Police Assistant Chief Constable David Phillips, who, as deputy chief constable of Devon and Cornwall Police, later provided a written report to the Hillsborough Taylor Inquiry.

The use of specialist police football intelligence officers/spotters had already been introduced but, as with all new developments, the ACPO guidance on the introduction and use of such officers was advisory only and introduced on an *ad hoc* basis by forces.

The National Football Intelligence Unit (NFIU) was introduced by the Home Office and ACPO in November 1989. Its primary objectives were: to provide a central point for the collection, analysis and dissemination of football intelligence; to provide for better co-operation of police operations in relation to serious and persistent football hooliganism; to promote effective collation of intelligence by individual forces; for the first time to provide a channel for communication with foreign police forces on intelligence and supporter traffic; to assess the extent and nature of football hooliganism and its criminal associations nationally; and to provide technical and operational support, where appropriate, on the use of optical evidence gathering and the presentation of such evidence before the courts.

The NFIU also became involved in developing and delivering the post-Hillsborough/Taylor training for police officers of all ranks. The NFIU became part of the National Criminal Intelligence Service (NCIS) when that organisation came into being on 1 April 1992.

Former PC Simon Pinchbeck recalls:

I was working on the Territorial Support Group in London between 1990 and 1995, and was based at Paddington. We were aware that hooliganism had moved on somewhat, and we had started to see incidents in Central London happening on a regular basis, before and after matches. A small group of us worked closely with the National Football Intelligence Unit, which at that time was working at Tintagel House. We developed a really good understanding of all the organised hooligan groups and I soon realised that there were informants in every group except for Millwall. We did a lot with Spurs, and a fair amount with Chelsea.

We had a good informant within the London-based Cockney Reds, and another within the Arsenal group. Most of the fights were now going on outside the grounds but, before the advent of the widespread use of mobile phones, only certain games were called on for an organised fight to take place.

Being on the TSG, we were out every weekend and would stay out late, trying to pick up firms who were operating around major train stations, such as King's Cross and Euston. Essentially we were there to provide intelligence to the NFIU.

I recall that, late one night, there were a few Spurs fans floating around. At that time they had one of the biggest firms, and a lot of them were down trawling the West End. Some of them were in a pub near to King's Cross. Oxford were coming back from a game and passing through. They found the Spurs fans and smashed the pub to bits.

On another occasion, three of us were out in a van. There was not that much going on, but Brighton was up playing Brentford.

We came round a corner in the van and saw some of the Brighton boys outside a pub in Brentford. A car with three Chelsea boys pulled up, and one of them had a conversation with some of the Brighton lot. It obviously didn't go well, as it resulted in him having beer thrown over him, and they drove off.

Brighton then moved on to a pub near to Victoria station and, shortly after, we found a big team of the Chelsea hooligans in another pub nearby. All the big names were there. We had a walk through; normally they would be pretty chatty, but not on this occasion. We walked outside and, within minutes, found ourselves facing Brighton on one side of the road and Chelsea on the other. Just the three of us, we did our best among the mayhem. You just couldn't afford to arrest anyone as pieces of wood were being used as weapons by the hooligans. We just had to survive until help arrived. In those days, it wasn't necessarily recorded as football violence, because it was so long after the matches had finished.

On yet another occasion, our Cockney Red informant gave us some information relating to a match between Manchester United and West Ham. It was quite a tasty fixture and was at the time when Paul Ince was coming back to West Ham as a Manchester United player, having previously vowed never to leave his old club. We were told that the Cockney Reds would be meeting the Salford Reds in a hotel at Euston. The information was correct and there were 200–300 present. There was only a few of us, but we policed them onto the Underground and stayed with them until we got to Green Street – West Ham territory. There used to be an underground market under an office block there, and it was from here that West Ham hooligans tried to ambush them. With good intelligence, however, we were able to prevent major disorder.

One time Arsenal was playing Millwall in the FA Cup. We got some good information, but it was not 100 per cent, and so we had to do some running around. We eventually found 200–300 Arsenal fans in a pub called the Blind Beggar, in Mile End Road. It's a famous East End pub, associated with the Kray twins. The game was at the New Den, Millwall's ground, and we corralled them all and took them on the Underground to the ground. As we were walking with them, we realised that a 'major call' had gone out, as we recognised a lot of faces. Basically, the organised hooligans would get a message to show up for a certain game. If they didn't show, they were shunned. The only problem on this occasion was that the Millwall fan who had called the fight on had given the Arsenal fans the wrong time and so, when we arrived, none of the opposition was there.

After the game, Arsenal made it back to the Blind Beggar and later some Millwall turned up. Flares were thrown and, as we tried to get the Millwall fans down Mile End Road, we were being attacked from side streets on all sides by Arsenal fans. Eventually we managed to get the Millwall fans on some buses to get them south of the river.

I was involved with a lot of football policing, but I can honestly say that the difference with them was that, when you charged at them, they generally wouldn't move. I've even seen dads from Millwall holding kids in one hand and trying to punch and fight with the other.

As police forces started to realise the importance of being one step ahead of the hooligans by gathering good intelligence, partly through the deployment of dedicated spotters working in uniform, Richard Shakespeare describes how he went on to play a key role in shaping the intelligence picture at a force and national level. Richard explains:

In 1989 I became a detective constable in the West Midlands Police force intelligence bureau, with specific responsibility for six clubs, namely Birmingham City, Aston Villa, West Bromwich Albion, Wolverhampton, Coventry and Walsall. I attended matches, did a lot of spotting looking for known hooligans, submitted intelligence reports, and acted as the link with officers working in London at a national level. Part of my role was to disrupt planned disorder. Sometimes we would go back to the police commander at the end of a match, and they would say, 'Well nothing happened, that was a nice quiet day', and then we would tell them what action we had taken to prevent something happening. A lot of it was about following certain people. They always led you to the others.

I remember one particular case where we were able to disrupt some fans in a significant way. I went to a local derby game between West Bromwich and Wolverhampton in the early '90s. The game was held at West Bromwich's ground, which I was very familiar with. I noticed some of the GROWTH hooligans hanging around, who were still the subject of five-year football banning orders not to enter stadiums. They thought that they could hang around outside the ground and we couldn't touch them. There was a whole group of risk supporters numbering more than 200 and, while the game was going on inside, they were marauding around. They thought that the turnstiles marked the boundary with the ground but, in this case, I knew better. I knew that, during the week at the away end, there were some roller shutter gates that closed the end to the turnstiles. On match days, they were opened to give access, which meant that some of this group were actually standing within the footprint of the stadium itself and, in my opinion, had therefore breached their banning orders.

I used to work on the Operations Support Unit; I liaised with them and a number of the group, possibly eight, were arrested. They pleaded not guilty but, when their solicitors were shown the map of the ground, they changed their plea to guilty. After court, I was threatened by some of the group, who were known as the Bridge Boys. They told me that, next time they saw me, I was going to get done over. I told them that, next time I was at the Molineux, I would be on the bridge on my own if they fancied their chances. Forty turned up, looked at me, and walked away. They just couldn't be sure whether we had them on camera and wouldn't take the chance.

On 1 April 1992, Richard Shakespeare went to the newly created National Criminal Intelligence Service, based in London, as a football intelligence officer with a national remit and operating within a dedicated unit.

He recalls:

After just a few weeks I went out to Sweden for Euro '92 to keep an eye on the England and Scotland supporters. I found myself in an office in Sweden, along with officers from each of the countries playing. Everyone had a little flag of their country on their desks and on mine I had two! We were allowed to take a day off after each of our teams had played, as long as there had been no incidents. Although the Scots were well-behaved, as I had two teams to cover I didn't get much time off. There was trouble with the English fans in Malmö, but it worked well, having British police officers abroad, which for one of the first times was properly coordinated.

I did five years at NCIS all together and, in the second year, I was given Wales to look after as well. That was a bit of an education. I did a report outlining my views on the current state of hooligan problems in Wales and circulated it. A local Welsh chief superintendent then rang up my boss, ranting about how I had got a nerve coming from London and trying to tell him what to do with his own fans. I took the bull by the horns and phoned him to try to arrange a meeting. Although he was initially very cold with me on the phone, we eventually met and, in fairness, I managed to win him over – so much so that they eventually raided some homes on the basis of some of my intelligence, recovering weapons and evidence of links to other hooligan groups.

One person of interest during this period was a German, who kept popping up all over the place and appeared to have links to some far-right groups. That was my experience of being adopted by the Welsh.

Richard Shakespeare concludes:

In relation to football hooliganism you are only as educated as what you see on the television. I'd like to think that we laid the foundations for change in the culture and, although it still exists, it's not like it was in the '80s.

Better intelligence, CCTV cameras, improved education of the police and proper coordination have all helped to demoralise gangs. Banning orders and the more effective use of legislation have also played an important part.

To some extent, football violence has been engineered out of the grounds but, of course, this has to an extent pushed the problem outside the grounds. I often used to get officers asking me what the game was like when I had been to a match. Most times the answer I gave was that I hadn't got a clue. I wasn't there to watch the game!

Professor Clifford Stott is a professor of social psychology based at Keele University. He has published over fifty articles, and co-authored three books. Much of his work revolves around research into crowd psychology, collective conflict protests, riots, hooliganism, and public order policing. His initial reflections for this book focus on his involvement in some of the steps that were taken to tackle the problems related to football violence, post 1990:

To understand what progress has been made in relation to football-related hooliganism, one has to look back at some of the historical factors that have helped to shape the problem over the years.

Much of my work has been focused on how to tackle issues of hooliganism among England supporters travelling abroad. In the days of Margaret Thatcher's government, the issue was acutely embarrassing, and trying to find solutions to stop the violence was high on the political agenda.

In June 1990 I went to the World Cup finals in Sardinia, Italy, and witnessed some of the interactions between police and fans at first hand. This was at a time when English clubs were still banned from European competitions following the tragic events at Heysel Stadium, Brussels, in 1985, when thirty-nine people died during rioting between Liverpool and Juventus fans. This resulted in a five-year ban for all English clubs from European competitions.

The Italian police responded with force to the slightest hint of trouble and, on Sunday 17 June 1990, up to 1,000 English fans clashed with police in Cagliari, who responded to a can being thrown with baton charges and volleys of teargas. It was this policing response that played a major role in the riot.

Riots are obviously not the preserve of football hooligans, but the very use of the word is enough to provoke headlines in national newspapers. Just a few months before Italia 90, I was present during the Poll Tax riots in London. I witnessed the development of that riot, and I had come to realise that, to comprehend why that riot occurred, you needed to have a very clear understanding of what police tactics were deployed at the time, and to understand the behaviour of the rioters. It was evidently the same in Italy.

One of the problems in Italy was not that all of the England fans there were hooligans but that the Carabinieri, the national gendarmerie, were treating all of them as if they were hooligans, which created a negative response among the fans. There was absolutely no scope for any de-escalation tactics to take place; my argument is that the police need to move away from the idea that such riots can be avoided simply by the identification and control of so-called hooligans. The problem is that the sensationalist media coverage of these big riots feed this agenda.

In 1996, the UEFA European Football Championship took place in England and, after England's defeat to Germany in the semi-finals, a large-scale riot took place in Trafalgar Square, while disturbances occurred in other UK cities.

In 1998 the FIFA World Cup was held in France and, yet again, England supporters became involved in serious clashes with the French police in Marseilles, who responded routinely with indiscriminate volleys of teargas. Large numbers of England fans found themselves being drawn into the problems by virtue of the impact of policing and out-group aggression upon the convergence of large numbers of people into relatively confined areas. Indeed, 95 per cent of those England fans arrested in Marseilles had no previous history of being engaged in football hooliganism, and so it is difficult to sustain the idea that these people were hooligans.

More than once, a scenario was played out whereby England fans in bars would be attacked by local youths, following which the French police would turn up and treat England fans as the protagonists, thus provoking a negative reaction. I personally witnessed a group of fifty local youths, who were armed to the teeth with baseball bats and bottles, attack a group of fans I was with. I felt frightened for my safety. The natural instinct on these occasions, whether you are an ordinary supporter or a determined hooligan, is to mob up and stick together for protection. The most violent within the group become the leaders, and so the cycle continues. The situation tells you to stay close to these men, because they are the ones that are going to get you out of trouble.

One of the problems is also that the English hooligans have a reputation that opponents in other countries want to match or conquer, and so successfully attacking England fans is seen as a significant achievement.

When you look at the events in Marseilles in 2016 at the UEFA European Championships, they were generally a mirror image, with a series of violent interactions between fans leading up to large-scale fighting between Russian and England supporters and, yet again, a police response that consisted of teargas. One could be forgiven for thinking that police tactics had not evolved with time, except perhaps later in Saint-Étienne, where there was more facilitation and less confrontation. No surprise, then, that there was no disorder in Saint-Étienne.

The 2000 UEFA European Football Championships were co-hosted by Belgium and the Netherlands; during the course of policing operations, the Dutch police adopted a different style, with officers patrolling in pairs, moving among crowds of supporters and positively engaging with them. It is widely recognised that the Dutch adopted a tactic that worked well. There is no doubt that England fans like to push the limits, but they also respect interaction and limit setting, which, when done well, contributes towards keeping the lid on things. It can also lead to self-regulation, where fellow supporters will discourage others from going too far, which gives them a sense of empowerment.

What has also to be remembered, though, is that, during this period, there was also significant investment in the UK National Football Intelligence Unit and a British policing strategic approach that, at the time, focused on increasing the number of 14(b) football banning orders within the UK. Police forces were actually provided with extra funding to achieve this; hence the focus was on enforcement, using police spotters to look for troublemakers, and managing risks, and less on liaising with ordinary fans.

During the 2004 UEFA European Championship in Portugal, the police implemented, in the main, a similar approach, which was massively successful. Where it wasn't implemented, however, was in the Algarve, where GNR – the gendarmerie – were deployed in Albufeira during confrontations, one of which involved up to 400 England fans, as bottles were thrown during two nights of trouble.

In 2006, Germany hosted the FIFA World Cup, and there were clashes between Germany and England fans. In Frankfurt, however, the police adopted a graded response and used 'dedicated communication officers' to interact with fans, which worked well. This approach was supported by the British policing leads at those times – David Swift and then Steve Thomas – who worked closely with the German Federal Police to encourage good communications.

In 2008, the UEFA European Football Championship was co-hosted by Austria and Switzerland, and in 2012 the championship was co-hosted by Poland and Ukraine. At both events, patterns of variability were deployed by the police, so as to take different crowd dynamics into account, and interaction with fans was successfully encouraged.

The reality is that most football-related violence is spontaneous rather than being pre-planned. Hooligans are not so much a phenomenon as a virtual industry.

In recent years, police forces have become more confident about entering into information-sharing agreements with other bodies in an effort to contain hooliganism. In one such example, in 2007, an effort to combat football hooliganism at matches played in York saw British Transport Police, North Yorkshire Police and York City Football Club join forces. Hooligans regularly caused trouble at KitKat Crescent and other areas around the York football stadium. In a first-time agreement, the three parties signed up to a protocol known as PACT (Police and Clubs together). To help secure football banning orders against the hooligans, they agreed to share information and intelligence about offenders. The three parties have worked informally for a number of years, but this new, formalised system would assist in the fight against hooliganism in the locations around the stadium and on the railway network.

Violence and racist behaviour caused by a small minority were identified as being significant issues for York City FC and the police. Over the years, a number of initiatives have helped, in varying degrees, to stem the tide of hooliganism. Some of them can be categorised in the following terms:

- A ban or restrictions on access to alcohol in licensed premises, locations and on trains – the so-called 'dry policy'
- Changes in kick-off times for matches
- Empty stadiums
- Segregation of supporters
- Mentoring and education
- Enforcement through pro-active intelligence gathering
- More effective use of CCTV and other technical overt/covert options

Restrictions on the sale of alcohol have experienced mixed fortunes over the years, and have frequently been combined with changes in kick-off times for matches deemed to be high risk, in an effort to prevent excessive drinking by fans prior to matches taking place. The reality is that fans who are determined to find alcohol to consume will always find ways to circumvent bans and, in any event, there is evidence that determined and organised groups of hooligans are not motivated by alcohol as a means of driving their activity.

During the 1990 World Cup in Cagliari, Italy, alcohol sales were banned throughout the city, but it did not prevent large-scale disturbances involving up to 1,000 England fans taking place. Likewise, during the Euro 2016 games, there was no evidence to suggest that the organised Russian hooligan element were acting under the influence of alcohol.

Certainly the experience of co-author Michael Layton during Operation Red Card was that, while many of the hardcore Zulu Warriors used certain pubs as bases in which to meet, they were in the main not hardened drinkers. As such, the timing of matches became irrelevant and were made even more pointless by the fact that most organised fights took place outside stadiums to avoid CCTV cameras; many hooligans actually never went to the games at all. In more recent years, there is evidence to suggest that the casual use of controlled drugs prior to matches has increased and that, by inference, the restrictions placed on alcohol, while still an important factor in combatting anti-social behaviour, do not provide the 'golden thread' in terms of prevention.

The same principles apply to playing matches in empty stadiums, in that hardened groups intent on causing trouble will simply arrange to meet to fight in the vicinity of travel hubs or city centre bar areas. Here, the fluidity of their skirmishes and the speed with which they move make it far harder for the police to contain and control than if they were within the constraints of a stadium.

As importantly, such measures penalise the vast majority of decent supporters, who then become disaffected and therefore less engaged in wider preventative measures proposed by organisations in authority. Demonising the masses makes it much harder to win over the silent majority.

Post-Hillsborough, the move away from an emphasis on public order to that of public safety has professionalised the way in which grounds approach segregation and the use of sterile areas, but it is clear that the creation of such areas has to be complemented with the effective use of well-trained stewards who can respond quickly to incidents, in addition to the availability of police public order trained resources. The incident with Russian fans at the Stade Velodrome in France during Euro 2016, wherein they breached a sterile area in an effort to attack England fans, is a clear illustration of how treating law-abiding fans with dignity and respect has to be balanced with being able to robustly deal with the lawless minority.

Control is an extremely important issue in the battle to prevent rival groups from clashing. In the UK, there is a long tradition of the police and stadium staff exercising a high degree of control over the movements of fans on the terraces. In contrast, in some European countries, such as Cyprus, for example, once the Ultras establish their territory in a specific area of the ground, it can become virtually a no-go area during the game for the police and officials.

Diversion away from criminal activities related to football through the effective use of mentoring schemes, using role models and reformed hooligans, has proved to be an effective tool. The so-called up and comers provide the next generation of hard-core hooligans and, until that cycle is broken, new recruits will enter the fray every year.

Renton Baker is one well-known reformed football hooligan who now seeks to divert people away from violence and towards Christianity. After the death of his father from cancer, Renton was drawn into football violence connected to hooligans who affiliated themselves with Arsenal FC. In the past, he has described using baseball bats and knuckledusters, and also ammonia to temporarily blind victims. During one of his talks, designed to deter offending, he describes leaving a game early in the 1980/81 season in order to ambush visiting Manchester United fans. After a fight on the Holloway Road in London, he found himself heavily outnumbered by the opposition and was hit with a bottle. As he was about to receive a severe beating, he was saved only by a police officer wielding a truncheon, who burst through the crowd and forced fans to back off. At the height of his activities, he was at one stage known as 'Chopper' and, although of short stature, he was well-known for the level of violence of which he was capable.

Renton now works with Christians around the UK to deliver messages of faith, in an effort to bring about changes in values. He has worked closely with Simon Pinchbeck, the former police officer, who witnessed violence from the 'other side of the fence'. They now see themselves as 'once separated by violence and now re-united by faith'.

Simon Pinchbeck reflects:

In 2002, having left the job, I became a Born Again Christian after seeing the difference that it had made to a former Arsenal football hooligan. I was at a low point in my life. I had made some bad decisions and was facing either prison or death at that time due to what I had got myself involved in. I was a very angry man. If I look back at it now, although I didn't realise it at the time, being constantly exposed to violence affected me greatly and I have no doubt that I was suffering from some form of post-traumatic stress.

I walked out of a gym one day and saw this guy who I knew had been extremely violent but was now a Christian and seemed to be genuinely at peace with himself. I had a coffee with him and we discussed his life as a hooligan. I told him who I was and he told me that he already knew me. He reminded me that Arsenal had played in the final of the Cup Winners' Cup in Copenhagen in the early '90s. I was off duty but acting as one of the stewards on one of the coaches. I walked into a pub over there and it was full of Arsenal boys, who started shouting, 'Here's the Walrus'. He, however, was with the main crew and, as I walked in, they walked quietly out.

This guy took me to his church and it worked for me. I embraced the Christian faith and I have never looked back.

Since that period I've involved myself in giving testimonials as part of my life story to try to encourage people to be able to see that the Christian faith has the ability to turn people around. During the course of those meetings I have met many former, and current, football hooligans as well as visiting prisoners serving sentences for football violence. I have even sat down with sons of hooligans, who have themselves got involved in violence, and once spoke to the son of a prominent Nottingham Forest hooligan who was himself serving a sentence at a prison in Newcastle.

About six years ago a well-known Arsenal hooligan came along to one of my talks. I think that he actually came to see if I was going to make a fool of myself. At the end of the meeting I noticed that he was no longer in the room and I presumed that he had just left. A woman spoke to me and told me that I needed to go outside and that the guy wanted to speak to me. As I walked outside this guy was slumped against the wall of the church, crying his eyes out. He said to me, 'I never cried at my dad's funeral. I don't know why I am crying now but I don't want to be angry anymore.' He gave his life there and then to the Church and said that it felt like a weight had been lifted from him. For me if I can change someone's behaviour for the better then it's all worth it.

Simon Pinchbeck concludes:

Football violence is still very much alive and happening but, because of surveillance inside grounds, it's less now, unless spontaneous violence breaks out. It's still very organised, but the general public don't see it. This year I was told about a game where Arsenal played Tottenham. The rule is that you normally leave the so-called 'bobble-hats', the ordinary fans, alone but in this case the Spurs fans carried out indiscriminate acts of violence. Next time Arsenal played Spurs the Arsenal firm did the same to exact retribution, and so it goes on.

In the end though, unless committed perpetrators also understand that there are consequences to their actions, and that their anonymity is likely to be exposed, the likelihood of football violence continues to be high. With reduced policing resources in the UK as a whole, and ever-competing priorities, the effective use of intelligence to mount coordinated operations and being in the right place at the right time, in order to be one step ahead of the determined hooligan, remains a priority for the future.

THE FUTURE

David Deakin was responsible for an investigation, on behalf of the BBC, into violence at non-League football matches, and his findings were aired in a programme called *BBC Coventry and Warwickshire Investigates: Non-League Football Violence* on 23 May 2016. During the course of his enquiries David conducted research into the historical nature of the problem, as well as speaking to individuals about the current situation.

His enquiries at that time revealed that there were more than 250 football banning orders in place at League clubs across the West Midlands – compared to just twenty-one at non-League clubs.

The question as to whether non-League violence was on the increase was put by him to a West Midlands Police officer, PC David Houlson, who is the dedicated football intelligence officer for Wolverhampton Wanderers FC. In response, he confirmed that they knew that hooligans in possession of banning orders had attended non-League matches in the previous season – but made the point that they didn't routinely police these games.

He concluded his remarks by saying, among other things, 'Every season I'll have fifty new lads come and you have to get to know them; don't get me wrong, forty might disappear, which they usually do, but ten stay. Then the next season another ten stay, so you're always evolving ...'

A self-styled football hooligan, who attaches himself to Nuneaton Town, said that he felt that he could get away with his activities because of a lack of police presence. David Deakin interviewed him on the basis of anonymity:

> If anything goes off we don't personally go looking for it. If it goes off then we all know we've got each other's back, no matter what happens. It's not in front of you that matters it's behind you and knowing you've got your mates' backs is one of the best things going. This season there was Worcester at home, none of it was organised, we saw their lads in the ground giving it a bit big had a chat with them, like what you going on about and that, saw 'em after the game and chased 'em, nothing malicious but it's just defending your team I guess at the end of the day. People see it as looking for violence and that but I don't, I see it as looking out for your team and your mates ... the feeling is belonging but the rush and the buzz you get from it is unreal, you don't get it with anything else there is nothing else you get that lives up to that level of that buzz you get that rush of adrenalin and you're ready to go.

When asked if he was worried about getting caught, he responded,

> I know yeah, it's one of the things you live with really you can go jail for anything these days but it's just one of them, you know it's gonna happen but it don't happen often like ... I don't know many people that get caught ... we know like at local games there's not many stewards there's not many police. Especially non-League there's not man ... Most I've seen police is Tamworth and Lincoln and they're obviously rivals 'cause of what happened in the past you don't really see many police around so you think you can get away it. There's cameras left right and centre so you've just gotta keep your face covered.

David Deakin concluded his interview by asking him whether he would continue his activities and he responded, 'Oh yeah I'll always fly the flag for Nuneaton and I'll always have my mates' backs and that. I'll always carry on doing that.'

Nuneaton Town currently has seven football banning orders in place, most of which stem from a violent episode in March 2013 as drinkers in the town centre clashed with Lincoln City supporters before a game. Some fans were corralled by police inside the Granby pub, which they vandalised, before using the wreckage as missiles to throw at officers. Twenty-one people were later jailed for their part in the incident – the majority of which were supporters of Nuneaton Town.

By way of example, another serious incident took place in the same year when, in October 2013, a crowd of around 1,000 supporters gathered to watch an FA Cup qualifying match between Atherstone Town and Barrow AFC at Sheepy Road.

Before the game had even started, smoke bombs and flares were let off, and, at half time, with Barrow winning 4-0, Atherstone fans invaded the pitch, before running across to the Barrow away section. Violence followed, wherein supporters, including women and children, were indiscriminately punched and kicked. A number of men from Warwickshire were eventually sentenced to more than forty-five years in prison for participating in the disorder, which left ten Barrow supporters suffering from injuries including burns, cuts and bruises.

A Leamington fan, who was assaulted by a teenage hooligan at an away game in 2015, commented:

> I think there's a subculture coming into football again, sort of glorifying violence and casual culture, you look on Facebook and you see many, many groups showing examples of supporters fighting. I think it's become quite popular as a culture. You've got to remember at non-League for someone who's sixteen, under eighteen, it's a couple of pounds to get in, there's no segregation, often there's very little stewarding. It makes it quite accessible for them to act out.

Leamington FC fan (AC) says that he was attacked by a teenager while watching the Brakes play away at Rushall Olympia in November 2015. Despite what happened, he decided not to report it to the police.

He recalled, when interviewed:

> At non-League football, you tend to go behind the goal that your team's attacking but there were quite a young group of people,

about anything from about twelve to eighteen, and all through the game they'd just been giving abuse towards us, which again you can live with, it's nothing major. We exited the terrace at the left and we sort of expected them to go to the right and filter out that way but I was the last one to leave the stand. Somebody pulled my hoodie so I turned around and looked around and there they all were. One sort of came running in behind from his mates and head-butted me then ran out back behind them.

The chances of getting a prosecution, or maybe a banning order on the individual, was very, very low because there was no CCTV. Essentially it would just be our supporters' words against theirs. It was a tough one, really; people from the club did urge me to report it but you know, I felt it would just be a waste of energy to report it ...

At Leamington FC, they are now addressing problems by employing paid stewards to deal with a small minority of potential troublemakers, recognising that they simply would not be able to afford to pay for police officers at games. The incidents referred to in David Deakin's investigation are by no means isolated.

On Saturday 24 October 2015, Sporting Khalsa FC played FC United in an FA Cup fourth-round qualifier in a match that Khalsa subsequently lost 1-3. The match was held at the Aspray Arena, Noose Lane, in Willenhall, with an attendance of 2,252 people. Prior to the kick-off, a number of fans clashed in one corner of the ground, and a flare was thrown. Hooded youths, who were said to be from the Wolverhampton Youth hooligan group, were believed to be behind the violence, as stewards struggled to maintain order. Twenty-two minutes after the match started, another orange flare was thrown on to the pitch and during the disturbances a barrel was thrown.

On Saturday 9 April 2016, Whitehawk FC played at their home ground, just outside Brighton in East Sussex, against Wealdstone FC. A crowd of 724 people were in attendance, compared with a normal attendance of just over 500. The match was being played in the English League's sixth tier, in the National League South, and Whitehawk won the match 3-0. At some point towards the end of the game, up to twenty men started fighting, and punches and threats were exchanged. At one stage, a well-known forty-nine-year-old Wealdstone supporter, described as 'pint-sized', was heard to shout his well-known catchphrase of 'You want some. I'll give it ya', at opposing fans, as he was held back by two friends. Police officers were called to the scene but no arrests were made.

On Wednesday 27 April 2016, Redditch United played at home at the Valley Stadium, Bromsgrove Road, Redditch against Leamington FC. The game was a Southern League Premier play-off semi-final, which Leamington eventually won 3-1 on penalties. During the course of the game, security staff were deployed to the Cedar Road Stand, after scuffles broke out. At the end of the game, some of the Brakes fans got on to the pitch, where one of them was confronted by a Redditch fan, who punched him in the face and pushed him to the floor. The offender was later arrested by the police, after fifteen police officers were deployed to the scene, as up to thirty fans from each side squared up to each other in the roadway outside.

On Sunday 1 May 2016, Cefn Druids AFC, based in Cefn Mawr, Wrexham, played Caernarfon Town at home. A brawl broke out during the match, as Cefn Druids were losing 7-0 after a Druid's player was sent off. As the player was walking off the pitch, a male member of the crowd appeared to gesticulate towards him. The player then climbed over a fence onto the terraces, and launched what appeared to be a head butt at one man; the incident escalated from then on.

It continued, with other members of the crowd and players rushing over, some of whom tried to calm the situation. North Wales Police officers attended and order was quickly restored, with the assistance of local club officials. An eyewitness commented that he had been to see Wrexham play lots of times and had never seen anything like it before. An investigation was launched by the North Wales Police.

In June 2016 the media released figures that had been obtained by the Press Association as a result of a Freedom of Information request to police forces. The figures revealed a so-called trend of 'schooligans', ready to follow in the footsteps of hardened football hooligans from earlier generations. The statistics also revealed that more than 100 under-eighteen-year-olds, the youngest being a boy of twelve years, had been banned from football in the preceding three years, with some suggestions that children were sewing 'casual' clothing labels into their school uniforms and posting pictures on social media of themselves 'looking hard'. Amanda Jacks from the Football Supporters Federation commented: 'There is no doubt that there is a glamorisation of football disorder and kids are attracted to it for the wrong reason.'

On Saturday 9 July 2016, a thirty-eight-year-old man, and a fourteen-year-old youth were arrested after a fight broke out during an under-fifteens football match. Bishop Auckland St Mary's were playing a team from Barnsley in a tournament in Bishop Auckland, County Durham. As Bishop Auckland were winning 1-0, with four minutes to go, two youths began pushing each other, at which point the father of one ran on to the pitch and grabbed hold of an opposition player. One boy was trampled underfoot as the disturbance continued, and several people needed medical treatment in what was described as a growing problem. In the months prior to this, co-author Michael Layton was approached by the media on two occasions for comment when lower-league teams in Nottingham and Coventry appeared to be faced with a rise in anti-social behaviour at games that did not normally attract a police presence.

In June and July of 2016 two football teams – arch-rivals Allmänna Idrottsklubben (AIK) from Solna, a suburb of Stockholm, Sweden, and Stabaek, from Fredrikstad, Norway – found themselves in North Wales playing two North Wales football clubs – Rhyl and Connah's Quay – who have qualified for Europe for the first time in their seventy-year history.

In their native Scandinavia the supporters of the two teams have a reputation for fighting among themselves. The fans from the two teams were staying in North Wales, and made it known that they would be travelling by train in North Wales to watch their respective teams in action. The British Transport Police officers from Bangor and Rhyl closely monitored the fans. Fortunately, there was no trouble.

On Saturday 23 July 2016 a so-called friendly game was played at Cleethorpes between Grimsby and Sheffield United.

Hundreds of fans travelled from Sheffield, and many of them spent the morning drinking in the town centre. Just after 1 p.m., violence flared as police tried to keep opposing groups apart and to safeguard families with children in the Market Place area, where up to seven public order vans were located, and outside O'Neill's pub in the high street. Police, with batons drawn and police dogs deployed, struggled to keep fans apart as several skirmishes broke out; bricks and stones were thrown in Grant Street and cars were damaged.

Later, a crowd of fans started pelting each other with stones in a violent running battle on a railway level crossing in Cleethorpes. Hundreds of fans ran along sandbanks between the North Sea and a railway line. Violent fist fights also broke out between the two sets of fans. Large missiles were used, and some landed on the railway line. Police eventually moved in and blocked either side of the level crossing to keep the rival fans apart. A police officer suffered head injuries and a suspected fractured ankle.

After the match, hundreds of away fans were penned in on a platform at the railway station, where the toilets were smashed and fans mingled with holidaymakers, many of whom had young children with them. One arrest was made at the station after a fan confronted an officer and then threw the contents of a can into his face before struggling violently. As injured fans started to fill up the local A&E department at the local hospital, many of them covered in blood, the local police reported making six arrests in total, with at least one further officer being injured.

Peter Craig is a crime reporter with the *Grimsby Telegraph*, and witnessed events on the day. This is his personal account of what he saw:

After the results of the Euro finals in France in the summer, and the behaviour of some of the team's fans, there was a sense of longing for a return to the friendly rivalry of the League games back home in Grimsby and Cleethorpes. Although Grimsby Town had a pretty bad record of football banning orders while in the non-League division, the club's triumph at Wembley in May 2016 to secure Football League status once again added an extra spring in the step of fans. They had a great sense of anticipation in hosting proper Football League teams and visiting bigger clubs' stadiums.

There had been an enjoyable series of warm-up 'friendlies' ahead of the start of the new season, with a mix of good and bad results. All of the other clubs in the area had home games on Saturday 23 July 2016, namely Scunthorpe United and Hull, while Grimsby Town FC had a friendly game with Sheffield United, due to kick off at 3 p.m.

On the day in question, it was soon clear that hundreds of The Blades fans had arrived early, either by coach or train, with most arriving in Cleethorpes for some pre-match drinks. All the bars were open and there was a large number of tourists and day visitors, with their families all enjoying a sunny day in the resort.

It soon became apparent that there were large groups of football fans gathered outside bars. It had been anticipated that Sheffield United would bring 2,000 fans but, in my view, there were many more than that. Humberside Police had officers positioned at key points around the resort and, by lunchtime, the atmosphere in Cleethorpes was beginning to turn from pleasant, friendly and relaxed, to one of being tense and nervous, as Grimsby Town fans also began to mingle with the crowds, with Sheffield fans singing outside several of the bars.

Photographer Duncan Young called at about 12.20 p.m. to say that he could sense there would be trouble and, sure enough, at about 1 p.m. rival fans clashed at the junction of High Street and Alexandra Road in Cleethorpes. Police officers, with truncheons drawn, moved on a small group who had been scuffling near to the redundant O'Neill's Bar. Minutes later, groups that had been gathered outside bars in the Market Place began moving closer together; this resulted in a throng of people running towards a handful of Town fans nearer the seaside end of the Market Place. It turned nasty, with bottles being lobbed, forcing holidaymakers and visitors to run into shops, salons, and out of the Market Place.

Aware of the dangers, I parked my car in a public car park hundreds of yards away, and walked into the Market Place. I arrived to see a salon owner sweeping up broken glass. One of the salon owners showed me footage she had captured on her mobile phone and described the terrifying sight of scores of fans running at a line of police officers.

For a while some calm was restored but more officers arrived, and police dogs were brought in vans; there were more police on the streets than before. Traders were complaining to me as to why the game had been allowed to go ahead as a 3 p.m. kick-off when the town was full of holidaymakers. I spoke to a number of pub landlords, who had welcomed the visiting fans; then there was another small skirmish, this time between Sheffield United fans and police on the High Street.

More United fans began running to the scene from several streets leading to the High Street. These were not your archetypal young football hooligan, but adult males, most in designer wear, egging each other on and heading to see what was going on or to support their fellow fans against the police.

At this point more police in full riot gear began to appear. There was some chanting heard near to the junction of High Street and St Peter's Avenue, where some fans had begun to head off to the stadium, which was about half a mile away. It was a very large group. What should be a road into the heart of the resort, usually with lines of cars, became a mass of football fans.

More and more bottles, and cups of beer, could be seen flying through the air. Mums with prams could be seen fleeing in the opposite direction, looking terrified. Lines of officers were trying to corral the fans and trouble spilled into a council-owned car park as police tried to disperse the crowd.

Traders had begun to put their steel shutters down and lock up, as there were a series of pitched battles in different directions. At the same time, a number of pub landlords, who were linked to the PubWatch scheme began to close on police advice. There were further reports of trouble at the stadium gates and unconfirmed reports of an incident inside the ground.

As preparations got underway for fans returning for trains after the match, a lot of police officers were on the streets, with many more waiting in vans nearby. I spoke to the landlady of the Number 1 bar, next to the train station, who showed me the damage to her car that had been caused by fans lobbing lumps of concrete and bricks.

The tension was electric as we waited the fans returning after the final whistle. The result of the game seemed irrelevant, as the force helicopter circled overhead, filming the action on the ground. At that point holidaymakers, seemingly unaware of the potential for violence, were waiting on the railway station platform, as more officers in riot gear arrived there. Young families, having had a fun day on the beach and at the resort's amusements, seemed out of place in a scene more often seen in riots.

But, this was their resort and they had come to the traditional season, holiday season after holiday season, for fun. This was, after all, the height of the summer and it was a beautiful day. There were still thousands walking on the prom and enjoying the arcades and stalls and donkeys. I had been to a celebration at a nearby sports club, where a family had honoured their ninety-year-old matriarch Pearl, the head of a five-generation family. The laughter and warmth and love was a far cry from the violence about to be unleased at Cleethorpes station.

By now, pubs in the resort were still closed, with the aim of getting as many fans as possible back on to coaches and the only train out of the town. Hundreds of fans began making their way from the stadium along a path that goes along the seafront. In previous derby games, police deployed their 'kettling' tactic but, this time, they were in static positions at strategic points.

There were reports that some of the hooligans had arranged to have a fight on the prom, but this did not happen; however, trouble did flare at the prom's north end.

Some Sheffield United fans were clearly intent on hunting down Grimsby Town fans, and some of the Town fans had made their way to the streets around the railway station to challenge them. There were a lot of Sheffield United fans who were in high spirits, but a few were intent on trouble, running around, leaping over barriers and encouraging people with them to follow them to find rival fans. There were reports of fans banging on the windows and shutters of arcades, frightening people.

Pockets of trouble broke out, which were quickly dealt with. Railway station staff had to close the toilets as they had been overwhelmed by fans, and someone had excreted in a urinal, making it unusable.

More police arrived and herded fans into the station. One Sheffield United fan drinking a can of Vimto was asked to move back into the station. He went 'face to face' with a police officer in riot gear. He was an inspector from the South Yorkshire force and tactfully waited for the United fan to comply. There were verbal exchanges as the officer patiently ushered the fan, who was with other fans, back under the archway of the station. The man pushed at the officer, who did not react but urged him back. The man used his hand to flick the officer's helmet visor down. The officer put it back up and the fan threw some of his drink at the officer's face. There were other officers who joined in and the fan put his drink on the ground and assaulted the officer. He was quickly turned over and laid on the ground and taken away to a waiting van. He had a gash to his head and shouted, 'I'm from Woodthorpe.'

The incident seemed to have a deterrent effect on the other fans gathered in the station, but it was another twenty minutes before a train packed with fans and holidaymakers was allowed to leave. British Transport Police mingled with Humberside and South Yorkshire Police before some of them left to escort the train.

We later heard that a Grimsby Town fan had been chased along a street near the stadium and seriously injured by a Sheffield United fan.

The 'Vimto' man subsequently appeared in court at Grimsby and was given a football banning order.

Duncan Young is a photographer with more than twenty-eight years' experience; for the last eighteen he has been working as a freelance, covering all aspects of general news, including road traffic accidents, murders and sport. These are his recollections of events on 23 July 2016:

I was out on the ground quite early on the day. I knew through social media and general chit-chat that there was likely to be trouble, following disturbances in Sheffield in April 2015 when Grimsby fans had caused problems in the city centre and at the railway station.

By midday I had parked up and got my camera out. I phoned Peter and told him that there was going to be trouble. After years of doing the job, I could just sense it. Peter came out and we stayed together. If there is a fight, I want to be in the middle of it because I want the shots. As a journalist, the picture tells the story and I want it. It's like an adrenalin rush, but with fear mixed in. I've been clouted a few times on the back of the head and, where I can, I now try to keep my back to a wall!

The violence throughout the afternoon was sporadic, ten to twenty seconds; somebody would get a kicking and then it would stop for a while. In parts, it was serious, and I have to say that, by the end of the day, I was affected by it. A lot of the police officers there were not local and I tried to help by telling them where the supporters were likely to gather, or from which streets they would emerge. Most of the trouble I monitored was in the Market Place, High Street, and at the railway station.

After the match, the fans walked back to the railway station, but there weren't any police at the railway level crossing, which had previously been a flashpoint for fights. Both sets of fans confronted each other there, and one Grimsby fan was seriously assaulted. A lady nearby actually filmed the violence and I have seen the footage, which showed a serious disturbance.

The fans were 'kettled' on the railway station for some time, and keeping them contained was obviously a challenge for some of the younger police officers there, a few of whom seemed quite timid in the face of the fans' behaviour. I photographed the assault on the inspector at the railway station and thought he was extremely patient. He was struck more than once before the guy was arrested.

While I was at the railway station I noticed this guy, who must have been at least seventy years old. I thought that he was trying to make his way through the crowd of fans but actually he was with them. Suddenly, from the corner of my eye, I saw him coming at me, waving a walking stick. He had a Yorkshire accent and was obviously a Sheffield United fan; he took exception to me taking photographs. A sergeant stepped in the way and then some of the younger element dragged him back. It was unbelievable.

It seemed to take ages for a train to arrive and all the time there was tension in the air.

While I was at the station, I saw a Sheffield United fan with his family. He had a head wound and, when I spoke to him, he laughed ironically – he'd just been assaulted by his own supporters for no apparent reason – wrong place at the wrong time!

I've also seen problems in non-League games but things have changed now. The days of skinheads, boots and braces have gone. The modern hooligans now are different; you could walk past them and not notice them until the trouble starts – t-shirts, shorts and trainers – urban-type gear.

It's never gone away from the '80s. I personally think that football violence is coming back, but on a different scale. Whereas before it might have been a trainload of supporters who wanted to cause trouble, now it's maybe forty who want to do it.

At the end of the 2015/16 Football League season, Blackpool FC, 'The Seasiders', were relegated to League Two, where their neighbouring seaside team Morecambe FC, 'The Shrimps', have been playing for a few years.

Following their first meeting at Morecambe on Saturday 13 August 2016, which Morecambe won 2-1, there were disturbances. Between 5.25 p.m. and 5.30 p.m., a car conveying several Blackpool FC senior officials was vandalised with scratches, dents and damage to the windscreen, as it was leaving the ground. Lancashire Constabulary officers used mounted officers to control the crowds and, as they were trying to prevent damage to the vehicle, a horse slipped on an uneven surface and partially fell on its rider. Fortunately there were no serious injuries to the horse or the mounted officer.

Blackpool fans were also asked to leave a pub in Morecambe near to Morecambe's football ground, shortly after the game at about 5.30 p.m. Violence broke out later some three miles away outside a Lancaster city centre pub, at around 7 p.m., when chanting Blackpool football fans, aged between thirty and fifty years, charged at the doormen of the pub who had denied them entry. The incident was witnessed by the mother of one of the doormen, who saw him disappear into a sea of rowdy fans. The doorman, who had suffered a broken nose and a bloodied shirt from a previous incident of violence, tried his level best to beat off a group of fans, many of whom were said to be old enough to be grandfathers. The fans were throwing punches and chanting about the owner of Blackpool FC. At one stage, there were about eight or nine men targeting one doorman. Shortly afterwards, officers of the Lancashire Constabulary arrived and began to push the fans back down the street until they dispersed. At the time of the incident, there were a number of families in the street out for a family evening.

Following the incident, a thirty-one-year-old man from Blackpool was arrested and later cautioned for assault. A fifty-three-year-old man from St Annes, near Blackpool, was also given a penalty notice for being drunk and disorderly. Further incidents were reported at the city-centre pub and police attended again, following which a group of twenty supporters were escorted to the city's railway station. The police also put in a temporary dispersal order, and four men were required to leave the area.

On 23 August 2016 a twenty-four-year-old Southampton fan appeared at Wolverhampton Crown Court for sentencing in relation to an incident on a train en route from Birmingham Snow Hill to the Hawthorns for a game with West Bromwich Albion at the end of February 2015. During the course of the journey, he jumped on the seats and kicked out at a West Bromwich fan, who received a cut to the head. The defendant was given an eight-month prison sentence, suspended for eighteen months, ordered to carry out eighty hours of unpaid work, placed on a curfew and made the subject of a football banning order for three years. A second Southampton fan, aged fifty-two, awaits trial for affray.

Commenting after the case, DC Tim Friend from the BTP made some chilling comments: 'As the CCTV pictures show, this man's aggressive and violent behaviour that day was completely unacceptable. The malevolence on his face throughout the incident is very disturbing and he shows no regard for other passengers as he clambers over seats to kick out at rival fans.'

Football violence does not only strike at League team games; it can also erupt at village matches as well! Llanllyfni, near Caernarfon in North Wales, is a sleepy Welsh village with a population of 450 people; the greater area has a population of 4,135. The village football team, Llanllyfni FC, plays in the Welsh Alliance Division Two.

On Saturday 27 August 2016, they played a home game against Prestatyn Sport FC, in a Welsh Alliance Division Two League match. Just before half time, when Llanllyfni were winning 2-1, fighting broke out between the Llanllyfni supporters and the players, which caused the match to be abandoned. A number of North Wales Police officers attended the scene and a Prestatyn Sport FC player was arrested by the police. One of the Llanllyfni players, who suffered a head injury, was taken to hospital at Bangor, where he was X-rayed and underwent scans. A number of children attended the match and they were shocked at the violence.

A Prestatyn Sport FC official, seventy years of age, commented that he had been involved with football since he was a toddler and that he had never seen anything like it before. He described the atmosphere as being very volatile and said that he was actually quite scared. The incident was reported to the Football Association of Wales. There have been no previous reports of violence when the two teams have met and, in fact, the two sets of supporters have previously enjoyed a drink together.

Following a two-day trial at Caernarfon Crown Court in August 2016, a twenty-six-year-old centre-forward, who played for Cefn Albion, near Wrexham, was jailed for twelve months for breaking the leg of an opponent in October 2015, when Cefn Albion played Brynford during a Welsh National Division One cup match. The tackle by the defendant was described as 'unlawful and maliciously inflicted'. The game had to be suspended after the attack.

Experienced FAW match referee Mark Stokes said, 'It was forceful. That challenge was probably the worst one I have seen in my time as a referee. It wasn't a challenge; it was a kick. There was no attempt to kick the ball.' The judge at the Crown Court, Mr Recorder Huw Rees, said, 'I take a serious view of this case. Because of your petulant and therefore violent act, the game was suspended.' The judge went on to say that unlawful violence on the pitch devalued the spirit of the game and that spectators did not need to be subjected to brutish thuggery.

Also on Saturday 27 August 2016, Everton played at home at Goodison Park with Stoke City. After the home side scored what proved to be the winning goal, complaints were made by a number of Everton fans that they had been hit with coins thrown by opposition supporters.

The father of one supporter – an eight-year-old boy – claimed that his son was hit in the neck by a twenty-pence coin, in what he described as appalling behaviour, and called for the persons involved to be banned from football grounds. He described another man receiving a cut to the head as a result of another coin being thrown.

Are these examples of what the future may hold?

* * *

Chris Hobbs, retired Metropolitan Police officer, concludes his thoughts:

Since the Hillsborough disaster in 1989, I've rarely attended matches. Indeed since the advent of all-seater stadia, I have been to one: England versus Ukraine at Wembley. The thought of sitting next to a beer-bellied tattooed moron, at great expense, who spends the match hurling abuse at rival fans, holds no appeal for me whatsoever. I do, however, occasionally visit the vicinity of grounds on match days to view the policing operation.

It would seem to me though that, although times have changed, the hooligan element have not left us. All-seater stadia; all-ticket matches for most Premier League and even some Championship games; improved CCTV and handheld cameras; banning orders; continued segregation and escorts: all have contributed to curbing the hooligans – yet, they are still there. In some ways, policing football has become even more problematic for officers on the front line of football, many of whom will be working on their rest days. Back in the 1970s and '80s, hooligans were mainly in their teens and twenties. Now, however, significant numbers are in their thirties, forties and even fifties, with relatively little fear of police.

They may not attend every match, but will turn out for their side's high-risk games, or matches of importance. These individuals, together with younger elements, can present considerable policing problems. Any football fan will be able to survey a fixture list and point to the matches at which there could well be problems that will necessitate a major policing operation. Such an operation invariably involves attempting to keep rival groups apart before and after matches. This can mean encouraging away supporters to congregate in designated pubs, from where they can be escorted to the ground, albeit perhaps the worse for wear.

Once inside the ground, there can be more bars on the segregated concourse, where fans will jump, sing and throw beer over each other. The scene is replicated at half time. At the conclusion of the match, the public-order-trained commander will decide whether or not to retain fans in the ground until the home fans have (been) dispersed.

Interestingly, it would seem that friction does sometimes occur between match-day, public-order-trained commanders, who go by the book, and the dedicated football-liaison/spotter officers, who attempt to utilise their experience to prevent violence.

Those members of the public intending to travel by train over a weekend during a season would do well to examine the fixture list. Complaints by passengers that can be seen on social media are legion, while BTP officers have to be aware of 'crossover' points where rival fans can clash, even if their respective teams are not playing each other.

Some grounds rely on stewards to enforce segregation, and others on a mixture of stewards and police. At West Ham's new Olympic Stadium, it would appear that police are no longer required to support this task, whereas, at the Boleyn Ground, officers stood between rival supporters on the South Bank. Interestingly, there have already been some challenges for the Olympic Stadium stewards, following disorder between home and away fans. YouTube footage recently appeared showing fighting between a group of West Ham and Bournemouth supporters on the concourse outside the ground at West Ham's first League game of the 2016 season, on Sunday 21 August.

At Wembley, there appears to have been some form of agreement between stadium officials and police that stewards are to be solely responsible for maintaining good order inside the ground. The Millwall versus Wigan semi-final in 2013 should perhaps have caused that policy to be questioned. Millwall supporters began fighting among themselves and, as the fighting escalated, BT Sport commentators became more concerned at the level of disorder. Stewards would appear to have, not unreasonably, hung back. It was some considerable time before police officers appeared on the relevant terrace, and even they were initially beaten back.

Three years later, it was again left to stewards to segregate Millwall and Barnsley supporters in a Wembley stand. As Barnsley took an unassailable lead, Millwall supporters attempted to break through the line of stewards, who, it must be said, valiantly tried to hold their line in an unpleasant situation, fully captured on YouTube. Police arrived six minutes later, just as Millwall supporters broke through the line of battered stewards; Barnsley supporters, who included families, fled.

Occasionally a policing operation will be breached by hooligan elements. This was seen outside Tottenham's ground last season (2015/16), when hundreds of Spurs fans attacked those from Arsenal who were attempting to enter the ground, despite a large police presence. Manchester United's Europa leagues match with Liverpool saw fighting inside the ground, as Liverpool supporters announced themselves in stands occupied by the home side's fans. West Ham's final Upton Park home fixture with Manchester United saw serious disorder in the streets before the game, with the Manchester United team coach being attacked.

A scroll through social media and local papers covering areas where there are medium-, or high-risk, games tends to give more than a useful indication of where problems have occurred. Searching on Twitter under 'trains fans', 'trains police', 'trains drunk' or 'trains drunken' will often produce a litany of boorish behaviour on the transport system.

Trouble isn't confined to the Premier League; even non-League matches can attract football-related violence. On Saturday 3 September 2016, during a Vanarama National League North match, Stockport fans caused their match at Altrincham to be held up after they threw smoke bombs on to the pitch. There was also fighting at AFC Fylde's match versus Gloucester; some Gloucester fans were ejected after just fifteen minutes of play.

It's only a minority, they say – really? Sky and BT Sport have both seemingly given up trying to muffle the four-letter chants that echo around grounds when sung by thousands. Who, with access to live televised football, hasn't heard, 'Your support is fucking shit,' or this delightful Spurs 'ditty' concerning Arsenal, which could be clearly heard at their opening home game against Liverpool:

'When I was just a little boy,
My mother gave me a little toy,
An Arsenal fan on a string,
She told me to kick it's fucking head in ...'

Thousands of Manchester United fans can also be heard frequently singing how they would like to be 'kicking a blue'. Equally obvious on television are foul-mouthed, gesticulating fans that spring into action simply when a visiting team member trots across to take a corner.

The fact that football hooliganism is still very much with us was clearly illustrated by the reprehensible behaviour of hundreds of England supporters in France. Yes, this was the behaviour of a minority, but a significant one, with social media full of boasts of what the England fans would do to the Russians. The result was a rout of the English hooligans, but it was rout that also drew in the thousands of decent England supporters, who must have feared for their lives. More trouble in Lille saw England supporters roaming the streets looking for Russians.

Organisations like the Football Supporters' Federation are quick to seize on any alleged transgression by police but, in my opinion, rarely praise any successful policing operation. They have previously criticised the police for kettling, segregation, cordoning or retaining after matches, and also for not being there when trouble occurs, and fans are attacked by rivals. Those who feel police shouldn't be at matches at all would do well to remember the virtually unpoliced Wolves versus Watford game at the end of the 2014/15 season.

Wolves have a known hooligan element and Watford fans, who took several thousand to this game, had also been involved in incidents earlier that season. After the match, a group of Watford fans were attacked on the way to the station and one, Nick Cruwys, was left fighting for his life. In fairness, Wolves fans responded with fundraising that raised thousands of pounds. Nick is now on the road to recovery, while several individuals have been convicted.

In my opinion, little will change this season. Sports writers will ignore the foul-mouthed chanting of thousands and any outbreaks of violence away from the ground, instead commenting only on disorder inside the ground if it is literally so serious that it cannot be ignored. As for me, I may make a belated pilgrimage to Leyton Orient. I just hope I won't be sitting next to a foul-mouthed, shaven-headed, tattooed moron!

On Saturday 10 September 2016, violence again erupted at the London Stadium as some West Ham fans started fighting among themselves during the club's 4-2 defeat to Watford, while others clashed with away fans. Ten fans were ejected and three handed over to the police, as urgent calls came for police officers to be reintroduced into the ground itself, with young children caught up in the violence. Video, circulated on social media, showed terrified parents trying to shield their young children, while men fought among them, with fans swearing and jostling each other.

In addition to the potential for increased violence at non-League games, the perennial problem of policing so-called friendly games (which can sometimes be anything but) and the inevitable outbreaks of violence that many local derbies attract mean the police in the UK are also facing new challenges.

There is some anecdotal evidence to suggest that fans are now making greater use of pyrotechnics both inside and outside grounds. With reduced policing at many grounds, without the strictest of search regimes, the use of powerful fireworks increases the potential for injury, as well as adding a potentially dramatic ingredient to the sense of disorder and loss of control by those in authority. To a degree, this is a European phenomenon that is being copied by English fans.

Mark 'Snarka' Whitehouse concludes his story with his own contrasting thoughts:

I don't think it's the same as in the '80s. When I see things in the paper, I always look at the ages and, when it's someone in their forties and fifties, I can't understand why they are getting involved. Some of us grew out of it and others went to prison!

I did it when everyone did it but, in the '80s, if something happened nobody would point the finger at you. CCTV stopped a lot of the trouble inside grounds but the football brand is different now and it's not just working-class lads. It's a different set of people now and people are more prepared to say, 'It was him!'

We do still get criminalised by the police on occasions. I remember in 2014 going to Stoke on a coach for a match. We had arranged to go to a pub in Ettingshall in Staffordshire before the match, and the licensee had arranged to put some food on.

I accept that the coach would have had some people on it who would probably be classed as a 'risk' group, but someone had put something on Facebook like, 'No pyros, no party', and that was enough for the police to respond. There was a police reception committee waiting for us; they put a dog on the coach, looking for explosives, and took our details, even though they didn't find anything. They refused to let us go into the pub where we had arranged to go and insisted on taking us to another one that was just 400 yards away.

Professor Clifford Stott from Keele University concludes with his thoughts on the future of football-related hooliganism in the UK:

It's difficult to say what the future is because it is so dependent on policing tactics. Anecdotally, some years ago I did some work with the police in India, which has a huge numbers of police officers, and has retained many aspects of colonial policing. The reality is, though, that up to 85 per cent of officers are engaged in public order duties and relatively few are engaged in dealing with day crime, which puts them at a distance from their communities. My view is that you can measure the democratic status of a police force by the number of officers it has engaged in public order roles. In this country, as you see cutbacks continue to bite, especially in local policing and engagement, I think that this will become more of an issue for us.

If we don't see changes in British policing approaches to managing football, my prediction is that the problem may well get worse. If we do see change, then we could embrace a positive future. You achieve control through facilitation. Currently, the dominant agenda is about 'getting a grip' and, if that continues, there will be no change, with the police still locked into the use of resources and banning orders.

In 2013 a total of 1,500 football supporters, from across the UK, responded to an online survey regarding their experiences of football-related violence. The findings from this survey were published in 2015 in a document titled 'Football Fans' Views of Violence in British Football: Evidence of a Sanitised and Gentrified Culture', by Jamie Cleland and Ellis Cashmore. Some 89 per cent of fans said that violence had decreased since the 1980s, and highlighted better policing, better stadia, the use of CCTV, football banning orders, and alcohol restrictions as being some of the reasons as to why this had come about. Interestingly, they also pointed towards higher ticket prices, and the fact that there was a more civilised supporter base, as being supporting factors.

One enlightened respondent highlighted the link between disorder and an increase in the casual use of controlled drugs, and suggested that police drugs sniffer dogs should be deployed near stadia and at transport hubs. Unfortunately, while entirely logical, this approach is unlikely to feature as a major part of police tactics in future, as police forces, including the BTP, have cut back on the use of drugs dogs. A more cautious approach to the use of stop and search powers, following criticism from the Home Office, makes it an even less attractive option.

In contrast, some 11 per cent said that football violence remained an issue and the report quoted the opinions of a number of fans on the issue, which remain relevant to this day.

One Millwall fan reflected, 'Wannabe hooligans remain part of the culture of football, but the real hard-core element appears to have died out. That is not to say that violence does not happen; we live in a casually violent society, but the commercialisation of English football has limited its impact. There are too many people keen to protect "The Brand".'

A West Ham fan said, 'Violence at football will never leave. Better policing in England and banning orders have prevented disorder but the issue is still there. As older hooligans retire, a new breed is born. It's a British subculture and Britain are the kings of youth subculture.'

Two individuals who appeared to be closer to involvement in the subject matter commented, 'With not much excitement in your life, you latch on to a tribe who then become the focus of your life and you live and breathe it. I believe it's more to do with the poverty/boredom/mob rules, a need to release your frustration at what little seems to be going right in your life,' and, 'Violence is an essential part of the match-day experience. We go toe-to-toe with firms all over the country wherever we play. We've got each other's backs, we drink together, and we crack skulls together. We like to drink, watch the game, and fight. It's human nature.'

REFERENCES/
ACKNOWLEDGEMENTS

Every attempt has been made to seek permission for copyright material used in this book. However, if we have inadvertently used copyright material without permission /acknowledgement we apologise and we will make the necessary correction at the first opportunity.

Newspapers/Magazines

Argus
Blackpool Telegraph
Burnley Express
Burton Mail
Chad
Chronicle Live
Coventry Telegraph
Daily Express
Daily Mail
Daily Mail Online
Daily Post North Wales
Daily Telegraph
Evening Standard
Greater Manchester News
Grimsby Telegraph
International Business Times

Lancashire Evening Post
Lancashire Telegraph
Leicester Mercury
Midlands Express and Star
Newcastle Metro News
NiceOne Magazine
Nottingham Post
Oxford Mail
Peterborough Telegraph
Portsmouth News
Railnews
South Shields Gazette
Stoke Sentinel
Swindon Advertiser
The Birmingham Mail
The Blackpool Gazette
The Bolton News
The Chronicle
The Comet
The Daily Mirror
The Daily Post Wales
The Daily Star
The Guardian
The Herald (Oxford)
The Huddersfield Daily Express
The Independent
The Irish Mirror
The Lancaster Guardian
The Lincolnshire Echo
The Manchester Evening News
The Manchester Metro
The Mirror & Mirror Online
The Morecambe Visitor
The Northern Echo
The Plymouth Herald
The Railway Magazine, April 2014
The Railway Magazine, May 2014
The Scotsman

The Scottish Daily Record
The Scottish Herald
The Sentinel
The Sheffield Star
The Standard
The Sun
The Telegraph
Tottenham Journal
Witney Gazette
Yorkshire News
Yorkshire Post

Books/Articles/Programmes

Ben Carrington and Ian McDonald – *Race, Sport and British Society* (2001)
David Deakin – *BBC (Coventry and Warwickshire) Investigates Non-League Football Violence* – radio programme aired on 23 May 2016
Desmond Morris – *The Soccer Tribe* (1981)
Ian Bent, Richard McIlroy, Kevin Mousley and Peter Walsh – *Football Confidential* (2000)
Jamie Cleland and Ellis Cashmore – *Football Fans Views of Violence in British Football: Evidence of a Sanitised and Gentrified Culture* (2015)
Michael Layton and Robert Endeacott – *Hunting the Hooligans* (2015)
Norman Lucas – *WPC Courage* (1986)

Websites/Media

Albion Rovers Football Club official website
BBC News and Ceefax
BTP Media Centre and Twitter accounts
ESPN
EuroSport website
News Shoppers
Sky Sports

Soccer Lens
SportsMole
SportsVice.Com
Sussex Police website
Terrace Links
The anti-sectarianism website via www.fawndoo.com
TheCourier.co.uk
TheFirms.co.uk
Wales Online
Wikipedia
York Press

People/Organisations

Alan Beesley – critical reader
Andrew Hunt – retired Chief Inspector, BTP based at London Underground
Andy Baxter – retired Police Constable, BTP based at Manchester
Andy Bryson – Train Driver based at Edinburgh Waverley railway station
Bill and Sean McNeish – committed Glasgow Rangers fans
Bob Cook – retired Police Inspector BTP based at Hull
British Transport Police History Group
Bryan Drew OBE QPM – retired Director of United Kingdom Football Policing Unit
Carl Jarvis – Rail Enforcement Officer, Southeastern Trains
Caroline Gall – BBC Journalist and Author
Chris Hobbs – retired Detective Sergeant, Metropolitan Police Service
Clifford Stott – Professor of Social Psychology at Keele University
David Deakin – Former BBC Football Reporter
Dan Taylor – Policy lead on security with Transport Focus
Deirdre Cobley – retired Police Constable, BTP based at London North
Duncan Young – Freelance Photographer working with the *Grimsby Telegraph*, with a special mention for his support in providing a photograph used to produce the book cover
'ED' – London-based police officer

Education Scotland
Independent Advisory Group on Sectarianism in Football
John Lighton – retired Police Inspector, West Midlands Police
John Wallace – retired police officer from Scotland (Glasgow)
Kevin Marshall – retired Chief Inspector, BTP based in Birmingham
Mark 'Snarka' Whitehouse – committed West Bromwich Albion fan
Martyn Ripley OBE – retired BTP Chief Superintendent
Mike Cresswell – retired Police Sergeant, West Midlands Police
Mike Spoors – retired Postman and committed Sunderland supporter
PARK – cartoonist
Paul Robb QPM – retired Assistant Chief Constable, British Transport Police
Peter Craig – Crime Reporter for *Grimsby Telegraph*
Renton Baker – Christian Vision for Men
Richard Shakespeare – Former Undercover Police Officer
Simon Pinchbeck – former Metropolitan Police Officer
Stephen Burrows – retired Chief Superintendent, Warwickshire Police, and critical reader
The Press Association
Wayne Clayton-Robb – retired Inspector, BTP based in London

AUTHOR BIOGRAPHIES

Michael Layton QPM joined the British Transport Police as a cadet on 1 September 1968 and, after three years, was appointed as a police constable in 1971, serving at Birmingham New Street station. In 1972, he transferred to Birmingham City Police, which amalgamated in 1974 to become the West Midlands Police, where he eventually reached the rank of chief superintendent in 1997. On retirement from that force in 2003, he went on to see service with the Sovereign Bases Police in Cyprus. He then returned to the British Transport Police in 2004, initially as a detective superintendent (director of intelligence), and then, in his last two years, as the operations superintendent at Birmingham, where he continued with his passion for combating football violence. He finally retired again in 2011. In the January 2003 New Year's Honours list, he was awarded the Queen's Police Medal for distinguished police service.

He is the co-author of a book entitled *Hunting the Hooligans – the True Story of Operation Red Card,* which was published in July 2015 by Milo Books, and the author of *Violence in the Sun – a History of Football Violence in Cyprus*, which was published as an eBook, also by Milo in May 2015. More recently, he has co-authored a book called *Tracking the Hooligans: The History of Football Violence on the UK Rail Network* and *Police Dog Heroes*, both with Amberley Publishing. He is also the author of *Birmingham's Front Line – True Police Stories*, also published by

Amberley, and the co-author of a crime fiction eBook, *Black Over Bill's Mother's*, available on Amazon UK.

Michael is a self-employed consultant, engaged predominantly with crime and community safety issues.

Bill Rogerson MBE is a native of Morecambe, Lancashire, and began his career with the British Transport Police on 5 April 1971 at Birmingham New Street, serving at Coventry, Leicester, and Heysham Harbour in the rank of constable. On 3 September 1979, he was promoted to uniform sergeant at Crewe. In October 1985 he transferred to Holyhead. While serving at Holyhead, he also performed duties at Dun Laoghaire Harbour, which was a British Railways Board harbour in Southern Ireland, in connection with sporting fixtures and thefts. On 1 February 1989, he became the officer in charge at Bangor, North Wales. He was appointed an MBE in 1995 for charity and work within the community in North Wales, something he described as 'a huge surprise and quite an honour'. He retired from the force in September 2001. However, four years later, he returned to the force after being offered the position of community partnership co-ordinator, which he filled until the role become redundant in July 2011. This did not deter him as, in September 2011, he returned to the force for his third career, as a volunteer, visiting schools and delivering safety messages. Bill is also a founding member and current secretary of the British Transport Police History Group. He edits the group's monthly newsletter, *History Lines*. Bill devotes the majority of his spare time to charity work, assisting a number of organisations in North Wales. He is the co-author of *Police Dog Heroes*, published by Amberley.

DEDICATIONS

Michael Layton – to my wife Andry for her continued support, and to my mother Gladys. Also to the men and women in the police service in the UK who have put themselves in harm's way over the years to combat football-related violence and protect the public.

Bill Rogerson – to Shirley, my wife, for her patience and understanding while writing this book. Also to my former colleagues, who unstintingly manned the thin blue line, through thick and thin, while dealing with football hooligans week in and week out to keep the general public and railway staff safe.